Planes, Trains and Automobiles

Also by Dan Kieran

Three Men in a Float (co-author)
I Fought The Law
Crap Towns I and II (co-editor)

Planes, Trains and Automobiles

Why Men Love Things that Go

DAN KIERAN

JOHN MURRAY

First published in Great Britain in 2009 by John Murray (Publishers)
An Hachette UK Company

2

© Dan Kieran 2009

A CIP catalogue record for this title is available from the British Library

ISBN 978-1-84854-014-9

Typeset in Bembo by Servis Filmsetting Ltd, Stockport, Cheshire

Printed and bound by Clays Ltd, St Ives plc

John Murray policy is to use papers that are natural, renewable and recyclable products
and made from wood grown in sustainable forests. The logging and manufacturing
processes are expected to conform to the environmental regulations of the country of
origin.

John Murray (Publishers)
338 Euston Road
London NW1 3BH

www.johnmurray.co.uk

For Rachel and Wilf

Contents

Introduction

I WAS SITTING in a treatment room with my trousers round my ankles when I asked my GP how he would account for men's fascination with machines. He stopped writing for a moment, looked up and muttered 'Asperger's?' and then continued to scrawl something down on his note-pad. 'I had one patient so obsessed with washing machines that he had to be sectioned for trying to climb inside them every time he walked past a laundrette.'

Now that was an unhealthy, although you'd assume clean, machine obsession. I pestered him a little more. 'What about train, car, motor-bike, aeroplane, bicycle and tank enthusiasts – ever had any odd versions of those?' The doctor looked up again, shook his head, stared intently at the red sores and flaking skin on my outer thighs and handed me a prescription for a particularly potent skin cream. 'Who knows? Now try this. You may be allergic to oil and coal.'

I pulled my trousers up and reflected that this discovery was not, perhaps, the ideal start for my journey into man's obsession with the machines of the industrial age (I'd spent the previous day learning to drive a steam train and had come out in hives).

It was rather like discovering you're allergic to salt water the day before setting out on the Round the World Yacht Race. If nothing else, though, I was quite impressed by the way my body had begun to exhibit symptoms I'd previously thought were merely psychological. I've always been, shall we say, *reticent* in the presence of machines, but the knowledge that I could actually be allergic to them made a great deal of sense. That would account for the fact that I hadn't learned to drive until I was thirty, or set foot in an aeroplane in eighteen years (having become a bit of an eco-worrier too) and had always found the slightly bizarre language of engine cylinders and speeds – whether for boats, cars, unicycles, whatever – as baffling as the appeal of those vile little dogs blonde daughters of billionaires always seem to carry.

Ever since I can remember, I've been left completely dumbfounded by the way men salivate over machines. I hate going fast myself. Even on swings. I don't know what the 'point' of a 'three-point-four' litre engine is, and I don't know what my 'camshaft' is, or even if I've got one. I'm so clueless, in fact, that I once had to call out the RAC because I couldn't get the bonnet of my car, a Renault Laguna, to shut properly. Apart from 'The Mighty One', the carbon-neutral 1958 electric milk float I used to drive across England in with two friends last summer, machines and I have never got on very well at all.

On the other hand, I'm an enormous fan of enthusiasts. Anyone described as an *aficionado*, expert, connoisseur, authority, pundit, buff, fiend or geek is someone that I want to meet. I've always imagined that being an enthusiast about anything is like discovering the keys to a magical world. Life is short and if you've managed to find the thing within it that you use to interpret life's meaning then you are wise indeed.

And so it was that I set out from my local chemist later that morning (lathered in a steroid cream called Betnovate) to try and bring an end to my incomprehension, not to mention psychological and physical revulsion, about the machines of the modern world.

Dan Kieran
Fishbourne, winter 2008

I

Escape

Narrow Boats

A PPROPRIATELY FOR ME, my journey into the world of machines began at a very slow pace indeed. Barely walking pace, in fact. But as the great Mr Lazy once said, you should never walk when you can sit down and never sit down when you can lie down, so I was doing a combination of the last two, while scoffing a cream tea, on a boat dawdling along a canal. You may not think that a journey into the history of industrial progress and mankind's obsession with things that go has any business beginning in such a serene setting, but I thought the best way to explore the world of transport machines – both the history of their invention and the lives of the men who are obsessed with them – was in the order in which they were invented. If you want to know where modern machines and our obsession with speed began, then you must amble back to the dawn of the industrial age and glide along Britain's canals.

I had two companions on the narrow boat with me that sunny winter afternoon. Dennis, the man driving up and down the 4-mile stretch of the Chichester Ship Canal that is still navigable, and Lionel Thomas Caswall Rolt – the latter in the form of his book *Narrow Boat*, an account of the honeymoon he and his first wife, Angela, took on England's canals in the summer and winter of 1939, just before the outbreak of the Second World War. I soon came across a passage that immediately pointed out the curious contradiction about the men and the machines I was hoping to meet. 'There are two courses open to each man in his brief lifetime: either he can seek the good life, or he can struggle for wealth and power; the former emphasizes spiritual, the latter material values.'

This question of how to live was not something I'd expected to read in a book about life on Britain's canals. Looking back, of course, it makes perfect sense. We live in the age of machines, so it is to be expected that they have profoundly affected the lives we now lead.

Rolt saw canal-lovers as those seeking the good life, something reflected in their respectful relationship with the landscape itself, but, I began to wonder, what of other machine enthusiasts? Considering they spend so much time and money working on their contraptions for no apparent status or financial benefit, it would seem that their motivation was of the spiritual form too. But before I get too carried away with this philosophical meandering, without the quest for 'wealth and power' surely none of these machines would have been invented in the first place? I was confused already. It was to be the first paradox in a journey of many.

The idea of people bustling about in sheds being 'spiritual' was rather strange too, until I discovered the word 'enthusiast' has an interesting metaphysical origin. According to the dictionary, enthusiasm means 'having the god enter into the worshipper, who believed that he became at one with God' (from the Greek word *entheos* – 'inspired by God'). Today we tend not to think of it in a biblical sense, but in early Christian times the word 'enthusiast' was used to explain the moment of salvation ('Hallelujah, I'm saved!'). Now we think of enthusiasts as people who have an obsession with something, and for men that something is usually a machine.

It is curious that in this sense men have become less inspired by God and more inspired by mankind's own ideas and achievements; but, as I was about to discover, that's a neat and tidy encapsulation of a way of thinking that preceded and paved the way for a group known as the 'Lunar Men' to begin the journey that led to the machines of the modern world. More on them in a moment. While we're on the subject of the religious overtones within the term 'enthusiast', it's also interesting to note that it was around the time the canals emerged that people began using the word – in a specifically religious sense – as a pejorative term, much in the way that we use the word 'fundamentalist' today. The religious battles between Catholics and Protestants that dominated the reign of Henry VIII and culminated in the civil war of the 1640s, along with the emerging scientific mode of thinking we'll come to in a moment, meant that overt displays of religious obsession were becoming rather frowned upon in polite society. The previous century had been characterized by religious fundamentalists of one persuasion seeking the blood of another, in brutal and violent episodes that had threatened to rip the entire nation apart. A new habit of quiet respect for people's religious and political views was gradually beginning to emerge, in the hope that it might prevent such mindless brutality surfacing ever again.

As we chugged along that afternoon, the contradiction at the heart of the machine enthusiast began to fizz away merrily inside my head. The perception most people have of machine enthusiasts today is of slightly gruff men disappearing into their own little world. A world that is accessed through a portal that appears to the rest of us to be little more than an old and battered shed. None of us really knows what goes on inside those sheds. They are usually filled with bits of machinery that don't work, screws, tools, a faulty gas fire, balls of twine and hundreds of rusted nails. I was pondering this while trying to work out what my entry point into the subject of men and machines should be: I know practically nothing about machines myself. Even my sense of being a man seemed rather out of place in comparison with the kind of bloke who is 'good with his hands'. Then it hit me. These men clearly want to get away from the modern world. For one thing, they rarely like new machines. It's always the old, hopelessly outdated ones that seem to get them most excited. As though it's only once a machine has outlived its actual usefulness and technology has moved on that its particular allure can come to the fore. These sheds and these machines, then, were surely a refuge that reflected a different set of values not apparent in the modern world. But if that was the case, it proposed a rather startling irony: that in order to get away from the modern world they had found solace in the machines actually responsible for creating it. I found that problem, or idea, enormously intriguing. It hinted at a paradoxical pathway, and they are always fun to try and navigate. It also made my decision to start with narrow boats appropriate, because, of all the machines I had chosen to investigate, the narrow boat is surely the one that offers the greatest sense of escape. They are practically floating sheds.

Britain's first purpose-built modern canal, which would lead to narrow boats eventually criss-crossing the entire nation, was built in 1761. Britain at that time was a country still coming to terms with the ideas and arguments that have retrospectively been pulled together and called the 'Enlightenment' and with the impact these new scientific ideas would have on a more traditional way of life. Conventional wisdom has it that before this flurry of rational thinking, which swept the old mode of living clean away, people led incredibly primitive lives: in terror of religious doctrine, in squalor and filth. According to the history books I read at school, these poor people rarely had enough food to eat and were largely ignorant about the laws that governed the world around them. To modern eyes they seem like oblivious children, somehow enduring before the patriarch of modern science emerged to guide them to the light. With no modern healthcare or the machines that we rely on today, the pre-Enlightenment era seems a dark and foreboding place, but the new scientific age – which had begun to emerge after Copernicus proved that Genesis, the word of God, was wrong because the sun did not move around the earth after all – represented a new epoch of rational thought that promised a brighter and happier future for all. These principles of scientific discovery then took physical form during the Industrial Revolution in the machines of the modern age, and life as we know it had begun. Today science and the machine have become the primary motivators for human progress. So wholeheartedly have we embraced the scientific world-view that any way of thinking that is not scientific is condemned as 'emotional' or 'irrational'. The machine age has given us the overwhelming sense that life has never been better, and those of us in the West now consider it our duty to spread this knowledge and this approach to life to every scrap of land where people are denied this outlook today.

This is the view most books about the Industrial Revolution, machines and the scientific age will express, at any rate. As you may have sensed, my own opinion is not exactly the one I've just described, but this is undoubtedly the perspective that permeates our culture as keenly as the religious doctrine of the pre-Enlightenment past. We'll look into this in more detail a little later too.

Despite the frontiers being reached by a new way of thinking in Britain during the mid-1700s, getting around the
country, on the other hand, was still a rather primitive affair.
The era of the highwayman terrifying the great and good as
they stuttered and lurched through a sprawling countryside
in horse-drawn carriages was coming to an end thanks to the
new safer, dusty turnpike roads. But a journey from London
to Edinburgh still took eleven days in a coach with little or
no suspension. It was expensive too, costing up to £5 (one
way), and, in a move that would be repeated centuries later
by Ryanair, you had to pay extra if you wanted to bring any
luggage. (To put that ticket price into perspective, a doctor
of this time could expect to earn £62 in a year.)

It is when you apply this cost of transportation to coal,
however, that you begin to grasp how the nation's commercial hopes were being strangled. The new cotton mills in the
cities of the north were largely water-powered, but their
workforce required coal to heat their homes. Having duti-
fully left villages for the miserable working conditions of the
industrial mills in the aftermath of the great enclosures that
had robbed them of their life on the land, they could no
longer rely on collecting wood from common land to use as
fuel. The oceans of coal in the north-east were shipped down
to London, from where navigable rivers serviced towns and
villages where they could, but out to the west any town or
colliery without access to a river or a port relied on pack-
horses, carts and wagons to get fuel to the people over unreliable and dangerous roads. Coal became vastly more
expensive the further from the colliery you happened to be.
It was this that inspired Francis Egerton, the 3rd Duke of
Bridgewater, to employ a millwright called James Brindley
to build Britain's first modern canal to transport coal from
Worsley to his factories in Manchester. With his canal

Britain was not just on the verge of a new form of transportation – it was on the brink of a new way of life.

The Chichester ship canal, on which my journey had begun, is not part of a working network – not yet, at least – so I ventured to Pewsey in Wiltshire, on the Kennet and Avon canal, to meet Ben and Cath Fitch, a newly married couple who had decided to ride out the looming recession on a canal barge and live much in the manner of L.T.C. Rolt and his wife seventy years before them. I rang Ben during the early signs of the credit crunch to arrange meeting up, and his voice had the sound of someone living far below the modern hectic speed of the nine-to-five. I asked how things were, thinking of the impending global financial doom in the newspapers strewn around me, and he replied, 'Not bad actually. I've seen twenty-six red kites today already.'

Back in 1939 on his boat *Cressy*, Rolt had found the degraded state of the nation's canals that he discovered bewildering, especially when the tranquil and beautiful existence on the water was compared with the apparently purposeless chaos that had replaced it. There is no doubt from *Narrow Boat* that canals were a refuge from modernity for its author:

> To step down from some busy thoroughfare on to the quiet tow-path of the canal, even in the heart of a town, is to step backward a hundred years or more and to see things in a different, and perhaps more balanced, perspective. The rush of traffic on the road above seems to become the purposeless scurrying of an overturned anthill beside the unruffled calm of the water, which even the slow passage of the boats does not disturb.

I arrived in Pewsey to discover that sense of other-worldly detachment still intact. The idea of escape was particularly evident in the context of media reports wailing about financial catastrophe everywhere at the time. But on the Kennet and Avon canal you got the sense that, recession or no recession, things would simply remain as they always have been.

There was thick frost on the banks of the canal, with patches of ice floating between the reeds, and the serenity was undeniable. It was quiet, undisturbed and enchantingly beautiful. Ducks and swans eased carefully through the gloopy water with a backdrop of tall, motionless white grass and frost-flecked hills beyond. To the left under a sheath of mist a small bridge offered cars the continuation of another bland journey while the canal stalked slowly underneath, into a world of adventure and beyond. To my right a line of boats had stout plumes of smoke bubbling from their chimneys – the only source of fierce activity for as far as I could see. This was the ribbon of water that would be Ben and Cath's home until the spring.

Having travelled for five months through the nation's canals, they had settled on the Kennet and Avon because of its proximity to friends and family. The unspoilt, rural beauty seemed far removed from the industrial machines the canals would all eventually lead to. I walked slowly up the gravel path and saw Ben a little way down, clambering out to greet me. His and Cath's boat, *Constance*, was somewhat smaller than the vast 70-footers on either side of it. 'Narrow' boats were traditionally 7 feet wide, but today, thanks to subsidence, no boat wider than 6 foot 10 inches can guarantee passage throughout the canal system. Ben and Cath had chosen *Constance* with this in mind – she may have been less roomy than some of her companions, but no stretch of navigable water on the network, however narrow, was closed to her owners' curiosity.

I climbed down under a hoarding to find shoes and bits of general 'stuff' of the kind you'd see in anyone's porch before stepping down inside the boat itself and saw Cath, heavily pregnant, tending a cosy fire. The corridor of the boat had a sofa bed on its left, where Cath was reclining, with the fire opposite her to the right. A long window ran at eye-level along the length of the boat on either side. Behind the sofa I could see a small seating area around a table, a bookshelf and, beyond that, a small kitchen with a kettle proffering steam. It was astonishingly warm inside, which is not the first thing I had imagined about the inside of a canal boat. Cold and damp were what I had expected, but this was more like a hobbit hole than a shivering cellar. I soon discovered Ben saw it that way himself, something that no doubt added a new dimension of wonder to the heavily crumpled copy of *The Lord of the Rings* he'd been reading by the side of the fire before I arrived. Someone had told me that the inside of canal boats, and the people who live in them for that matter, always smell like ponds, but that myth turned out to be utter nonsense too. It was very homely indeed. Much more homely, in fact, than many large houses I've been to. Over a cup of tea around a small table it became clear very quickly that for Ben and Cath living on a canal was the perfect way to opt out from the chaotic mechanized world that the canals had helped create. Not for the first time I found myself in the presence of people who felt they didn't 'fit in' with the values of the modern world. I wondered whether this is what led them to choose life on the canal in the first place.

'It's been a happy discovery, but I don't think it was intended to be like that,' Cath explained. 'We spent three months travelling in New Zealand at the end of last year and realized we knew that country far better than our own. So we thought we'd come home and travel here for a while, and, well, you can't do it in a camper van and really escape, but a narrow boat seemed perfect. We spent most of our savings on the boat, and we've been living off the rest for the last five months. A lot of people think that if you're a boater you must be some kind of scrounger, but we're just very careful with what we have.'

I asked whether the rural idyll that L.T.C. Rolt had written of was still available, and Ben nodded. 'Definitely. The guy we bought this boat from said, "You'll love being on the canals; it's like being in this country fifty or sixty years ago." He was about seventy, so he knew what he was talking about, and he was absolutely right. If you break down or run out of fuel, somebody will always come by and say, "Are you all right?" and give you a ride to the boatyard if you need it. It's a nice way to live.' He grinned broadly. 'The sense of community is very real. You get lots of warm, friendly smiles, and when you're not on the water you immediately feel the loss of that. Even people in big, huge boats on the weekends that look down on you and perhaps think that they should have their own canal to go on and I should have one that's not quite so nice, even with them you're not completely cut off in the way you are on land. You still communicate. So it's a good leveller.'

I asked how living at such a slow pace had altered their perspective on life. 'In huge ways,' said Cath. 'Although we have always had different priorities from other people. When we got married, we agreed on the philosophy that time is more important than money. That's something that we both absolutely believe in, but living on the boat has made us realize we can actually live like that. Even when our stowaway comes,' she stroked her bump, 'and we end up back living on land, in the future we know you can live the way you want to if you are determined. We saw some friends last week who have two babies, and the husband doesn't see them from Sunday night through to Saturday morning because he works such long hours. He's on silly money, and they live in a huge, beautiful house. So you could look at them and say they're doing really well, but that's not for us. We're so glad to be away from looking at life in those terms.'

Ben nodded. 'It's definitely given us the chance to look at life differently. I've done lots of work in the building trade up till now, but I've never known what it is I really want to do. Being able to take the time out and get away from all the mania of "normal" life has been so beneficial and actually having time together without "work" rubbish being there as well. I'm now looking forward to getting back to earning money because I've worked out what it is that I want to do and not just because it's a job that pays X thousand pounds a year. Obviously a job has to pay the bills, but it's my life so it's got to be about more than that. So while we've been drifting along the canals, I'd say we've learned "how to live" stuff, and it's much easier to do that on here where you're in control of your own time than if you're spending every day thinking, "Oh, this job is doing my head in, but I can't be bothered to go home and think of something else I could do because I'm too knackered", so you just collapse in front of the TV, and the years race by.'

Having spent five months drifting around the countryside, they had, I imagined, enjoyed some interesting experiences. Ben moved forward and leaned across the table as though he was about to share a tantalizing secret.

'In many ways you're travelling through a lost country most of the time. We've been through some places where you stumble upon a huge estate with land that comes right down to the canal. The kind of place you'd never normally get to see. So not only is it amazing architecturally, to see these beautiful period houses in the country, but you're going through areas that you can't get access to in any other way. We'd be cruising all day and not see another boat moored up, let alone one moving. It was like we were in our own private world, and it just feels *so* special to be able to experience this country in that way. You're living much closer to nature too, which has been incredible.'

They began showing me pictures on a laptop of some of their most enjoyable moments. A picture soon flicked up of a mooring inside what looked like a city park. 'Going into Leicester was really amazing,' Ben continued. 'The day before we were in the middle of nowhere. You couldn't hear anything, it was so quiet, apart from owls in the night, and we didn't see anyone. The next day we took the boat right into the city. The outskirts, where the football ground is, are very industrial. There were kids tagging the bridges going "Give us a lift!" and we were "Er, no, it's OK", and they started shouting, "Don't tell anyone you saw us or we'll nick your boat!"' He laughed. 'But in the centre we found a secure mooring. There's a public park and at the back of the park there's a gate with steps down to the wharf where it's free to moor for up to forty-eight hours. You can buy a British Waterways key to access the water-points, refuse compounds, that kind of thing, all around the network. So our base was secure, but at night they lock the park from the outside too but, of course, we had a key to get into the park from the wharf while everyone else was locked out.' He shook his head nostalgically. 'It was such a great way to experience a city. We were in it but apart from it at the same time. That pretty much sums up being on the canals really.'

It certainly did sound as if they were living in a totally different country from the one those of us with jobs, mort-gages and televisions have got used to. It was apparent not just in the words they spoke either, but also in the relaxed and content demeanour they both radiated in front of their toasty fire. The small details about the way they had been living for the last five months that held self-evident wisdom to them came across to me as a series of epiphanies about the topsy-turvy values of the modern world. Life experience itself had become a kind of currency that they were now rich in. As if to reaffirm this, Cath smiled proudly and pointed out, 'Ben records all the birds he sees every day.'

Ben looked slightly embarrassed for a moment. 'Well, birds of prey mainly.'

Cath interjected '. . . and unusual things, like when we've seen water voles and otters.'

Ben became more relaxed. 'I've been doing it for a couple of years actually. I was working as a builder on places in the Sussex countryside and kept a note of buzzards, that kind of thing. But on here there's been so much more to look out for, like kingfishers. I remember when I opened my first bank account with Portman, and they did those wildlife calendars. I've always loved the kingfisher. But I never knew until recently, or I had never taken in before, the sound that it makes. Now that sound is second nature to me, it's a very comforting sound. We hear it so much. Before doing this I would never have thought I'd be able to identify a kingfisher by its sound. You just absorb the world so much more, I think, when you slow down.'

'We've slowed down so much that getting in a car now is terrifying,' Cath added, laughing.

Ben grinned. 'There's a boater's handbook you get from the Waterways Agency and it says that overtaking is banned! Well, not quite banned, but it's certainly frowned upon. If you come up to someone you should keep 500 yards back. Most people keep to that, but you can see people who are in a hurry, and we just pull over and let them go by. You do see some people going way too fast, hitting other boats and crashing into bridges. I don't think they've quite got the philosophy behind it. Hiring a canal boat so you can go fast – it's ridiculous!'

Fearful that their rosy picture of life on the water might sound smug, Cath then mentioned that, as August approached, the tranquillity became harder to find. 'In the summer the weekends can be pretty horrific, people go so much faster then, but the weeks are still quite pleasant. We would always find somewhere nice to moor by Thursday night or Friday lunchtime, because by the second part of Friday you'll get people dashing out and zooming up the canal to get somewhere by a certain time. So we'd just stop somewhere nice and let them get on with it. Maybe go for a walk to the nearest village, or just chill out and enjoy each other's company.'

Getting up to refill the kettle, Ben stopped to collect the mugs. 'But living slower is so much better than racing about. It's much easier to know what you want to do with your time, for one thing. Other stuff used to interfere with that when we were both working. Like you're too tired after work to make the effort to go out somewhere and do something. I mean, we both enjoy nature and wildlife, and this lends itself to that hugely, but now we're always open to it. Lying in bed at night, we sometimes get woken up because there's a little owl or a tawny owl a few metres away. Now if you're really busy working and you need your sleep and that woke you up, you'd be really annoyed and probably get cross about it. But for us that reaction just seems ridiculous. It doesn't matter what time of day or night it is, hearing something like that is just amazing, whenever it happens.'

Cath nodded, concluding 'We've learned that whatever happens in the future – if we live in a boat or not, with the baby coming we're thinking of other options now – we know that we always want to be somewhere that allows us to engage with life in the way that means something to us.'

I left with the smoke from their warm fire filtering the light of a bright full moon. I was completely unable to shake a question turning over and over in my mind. 'Why am I not living in a canal boat?' Although, to be fair, they did mention a few dark moments. Getting caught in a flood and stranded for a week didn't sound like much fun, although Ben confided in me that with hindsight it was 'awesome'. On a practical note, they had to empty their toilet every day, the shower was slightly basic and apparently the nights were getting chilly once the fire had gone out. But those downsides were surely offset by the benefits of living in such a wonderfully simple and poetic way.

The saddest part was the occasional bit of prejudice they had encountered for being 'boaters'. In their case it had come from a patronizing doctor rather than drunk passers-by. All in all, though, it seems that if you're looking for a machine that can help you escape from the rigid pain of the nine-to-five, then a narrow boat could well be for you. I was certainly very tempted by life on the water myself.

Of course, canals today are the exact opposite of the way they would have appeared when they were first built. For one thing most of the greenery around them, which gives them their quintessentially natural cloak, has sprung up since they were first carved through the countryside. To see them as they were requires us to imagine them like a brand new violent motorway being torn through the earth. It is because of this that boaters sometimes describe a canal as 'the cut', to reflect the difference between a man-made canal and a natural river. The building of the canals also meant that the age of localized services and industries was obliterated by mass transit and economies of scale. By 1820 there were over a hundred such canals in Britain, each as laborious and costly to build in its own way. Their existence meant that raw materials could be transported in bulk to and from factories all over the country. The comparative cheapness of coal this brought reduced the cost of living for the poor, while disease and famine within the new centres of labour diminished as fresh food could be moved around much more freely. Commerce began in a modern sense too, with the ease with which the wares from factories could reach the shops in towns and villages across the land. But, despite these improvements, it's worth remembering that the people that kept the new factories running in the new industrial towns still had a far lower quality of life than the rural generation that had come before.

Unsurprisingly, bearing in mind the nature of progress, very few working boats are still seen on the nation's waterways today, two and a half centuries on from the opening of the nation's first modern canal. Ben and Cath said they saw a fuel boat occasionally but that 99 per cent of the traffic was for pleasure. Initially the people who worked on the canals lived on land but as the railway age took hold, and fierce competition for transporting freight emerged, boaters moved their families aboard to save money. Wives and children could walk with the horses as they pulled the boats along and load and unload the freight, removing costly wage bills. One end of the boat became the cabin, in which the entire family lived, slept and ate, while the rest of the boat was given over to cargo. You can imagine how cramped the living conditions must have been, but you were still much better off squashed aboard a canal boat than working in the factories or living in the city slums that the canals travelled between. It was when the boats became homes that a totally new way of life began, an echo of which Ben and Cath were now enjoying. The canal community of families travelling up and down the country had to develop new ways of coping with such a transient life. The lack of education available on the cut created generations of canal folk who were largely illiterate. Combine that with a way of living that seemed remote from more conventional modes of life, and scorn and ignorance about boaters from the population at large began to emerge. This enforced separation from mainstream society led canal families to create and celebrate their own identity, traditions and values, which they chose to express in the brightly coloured decorative folk art that began to adorn their floating homes. The largely derided and 'dirty' perception of their way of life meant a tendency for fastidious cleanliness grew up. Every visible inch of their boats was kept polished, bright and clean to challenge the squalid stereotype in anyone who might be tempted to repeat it. These traditions of bright tidiness apparent on narrow boats are alive and well today, as, sadly, is the prejudice that caused them to appear defiantly in the first place. But it is surely the values of freedom of movement, vibrant colour and the slightly mysterious other-worldliness of life on the canals that inspire people seeking to find a more relaxed pace of life on the water today.

Twenty years on from the completion and success of the Bridgewater canal engineers began imagining far more radical routes across the country. The plans for the Thames and Severn canal through the Cotswolds included a mind-boggling 2-mile tunnel, which at the time of its opening would be the longest in Britain (it remains the third-longest tunnel even today). Designed, surveyed and built under the instruction of Robert Whitworth (who learned his trade as James Brindley's assistant), the Thames and Severn was to be 29 miles long, with forty-four locks, and would include the vast Sapperton tunnel. The mammoth project was hindered by the obvious practical problems inherent in funding and building something of this kind, but it also required Parliamentary permission. Letters from Whitworth to his family bemoan the amount of time it took politicians to pass the required Act, but assent was finally granted for the Thames and Severn in 1783. The entire project was finished six years later. Early plans had included a path along the canal inside the Sapperton tunnel, but it had proved to be too expensive. The horses that pulled the boat along the canal would have to be walked over the top to the other end while a team of 'leggers' lay on their backs on each barge and literally walked upside down for 2 miles, pushing their feet on the roof of the tunnel to move the boat along.

Considering it was one of the world's greatest expressions of the new ideas of science and reason at the time it was built, the Sapperton tunnel is haunting and almost supernatural when you go and look at it today. The eastern end is easy enough to track down, as it sits beneath a rather nice pub called the Tunnel House Inn, once frequented by a famous enthusiast we'll come to later: John Betjeman. The pub housed the navvies who built the tunnel with little more than shovels and gunpowder. If you walk down from the pub car park to the base of the canal, the opening of the tunnel appears immediately on your left. It looks like a dwarfish entrance to a subterranean world, but the canal itself is so shallow you can wade right into the mouth of the tunnel. Off to the right, the canal becomes little more than a quagmire of grass, water and silt – with tall, bricked walls that extend on to another bridge – before it meanders towards Oxford and off to our recent past. A high blue gate prevents you from walking into the tunnel itself, even if your nerves could take it. Of course, many men died building it, but little information remains of exactly how many or who they were.

Once you've seen where a tunnel begins, it becomes incredibly important to go and see where it ends. So I hopped back in the car with some companions, and a historical treasure hunt began. Sadly you cannot retrace the steps of the horses that would have ambled above ground while the leggers exhausted themselves some 65 metres below, because the wood it passes through is private land. But I knew that another pub, The Bell at Sapperton, lay not far from the opening, so we headed for that, and it was from there we began to slip and slide our way down the valley in the hope of finding the pinhole of light that signalled the end of the leggers' toil. We found a small school and followed the road, which fell sharply until we spotted a sign for a footpath called the Wysis Way. The path quickly disintegrated between overgrown banks of stinging nettles and grass before coming out by a horse trough and an undulating field of soft, wet grass. A path of silver green had been worn down through emerald surrounds, and at its end we found a stile, and beyond that, almost completely hidden under huge trees, was what looked like half of an ornate stone bridge at the base of a huge muddy bank. We were above and behind the opening and could only see the promontory of the tunnel rather than the mouth itself. So we were uncertain whether or not we'd found it, but the structure at the bottom of the large steep hill certainly looked promising. Our company included a three-year-old and a five-year-old, but I think I was even more excited than them at the prospect of finding our goal. It's always thrilling when you try and find your way around the countryside with a map and discover you are exactly where you thought you were and not unfathomably lost.

We walked over the top of the hand-hewn stones and down behind them to find an even more overgrown and dishevelled sight. I have to admit that I gasped. It was the nearest I'll probably, hopefully, come to understanding Charlton Heston's expression in the final scene of *Planet of the Apes*, when he comes face to face with the Statue of Liberty up to its waist in sand. There's something about the sight of a structure once heralded by men for its magnificence – in this case an engineering miracle – being devoured and reclaimed by the natural world, supplying a sense of ultimate irrelevance, despite our own ideas of grandeur, that we would all do well to remember. Here the 'canal' was just a boggy trench with full-grown trees reaching out of its base and up to the light, which made the sight of the tunnel even more mystifying. Then there was the opening itself, which was more awe-inspiring in its simplicity than the grand entrance 2 miles to the east. The blue gate at this end was broken and lay like a ladder down to the mud so that you could actually walk down and in, inviting you back 220 years to the sounds of explosions, rock falls and the jokes of the hard-working men – frequently to be found drunk on the job, with often tragic consequences – who gnawed their way through the rock. Discovering this end of the tunnel was thrilling and yet somehow rather mysterious and strange. It felt wonderfully liberating that such an immense thing could be 'lost' in this day and age. Now every scrap of land is accounted for on deeds in a plethora of bank vaults, and all the magic of this country where there was once space for the landscape to dream has seemingly vanished for ever.

The tunnel is part of a stretch of the Thames and Severn that is known as a 'ghost' canal, having been filled in many places and simply left to nature. We were so inspired by the mysterious possibilities of the canal bed winding its way further on through the over- and undergrowth that we left the cars at the pub and dived deep into a mix of history and our own imagination. Convinced we would all become Gullivers, for a few hours at least, we set off to discover where this ancient canal would take us in our own minds. In *Narrow Boat* Rolt wrote of the Thames and Severn sadly, because even then it was disused and looked as though it had 'lain idle for a century'; seventy years on, age had consumed her almost completely. Of all the canals Rolt longed to journey through aboard *Cressy*, this was the one he felt the loss of most keenly.

> Most beautiful and most tragic of all is the old Thames and Severn Canal, climbing up the Golden Valley between great hills that wear their beechwoods like a mane.

Even now, with its way blocked, covered and in tatters, you can imagine how wonderful it would be to slip serenely through such a perfect setting. As we tried to get our thoughts around the brilliance of the engineers and the savage toil of the men who brought their vision to life two centuries ago, we soon came across a blue sign warning us of danger and decay. Immediately behind it the ground dropped away. The swamp of grass vanished, and 20 feet down brickwork was visible again – it was one of the forty-four locks. In places the 'canal' has been filled in so that the towpath is now the only reminder of the waterway that used to exist, but now and again another lock would appear, seeming as absurd as a dishwasher in an impenetrable forest, and we began to notice that the earth's memory of the canal had not vanished completely. It has become just a shallow trench between these old locks that runs alongside the River Frome. We had to climb over trees that had fallen across the pathway, and in places stalks and insects sought to deny our way altogether. A little further on we came across another devoured lock. Intriguing, almost frightening, it was a wonderful, evocative day of discovery and surprise. We were sucked into thoughts of the ephemeral nature of human 'progress', the wonder of the men who fought and trudged their way to build these enormous rivers and locks and the poetry of nature reclaiming what will always be hers – something that she lent us for a time, but on which our lease has long since expired.

The Cotswold Canal Trust has reopened parts of the Thames and Severn and raised funds to extend their programme further still. Apparently there are even plans to restart boat trips through a part of the Sapperton tunnel. One day it is sure to reopen in its finery, but I will always treasure the magic of the discovery we made that afternoon. I began to wonder whether preserved buildings and monuments give less a hint of their past than of our modern values in the act of their restoration. Perhaps some things should be left to slip away, because the awareness that they are adrift gives you a more literal window into long-forgotten days. Decay is the act of time, and these canals were built so long ago that to see them brittle and overgrown gives back their own temporal life, rather than the unreal but eternal life granted to exhibits in a museum. To walk along the ruin of that canal is literally to see the two hundred years of time that have elapsed in the formation of huge trees that have grown between the stones brought by men at the base of the canal itself. You can see the years of foliage climbing over man's memory, which he seeks to tattoo into the landscape for ever with his efforts, seeking immortality when such a concept gives the lie to the definition of time itself.

It was around the time that the Sapperton tunnel was being constructed that the practical British Enlightenment I mentioned earlier began to emerge. In the new industrial midlands and the north, miles away from prying metropolitan eyes, these pioneers had the luxury of experiment, failure and the camaraderie of being among kindred spirits. One particular group met every month on the night of a full moon. In keeping with the new age this decision was not, as you might think, linked to some kind of superstition. It had a purely practical application. A full moon allowed much safer and easier passage across the nation's primitive road network at a time when there was no form of street lighting. (Incidentally, every imaginable outdoor event at this time took place in the days leading up to and after a full moon for the same reason. An interesting aside that hints at how much closer people at the time were to the whims and rhythms of the natural world than we are today.) These men were inspired by a concept that seems odd to us in our specialized and compartmentalized world. To them science, art, philosophy and chemistry were all components of a single discipline: natural philosophy. They were the Lunar Men and included Matthew Boulton (1728–1809), Josiah Wedgwood (1730–1795), Erasmus Darwin (1731–1802), Joseph Priestley (1733–1804), Joseph Wright (1734–1797) and James Watt (1736–1819).

An Experiment on a Bird in the Air Pump, by Joseph Wright of Derby, can be seen in the National Gallery today. For an age of such excitement one of the most iconic paintings of the time seems incredibly foreboding. It depicts a man in a red dressing gown suffocating a bird by placing it in a jar and slowly pumping out the air. The picture has been explained as an expression of the fear in the public mind about the new knowledge shown by the experiment – something that begins to make sense when you look at the political events of the time. The new scientific era was undoubtedly an exhilarating one, but not everyone was convinced that the new empirical ideas of reason and experiment, which seemed to undermine the establishment of religion and monarchy, boded well for the future. The lessons of the Civil War were fresh in the minds of many and, while those of a revolutionary bent would soon welcome the upheaval in France, any potential loss of the monarch aroused uncertainty and fear, especially as the years went on and news of the horrific working conditions in the industrial factories that science and reason had led to began reaching the population at large. These days such a reaction to technological progress would be seen as absurd. Invention and 'progress' are considered by definition a good thing just as long as they provide military supremacy or financial wealth. Back in the late eighteenth century other things were valued too: things such as civilization, not to mention the human soul.

In the National Gallery Wright's picture sits opposite a painting by Turner, appropriately of a steamship and a sailboat at war. Elsewhere in the gallery, Room 13 to be precise, you'll find a small room that contains portraits of some of the Lunar Men. Erasmus Darwin looks the happiest of all, in his portrait by his friend Joseph Wright. He is so fat he is literally bursting out of his blue jacket, but the table hides much of his girth, along with his wooden leg. The grandfather of Charles Darwin, Erasmus was a doctor of great repute and something of a biologist himself. One of his books, *The Botanic Garden*, was particularly well received and featured an engraving by another contemporary: William Blake. Darwin was an inventor too: he devised a machine that was able to speak, but not sufficiently well to recite the Lord's Prayer and thus win a bet with another man on the wall, Matthew Boulton. Boulton looks like he has lots on his mind: debts, probably. Despite his huge success in building the Soho Manufactory in Birmingham, which made everything from buttons and toys to, eventually, coins for the Royal Mint (spies regularly came from all over Europe to try and copy the vast machines that punched out his wares), not to mention the money earned with the steam engines he funded and co-owned with his friend James Watt, Boulton was always working on something bigger and better. James Watt, too, seems to be worrying about something. Perhaps it was the end of his patent, which prevented anyone from improving the design of his steam engine. It would expire in 1800, eight years after the portrait was painted. (As soon as the patent ran out, Richard Trevithick was waiting in the wings, as we'll find out in Chapter 3.) After a lifetime worrying about money, workers destroying his engines in the Cornish mines and the cavalier attitude of his business partner, Watt eventually acquired enough security from his invention to blossom into a happy and contented retirement. Joseph Banks, the great botanist who worked with George III to improve the Gardens at Kew, sits there on the wall as well, painted after he had sailed on *Endeavour* with Captain Cook. Joseph Priestley's portrait is smaller than the others. He looks a little self-righteous, but perhaps had a right to feel proud having discovered oxygen, or 'dephlogisticated air' as he called it, before creating carbonated water for the first time. After that he began preaching his way into a self-imposed exile in America in 1794. Inspired by events in France, which the Lunar Men all largely welcomed, he rather fanned the flames of revolution at home. An angry mob took exception to his views and burned his house to the ground in 1791. Priestley fled to America for his own safety. The public's fears of a French-style revolution following the scientific revolution in England turned on the advancements of the Lunar Men in the end.

More peripheral Lunar figures are on the walls with them, including James Brindley, with one of his viaducts in the background behind him. John 'Iron Mad' Wilkinson is there on the wall also. He spent years perfecting techniques for boring more precise cannons for the army but quickly diversified into making incredibly accurate cylinders which he supplied for Boulton and Watt's revolutionary steam engines. One of them was used to pump water to the highest reaches of the Thames and Severn canal, including Sapperton tunnel, when the water level fell too low for the boats to travel through. Wilkinson's love of iron extended to his coffin and a huge obelisk to mark his final resting place. Bizarrely, his coffin was later pinched.

Many of the Lunar Men are missing from their small room in the National Gallery, but perhaps the most well-known absentee is Josiah Wedgwood, the potter and entrepreneur, who pushed not just the boundaries of production, taste and design but also the world of commerce with his catalogues, door-to-door salesmen and – incredibly modern by today's standards – London boutique to sell his wares. Needless to say, the Lunar Men had enthusiastically backed the canal-building programme of the 1760s. Bolton and Wedgwood saw it as the opportunity they needed to move their products to wider markets and put up considerable quantities of money for their construction, while others, notably Darwin, fancied them purely for their investment potential. It was an extraordinarily bold action for Boulton and Wedgwood.

George III thought as much when he came to visit the Sapperton tunnel a year before it opened. He 'expressed the most decided astonishment at a work of such magnitude, expense, and general utility, being conducted by private persons'. But the actions of the Lunar Men give a hint of the idea they were all drenched in — that anything was possible. Wedgwood was to proclaim that they were 'living in an age of miracles, in which anything could be achieved', even if that meant getting boats to float deep underground or high through the air. To slightly misquote the phrase of Immanuel Kant's that has come to define the Enlightenment, they certainly dared to know.

Glancing between their portraits is a humbling experience. The men would meet every month when they could and dine together to catch up as friends before performing their latest experiments and explaining their latest scientific and philosophical ideas. Priestley's experiments with 'dephlogisticated air' led to them all inhaling vast quantities of pure oxygen and laughing gas, and Watt's iron dragons entranced them all, urging him to keep them all up to speed with developments as they were made. In 1783 they were so enthralled by the Montgolfier brothers' first public hot-air balloon flight in Annonay in France that they set about recreating it, with varying degrees of success. Boulton's attempt, with help from Priestley's experiments with hydrogen, exploded a few miles away from the launch site, causing confusion and panic in a nearby village. Watt later claimed that it was a serious experiment to discover whether the noise of thunder was generated by an echo from a single explosion or by a series, but you get the impression of a slightly eccentric group of men who can't contain their excitement in world that had suddenly decided to unleash some of its secrets. Jenny Uglow, who wrote the wonderful book *The*

Lunar Men, The Friends Who Made the Future, condenses their spirit thus:

> They felt the greatness of the cosmos and its limitless pos-
> sibilities, the beauty of the infinitely small – the bud, the
> grain of quartz, the microscopic animalcule – and the grand-
> eur of the vast, the thundering force of steam, the rolling
> clouds, the relentless flow of lava over aeons. They knew
> that knowledge was provisional, but they also understood
> that it brought power, and believed this power should
> belong to us all.

It is a sentiment that would not be shared by the men set to stand on their giant shoulders in the years ahead.

If you walk on past the portraits of the Lunar Men in the National Gallery, you are confronted with paintings of the great and the not-so-great that have come after them. The portraits of the Lunar men (some of whom even dare to smile) seem far less pretentious than the aristocrats, royalty and military and naval heroes that surround them – a small pocket of human triumph, perhaps, in endless halls of triumphalism.

A little further on you are spared the paintings of kings, dukes, queens, barons, Regency clowns and busts of politicians to find the reassuring faces of Turner, Coleridge, Mary Shelley, Percy Bysshe Shelley, Keats and Wordsworth (the Romantic poets, valuing intense emotions that had previously been seen as merely a threat to civilized life, released the word 'enthusiasm' from its chrysalis of religious suspicion to describe their rapturous appreciation of the natural world), and on the faces go. You then come to a portrait of a man called William Beckford and, despite his having nothing whatsoever to do with machines, I can't resist mentioning him quickly here. If nothing else, he gives a sense of the spirit of the times. Born in 1760 to astonishing wealth, he succeeded in wasting most of it building wonderful yet utterly pointless buildings, known as follies, most famously Fonthill Abbey, which had a 300-foot octagonal tower that was completed in 1807. Lord Nelson and Lady Hamilton visited when it was finished, but its foundations were no match for the ludicrous height of Beckford's ambition, and it later collapsed. It's fair to say that he was an eccentric when that word meant more than a person who collects garden gnomes. He did a spot of travel writing and also wrote a Gothic novel called *Vathek*, which is generously referred to on the paperback edition as 'difficult to classify', and generally lived a life of extravagance and scandal. He died at the age of eighty-four and left strict instructions to be put in a pink granite sarcophagus on the top of an artificial burial mound in the fashion of the Saxon kings, from whom he claimed to be descended. They don't make them like that any more.

Beyond Beckford I reached George Stephenson. But before we get to Stephenson's famous Rocket of 1829, we have to stop off somewhere more grounded and unexpected.

2

Integrity

Lawn mowers

I T WAS 2.30 in the morning, and I was driving in the Sussex countryside with the window down, attempting to summon the sound of engines from an eerie July night. I was on the trail of an invention from 1827 by a man called Edwin Beard Budding. Budding (who also invented the adjustable spanner) filed a patent in 1830 describing his latest innovation as 'a new combination and application of machinery for the purpose of cropping or shearing the vegetable surfaces of lawns, grass plats [plots] and pleasure grounds'. His patent continued: 'Country gentlemen may find in using my machine themselves an amusing, useful and healthy exercise.' He had no idea how far-sighted those words would turn out to be. Budding had invented the next machine on our list: the humble lawn mower.

I was feeling rather tired, having already driven for three hours to get back from an eco-festival in the Cambridge countryside. There I'd appeared alongside Jay Griffiths, author of a magical book called *Wild*, to talk about how to free ourselves from a tamed and mechanized world. The festival was full of people who were rather surprised to hear I had to leave early to go to an overnight lawn-mower race. 'That's not really you, is it, Dan?' one of them replied on hearing I had to scarper. As I hurried away, he shouted, 'You'll miss the discussion tomorrow about why Tesco is evil!' But I was already mentally somewhere else. My event with Jay Griffiths had been particularly interesting. She had talked about how it is a connection to the land that allows us to retain some of our wild spirit, even in the modern age. Lawn-mower racing seemed vaguely related to me. It was a connection with the earth, of sorts. My life was zigzagging between the natural and the mechanical words, and I was beginning to enjoy the contradictions and potential parallels I could find between these apparently opposite points of view.

I had a vague notion of where I was going, but the bright yellow AA signs I'd been hoping for hadn't yet appeared. I was on the audible scent of a particularly zany breed of machine enthusiast. Then at last I spotted a sign: '12-Hour Lawn-Mower Race This Way.' At last, I'd found the race-track for the lawn-mower equivalent of the Le Mans 24-hour rally. I pulled up off the A29 into what looked like a farmer's field and soon spotted two rather tired and bemused people sitting in fluorescent yellow jackets next to a small red moneybox. I asked if this was where I should pay the £4 entry fee. 'Yes,' the man grunted. I asked where I should park and he gestured at an almost empty field. I could see the yellow floodlights in the distance and drove the car slowly and unsteadily over the bumpy, heavily ploughed earth. As I got closer, the sound of lawn-mower engines began to become perceptible above the general hum, and I soon began to see machines themselves being flung around the track at speeds they were surely not originally designed for. The race had been going for four and a half hours by the time I got there and still had another seven and a half hours to go. The rules were simple. Whoever managed the most laps in a 12-hour period won the race.

I could see ten or fifteen cars parked up, but there didn't seem to be any conscious spectators, although there was a tea van, a carvery truck and a refreshment lorry. Despite having scoffed a Mars bar and drunk a pint of Coke in an attempt to wake myself up on the way down from Cambridge, I was drifting dangerously towards slumber, so I went to get a cup of tea. The lady running the refreshment lorry refused to sell me one, though, and ushered me to the 'tea van' further up. 'He only sells tea. We sell tea but we sell other things too, so you'd better buy your tea from him if that's all you want. Unless you want a pasty with your tea?' I wasn't really in the mood, so I thanked her for her wonderfully uncapitalist attitude and wandered up to see the tea man. Pleasantries with him soon turned into a conversation about the 'bloody mad' people driving their lawn mowers. It was the fourth year in a row he'd come to sell tea at the race, and I was lucky to catch him, as he was about to close for a few hours to get some sleep.

The track was in an enormous, stunted 'U' shape about the size of a couple of large golf holes, and we were in the bottom of the 'U', on its inside. The noise was astonishing. I had to shout into my Dictaphone in front of my mouth to get it to discern my voice above the cacophony behind it. On the track people hunched forward in sit-down lawn mowers thundered along. Then I spotted someone practically lying down in a makeshift seat behind what looked like a push-along mower. The speeds were terrifying, so that you could barely glimpse the drivers properly before they'd bounced and swerved away. I'd imagined it would all be a bit of a laugh, but they were clearly taking it very, very seriously indeed. Then I got a good look at another mower, number 71: apparently not going fast enough to use the track itself, it was bumbling along outside the hay bales that marked its edge. The driver was wearing a pink boiler suit and a helmet with deely boppers on it. Embroidered on the back of the suit were the words 'Boozy Birds'. They, clearly, were not taking it quite as seriously as some of the others.

To my right was what looked like a mini-version of an aircraft control tower, from where the commentators occasionally fed the audience news of the race over a Tannoy. All the way along the bottom part of the 'U' on the other side was the pit lane, where the competitors frantically tried to keep their lawn mowers alive. When I say 'pit lane', I mean marquees decorated with fairy lights full of family members and friends all drinking cans of beer and eating barbecued food, in front of whom were the technical crews, who I assumed were not partaking in the excessive drinking of beer because of the hard graft it clearly took to keep the machines running. There was an incredible smell of burning oil that seemed to waft in with or without the breeze. It was mechanical chaos under a sliver of a summer moon.

Number 13 came growling round the corner and went up on its two right-hand wheels before the driver began waving nonchalantly at the people in the control tower. It was all clearly very well organized, but that made the obvious battiness of it even more hilarious. Apart from the stewards, all wearing 1960s astronaut-like orange jump-suits, the people running the food and drink vans and the throng of people in the pit lane there were only about three paying spectators watching apart from me. Then again, it was nearly 3 a.m. – perhaps more people had come at the start and would turn out for the finish.

I went down to the control tower to try and talk to the organizers and spotted a scoreboard, which made very little sense to me but which I assumed gave out the lap times and the number of laps each team had managed. The teams had lots of grass-related puns in their titles – 'The Cutting Crew', 'Grim Reapers', 'Grass Bandits', 'Pain in the Grass Racing'

– but my favourite was definitely 'Mow-Claren'. I soon found a beaming man in orange trousers reclining on a floral sofa inside an enormous tent that looked out on to the track. The tent was empty apart from him. I waved, and he gestured for me to come and sit down. The noise here was intense for the brief moment when a lawn mower passed, but quiet immediately before and after. I introduced myself and discovered he was Charlie George, one of the race organizers. I asked him when and where 'lawn-mower racing' had come from. Inevitably perhaps, he began to chuckle.

'Well, believe it or not, lawn-mower racing was devised in a pub. Our chairman, Jim Gavin, was in the Cricketer's Arms in Wisborough Green thirty-odd years ago with some mates, and they were talking about motor sport being far too expensive. They wanted to find a cheap way of doing it, and they hit on the idea that everyone's got a lawn mower in the shed (apparently their first idea was to race combine harvesters). So it all started on the village green one Sunday morning with ordinary push-along garden mowers.'

The lawn mowers continued to zip past at ungainly speeds, far faster than any lawn mower I'd ever seen. I asked him what relation they were to ordinary lawn mowers.

'Well, every machine out there has been sold to cut grass on a domestic lawn, and that's the main rule. It started with the run-behind machines, but it rapidly progressed to the 24-inch ones for cutting the village green or a cricket pitch with a trailing seat. Then somebody got a ride-on machine, and it developed from there to the 36-inch-cut machines we've got here.

'We celebrated our 25th anniversary a few years ago with a 25-hour race. In a 12-hour race the teams can have a maximum of three drivers driving a machine for four hours each, but for the 25-hour race we allowed them to have five.'

I asked him why, he thought, people did it.

'Why not? It's one of those eccentric things, isn't it? What else would you be doing on a Saturday night at three in the morning in July? Only in England . . . But seriously, you can set yourself up racing for £1,000, which is not a lot of money these days. At our normal sprint races people come along, they have competitive racing and a nice social evening. We've done international races. There are some guys here from Luxembourg, so we've been over there to race against them. We've raced in Belgium, France, Ireland and even Chicago. There is an American Lawn Mower Racing Association run by a guy called Bruce, who's an absolute . . . well, I'm sure you can imagine.'

I wondered whether the attraction simply came down to the machines.

'With the 12-hour race it's the challenge of keeping the machine going through the night. That's why people do it. We run it from eight in the evening on the Saturday to eight in the morning on Sunday, and then we spend the rest of the day on Sunday clearing up. Just before you arrived, a girl came in, and she was explaining that their mower broke down at about one minute past eight and then the guys spent the next three hours fixing it. Once they'd got it fixed, they realized that the engine had gone bang at the same time and had a hole in it, so they've now changed the engine and they're racing again, but they think it's only going to race for about five or six laps.'

I told him it all sounded wonderfully hapless.

'It is a bit, yes. I mean, some teams are very serious about it, but others just want to be involved. There's a group of guys over there that bought a machine three weeks ago, and they've fixed it up for racing, so it's half-way between a racing machine and a normal machine, and they just want to enter and get that machine to the finish. They don't care about where they come. They just want to get to the end.'

I mentioned the origin of the word 'enthusiast' and asked what he thought these people were inspired by, but I should have known not to ask a serious question in such absurd surroundings.

'I don't know about that, but you go and find out what the word is for being inspired by petrol, because I'm probably one of those. I follow most forms of motor sport, but I'm actually an aircraft engineer, so I work on big machines all the time. Boeing 747s. I maintain them at Gatwick Airport. I should be on the night shift tonight.'

I left Charlie and staggered back to the car to try and get some sleep. It was 3.30 a.m., and the drivers still had another four and a half hours to go. After contorting myself in the driver's seat for a while, with the relentless thud of the engines all around me, I finally dropped off.

It turns out that Edwin Beard Budding's invention of the lawn mower was not entirely deliberate. He was working in a local woollen mill when the mill owner was commissioned to make guards' uniforms for the army. Unhappy with the end-product – the coats were covered with tufts, knobbly bits of wool and loose thread – he asked Budding to design a machine that would give the cloth a smarter finish. The machine Budding came up with used what's now known as 'the cylinder cutting principle' – a revolving blade moving over a fixed blade. The mill owner was delighted with Budding's contraption, and the inventor began to wonder what else he could use it for. He soon turned his attention to garden lawns but was concerned that those around him might think he was some kind of lunatic, so he carried out his tests in the middle of the night. His fears that a new 'lawn mower' wouldn't be taken seriously proved correct, conventional thinking at the time being that a professional scythe man, who was capable of getting a bowling green finish, was unlikely to be bettered by a machine, so Budding joined forces with a local engineering firm with more established agricultural connections and turned his attention to marketing instead.

This is where the phrase from his patent submission came in again – 'Country gentlemen may find in using my machine themselves an amusing, useful and healthy exercise' – and this principle, that the man of the house should take care of and have pride in his lawn, has been with us ever since. Most people will have memories of their father out on a Sunday afternoon taking an almost pathological glee in creating a perfectly manicured lawn with full parallel stripe effect. Unless, of course, he had a grass cutter and not a lawn mower, in which case the stripes would have been much harder to achieve. You see, grass cutters and lawn mowers are not the same thing, which I now realize is the reason I never managed to get stripes on our lawn when cutting the grass became my job. I discovered this mower/cutter distinction from Brian Radam, the owner of the world's only lawn mower museum, in Southport, Lancashire (and two-time lawn-mower racing champion in the 1980s himself)

You can get a glimpse of the lawn-mower world online (www.lawnmowerworld.co.uk), but in the iron the machines are fabulous to behold and much brighter and more colourful than you might expect. Brian began by pointing out a lawn mower made by Rolls-Royce as we walked beyond the 'lawn mowers of the stars' section. (Prince Charles and Princess Diana's, Hilda Ogden's and Joe Pasquale's stood out – no, I'm not making this up.)

Brian was bursting with knowledge about lawn mowers and with his passion for the excellence of British engineering, which he was convinced had all but slipped away.

'Lawn mowing is a very British thing. With cars and motor bikes, those sorts of thing, every country could be passionate about them, but Britain is very passionate about lawn mowers. We have the best lawn mowers in the world, and we also have the best lawns, although we're losing them both. As people go to replace their lawn mower, and perhaps go to the supermarket or something, they'll often come back with a grass cutter without realizing it. But if you're wanting a formal lawn – to have it rolled, striped and cut perfect – then you need a cylinder-cutting machine. That was the kind of blade that Edwin Budding invented, and it's still the same principle today. A grass cutter is like a rotary-type machine that just thrashes the grass like a propeller to keep it short. A cylinder cutter cuts like a pair of scissors and gives you a perfect cut.'

Brian seemed slightly pained as his lament gathered pace.

'We're living in a different social time, you see, whereas in the past your lawn and garden showed what class you were – it was much more important than it is today. To me lawn mowing is a relaxing form of exercise, but I do have a large lawn and I have several lawn mowers. I can use a 1926 APCO machine with a crank-handle start, but I also use a sit-on one. I've got a Robot one too. It's just something about cutting the grass that people used to love, and some, like me, still do. I heard on the radio the other day the nation's second favourite smell is freshly cut grass. It's part of our nationality, I suppose.' I asked what the nation's favourite smell was, assuming it to be cooked bacon, but I got the sense from Brian that I had missed the point.

'I don't know.' He collected himself.

'Lawn mowers are a very strange subject really. We get a

lot of people that visit the museum who've got lots of lawn mowers at home. All sorts of collectors. But the history of lawns is a fascinating one. I could go on for an hour without mentioning lawn mowers at all. Originally you'd have had gangs of eight men with scythes followed by eight women and children collecting the cuttings. It was a very labour-intensive job but they were very, very skilled – the scythe men – in those days. I suppose if you use a scythe eight times a day, you get good at it. The best time to cut the grass was early in the morning or late in the evening, when the grass was slightly moist.'

Staring around at the vast collection of slightly lurid green and red contraptions, some of which looked like monsters from a slightly camp, mechanical Hammer Horror movie, I asked Brian how he had become the world's foremost authority on lawn mowers, and he looked a little surprised, as though the thought hadn't occurred to him before.

'I suppose . . . we *are* the only lawn-mower museum in the world. We have all the original patents, blueprints, that sort of thing, and we restore vintage garden machinery here. Originally my father started Southport's only DIY shop in 1945, and he repaired lawn mowers. He ended up with lots of machines that were too expensive to repair There were no parts available for them, they were too old, and when it came to actually throwing these machines out, I said, "Well, perhaps this one by Royal Enfield shouldn't be thrown out, we could restore that one, and perhaps this one by Rolls-Royce", and it sort of went from there. A lot of companies that made lawn mowers aren't usually associated with lawn mowers, you see. You've got to remember that you're at a period of time where British engineering was the best in the world. Now everything is made abroad, and those prestige companies have all gone, which is a real shame.'

The sadness in his voice threatened once again, but then he looked at the machines surrounding him and his expression lifted.

'Now these, you see, they've all been handmade. They've all got character, a nice sound. The first mass-produced ones didn't really start until the 1920s. The companies then were building a machine that would last a lifetime. Unfortunately those companies are gone now because they only sold the one. But these days things are designed and built specifically to fail. They've all been manufactured with "serious economic restraint", and they're made to the lowest cost. You have to buy another one within a few years. But these old lawn mowers were made with what you might call old-fashioned values like integrity, that's the thing. Whatever you buy today is going to be out of date in twelve months, and that changes the production process completely. But these lawn mowers simply weren't made like that. One of the machines we have here, the Green's Silens Messor (*silens messor* is Latin for "silent cutter"), is in the *Guinness Book of Records* for not changing the model for seventy years. They made a product; it is perfect, so why change it? It was so well made there was no need to alter the design. You could still use it today. '

He pointed at the Rolls-Royce mower again.

'Take the Rolls-Royce machines. That was a company called Jerram and Pearson, and they just set out to make the best lawn mower it was possible to make, and when it came on to the market, they advertised it as the "Rolls-Royce" of Lawn mowers. Rolls-Royce was so impressed that they actually bought the company. The engineering was that good. They were very expensive, though, and in the end too costly to produce. But when they came out, at first people bought them because they thought, "We'll get that one because it's a quality thing. It's going to last a long time and it's going to do a good job." So back then it wasn't just about making things for the cheapest price. We've got one lawn mower here that when it was released was the price of a small house!'

I found it very interesting that someone could develop a fascination for a machine because of the integrity with which it had been built, which had largely disappeared in the nakedly commercial motives behind machine production today. I asked whether he thought this integrity might account for why men were so obsessed with machines, but he shook his head.

'Well, it's a man's toy, isn't it? Like the garden shed to some men is their castle. They like to show they can make something work, but even that seems to be slipping. We take a lot of work-experience lads from school, and they don't do metalwork any more, they don't do woodwork, they're not doing the practical skills. They're leaving school not knowing what a nut and bolt is, and never having had a screwdriver in their hand. You don't need the practical skills today. You used to need to know all these things, of course, but not any more.'

The idea that practical skills have been rather devalued reminded me of a conversation I'd had with a friend of mine who was a Design and Technology teacher at a secondary school in Wales. He'd been at the school for a year when he discovered from a pupil who had asked his head of year if he could take Design Technology that 'academically talented pupils do not waste time doing DT'. In that school this attitude had now been successfully challenged, but it makes you wonder how widely held this perception is. It seems practical skills are not considered appropriate for 'clever' people any more.

Brian, meanwhile, moved on to explain the lengths he was prepared to go to preserve the memory of vintage lawn mowers.

'The sounds are gone too. Like you will remember the sound of an old typewriter. Well, these kids at school now have never heard one. So we just professionally recorded the sound of each of our lawn mowers working to go into a sound archive. So people in the future will always be able to hear the sound of these mowers. If they want to.'

There was an undeniable twinge of regret in the way Brian spoke about his preferred machine. For him the philosophy behind vintage machines was slipping away. I've always wondered why old machines are the ones that men really salivate over, and perhaps it's because often they were designed and built with a completely different motivation from most made today. This is something everyone will have noticed. Only last year we bought a washing machine that illustrates this point perfectly. My little boy was rather fond of the machine's buttons, especially the lights and beeps it made when he fiddled with them, and so he pressed them frequently, despite my telling him not to (while going from one shade of red to, eventually, a particularly dark purple). One day the washing machine stopped working, and I called out a repair man as calmly as I could. He told me that the machine was perfectly fine, in great condition actually, but the computer inside it was broken. The cost of putting in a new computer was £250. The cost of the brand new machine was £230. There was nothing wrong with the machine mechanically, but it went to the tip because it was more expensive to fix than to buy a new one. (We would have paid the extra £20, but he said it would take months to order a new computer, and he wasn't sure how to install it if we did.) The manufacturer had done everything possible to deter us from fixing it.

The subject then turned to racing. Brian began to reminisce about his days on the circuit but found sadness in that subject too.

'To be honest, I don't think people who are into lawn-mower racing are really into lawn mowers; they're just into racing. It's the best you can get for the smallest amount of money. It attracts some interesting people, though. Stirling Moss is a keen lawn-mower racer, as was Chris Tarrant. But Oliver Reed was quite into it too. He drove a lawn mower into a toilet cubicle at a race I was at once and ran someone over a few weeks later. I think he was half-cut at the time.'

My visit to Southport soon had me reminiscing over my own experiences with lawns, neither of which had instilled in me a love of lawn mowers – quite the opposite actually. The first was a temporary addiction I'd developed to sniffing the rather pungent and mildly toxic smell of fermented grass cuttings when I was about nine. My dad used to leave the cuttings in a bin in the garage, and I became quite keen on lifting the lid and inhaling the fumes. It took some time for me to develop an interest in other, more intoxicating, types of grass. The second episode that comes to mind where my world and the world of the lawn coincided was a particular front garden up the road from where I lived as a teenager. Of all the lawns in the neighbourhood this particular one really stood out – not because it had the kind of lines you'd expect on a football pitch but because the man who tended it sprayed limitless amounts of water all over it in the midst of a hose-pipe ban, and, more importantly to me perhaps, his beautiful but seemingly frustrated wife used to stare out the window at him longingly while he tended his lawn. To my lascivious teenage mind it seemed that she'd have much rather he attended to her instead. For some reason my friends and I really took exception to his lust for his lawn, and so we resolved to do something about it. Happily for two of us, at the time we were working as weed sprayers, a humiliating and miserable profession, but it at least meant that we had large amounts of industrial weedkiller at our disposal. When I say 'weedkiller', I mean a chemical created in the laboratories of the world's most loathed chemical company and designed to destroy any living plant. (We'd spent the summer spraying around the brambles that smothered the tiny trees on the banks of the M3.) One night at about three in the morning, after large amounts of alcohol, we embarked, ninja-like – well, like shamefully intoxicated ninjas anyway – and darted up the road, giggling, to the lawn in question. Once there, we decided to graffiti his lawn with this industrial plantkiller. I won't detail the specific words we spelled out here for fear of legal action, but suffice to say his lawn was utterly and profanely ruined. As callous and awful as it clearly is to damage someone else's property, I think writing graffiti with industrial weedkiller that takes up to a week to take effect but is impervious to mowing (having penetrated into the earth itself) showed great creativity. By the time it took effect we were long gone, but three years later one of the words was still clearly legible. Now the irony of desecrating a garden in the name of preserving the environment seems much clearer to me than it did then, but I suppose it does illustrate perfectly the joyous and indefatigable paradox of the teenage mind.

There is one bit of perfectly manicured grass that does get me rather excited, however, and that's the hallowed turf of St Mary's Stadium, the football ground of Southampton FC. If I was to have any hope of understanding the allure of the lawn-mower enthusiast, then that was surely the bit of grass I had to visit. I contacted the club to see if I could go and see their award-winning groundsman, Andy Gray, and try my hand at mowing the sacred pitch. According to the press department, of all the people working at the club Andy did the fewest interviews, but they said it should be fine and, sure enough, a few days later I arrived excitedly at the ground.

Strictly speaking, Andy isn't a lawn-mower enthusiast, but he was a professional lawn mower ist, and that was good enough for me. In fine drizzle I got momentarily confused about which entrance I should go to, but a few apologetic mobile phone calls later I found myself standing on the edge of the pitch, feeling rather overcome. Here I was at the site of my only real 'male' obsession. I'm not *that* obsessive about Saints but, apart from my immediate family, my attachment to Southampton FC is the longest meaningful relationship I have ever had. People who don't understand the devotion of football fans never seem to grasp that this is the nature of the attachment. Since I started watching Saints, they have never been very far from my consciousness, and because I am now thirty-three, that adds up to a lot of years and, in the case of Saints, a lot of tears. All I know is that, when they score, it feels better than when England do, even if we're playing the MK Dons and England have just put one past Argentina. I began to wonder whether my love of football and the machine enthusiast's passion for machines were comparable. Brian had pointed out that his interest in lawn mowers was down in part to his father, and it was my dad who had taken me to the Dell (Southampton's old ground) when I was six years old. It was largely due to him that I have largely had the abject misery of supporting Saints loyally ever since. I spend a fortune on tickets, getting there on the train and beers before, during and after, and invariably see us get slaughtered, but that's strangely not the point, although I do feel a lot happier if we win. It's about being able to shout your head off in a totally unthinking, partisan way while catching up with old mates. Football is often portrayed in a kind of philosophically profound way, but I don't see any real evidence of it myself, certainly not these days. Like the production of lawn mowers, football has little or no integrity left any more, but supporting a football team does provide a powerful sense of belonging. I wondered whether the camaraderie of machine obsessives provided a similar thing.

Andy appeared to be slightly bemused about being interviewed, but I asked what had attracted him to the job, assuming he too was a Saints fan, only for him to reply, rather pointedly, 'Well, I like working outside, and I like working on my own.' I felt I had disturbed him. Solitude seemed an unlikely reason for working in a football stadium, but he was quick to correct me. 'Everyone says that, but it's just me in here most of the time. Every other Saturday there's a game and it fills up with people, but it's when it's full that it feels weird to me.'

Andy then kindly and carefully explained each of his varied grass-cutting machines, before admitting he didn't have a clue about mechanics himself. I think he thought I was a real machine head, so I was rather pleased to think I could be mistaken for an enthusiast so soon. I asked a few questions I'd always been desperate to have answered (the pitch is less than a foot deep, and it takes nine weeks to go from planting grass seed to having a pitch good enough to play on) and then asked about the patterns mowed into the pitch, for which St Mary's has become famous. Andy's face lifted. 'Well, some people just do the minimum, but I like to do that little bit extra.' Anyone familiar with *Soccer AM* on Sky 1 or who has watched a Saints match will know all about the patterns at St Mary's. Most grounds have standard lines that go up and down, but at St Mary's you never know what you're going to get: concentric circles, patterns, tartan effects in each box or even lines that are thin at the edges but get wider the closer to the middle you get. Andy said that he kept the same pattern every time Saints won a match for good luck but that up to that point in the season, as they'd only won a single game, he had almost run out of designs – a perfect example of the hilarious and typically hapless experience of supporting the mighty Saints.

Before arriving I had my heart set on getting on a ride-on mower and cutting my favourite piece of grass. Sadly that particular plan didn't materialize. Andy was rather protective of the pitch and confided in me that he shouted at anyone who dared to walk on it, even on the far corners. 'I won't have anyone going on my pitch unless they're here to play football,' he told me as he put up a chain along one edge. I could see he was keen to get back to work, so I left without the experience I had craved.

I woke up in brilliant sunshine just before the end of the 12-hour lawn-mower race at 7.15 a.m. A few more spectators had arrived, and the tea man seemed to have woken up, but most of the excitement was now emanating from the Tannoy. It appeared the race leaders had encountered a few technical problems, and a team called Promo Racing was eroding their eight-lap lead. A nasal voice from the Tannoy continued: 'I don't want to be the bearer of bad news, but if they finish in the top three now it will be a miracle.' Sure enough a few minutes later, 'Promo Racing is coming down the straight, and yes, they are now in the lead.' It then emerged that Promo Racing had been driving without breaks since midnight. When they changed their driver over for the final set of laps, you could see the men in the pit lane run up to the mower and grab the front of it before trying to push it to make it stop. There was now half an hour to go. A lady called Tracey began repeating over the Tannoy, 'You just couldn't write this!' Then I spotted someone driving along with a huge chunk of sponge between his back and the seat of his mower. It was then that I began to notice how staggeringly uncomfortable every driver looked. These machines were not built for 12-hour bouts of use. Another man was sitting right over to the left-hand side of his seat. I'm not sure whether this was for balance, to keep something in place or because the seat itself was now too hot to sit on. The endurance aspect was certainly coming through. Yes, it was all rather silly, but it looked incredibly tough at the same time. By now lots of the mowers were falling to bits. The chassis were coming off; wheels looked like they were only vaguely attached by bits of wire. You could see right into some of the engines: sparks, unsecured wiring and reams and reams of duct tape on seats or holding the massacred machines together. Then there were the drivers. You could imagine them all walking like John Wayne for weeks afterwards. There were the low-slung mowers, where the recognizable mower part was snaking all over the track, pulling the beaten-up driver along the floor behind it. None of these things had altered the speed, which seemed even faster than before, no doubt because the drivers were now so accustomed to every lump and groove in the track. The leader, number 7, wasn't taking it easy either. As he cut a huge corner to overtake another mower, raised fists were exchanged, and then members of his pit crew appeared to urge him on. The insanity of it seemed to be morphing into a kind of magic, though, and I found myself brimming with emotion about their utterly pointless heroics. Such a meaningless display of human endurance seemed strangely reminiscent of the Charge of the Light Brigade. The way the drivers seemed to revel in such futile torment and suffering was breathtaking. Either that or I was now in the grip of hallucinatory tiredness. Over in the pit lanes you could see people frantically trying to get their machines back on the track. Mechanics from other pit lanes seemed to be offering help too as the mayhem began to edge towards the end. I spotted Charlie going from pit lane to pit lane, presumably offering advice and assistance to revive the mechanical heaps now whimpering like beaten canines from an illegal dog-fight.

'You simply couldn't write this!' came from the Tannoy again. We were now a matter of minutes from the end of the twelve hours, and the leader was only half a lap ahead. The three commentators quickly did the maths and calculated that they could be overtaken in eight laps, but time for only three remained, thus dampening their attempts to suggest to the ten people in the crowd that we were in for an even closer finish. But then Tracey interjected masterfully, 'But this is lawn-mower racing! Anything could happen, even on the final lap!' This did the trick, and the two other commentators joined in with tales of past close shaves and had soon whipped themselves up even further. The exhausted spectators meanwhile, either on the verge of comas or having only just got up, seemed impervious to the excitement, but still the racers fought on and on.

And then, after twelve hours of the constant popping drone of lawn-mower engines, the field was serenely quiet. As number 7 crossed the line, the commentator had chosen the words 'Now I know he'll be crying in his helmet because he wanted that more than anything'. I wondered whether he used to be a scriptwriter for the *Carry On* films, but the nervous energy was clear to everyone when Matt Jones, of the winning team, made his victory speech a few minutes later.

'Thank you very much to everyone here. That has to be the hardest thing we've ever done. I tell you what, all those people who watch, if you actually had a go, you'd realize how rough that is and how terrible it is. You'd admire these guys so much because it is just incredible going round there.

'Now this win is for Jason. Jason Kanabus died a few years ago [tragically of cancer, at the age of thirty]. The night before he died we were getting ready for the 12-hour, and I said what's going to win it then, Jase? And he said, "My Honda's going to win it! Course it is, Matt." Well, Simon's been racing Jason's Honda for the last two years, so I'm afraid that's the end of it; it's in the scrapyard up the road, and it's had it. So we built another one and this one's for you, Jase.' He pointed up to the sky. 'This one's for you, buddy.' Behind him his fellow racers began clapping. One of them shouted out, 'Good on you Matt!' One of the other drivers was then too tearful to speak and the other, called Tiff, seemed to have disappeared. Someone shouted, 'He's hiding, his wife doesn't know he's here.' And with that, in the most anticlimactic, matter-of-fact way imaginable, everyone there – and by that I mean every single person apart from the few of us in the 'crowd' – began dismantling the track. Hay bales, fences and bits of rubbish were all collected and packed away by drivers, team members, kids and officials alike. By the time I got back to the car the track had almost completely vanished.

There was definitely no sign of wealth and power being the motivation when it comes to lawn-mower racing. What greater thing is there to be inspired by than the loss of a loved friend? I later discovered that the British Lawn Mower Racing Association has a motto, *Per herbam, ad astra* – 'through the grass to the stars'. I imagine Edwin Budding would heartily agree with that.

3

Curiosity

Steam

'YOU'RE A BAD driver if your fireman's always got his head down and his arse up.' These were the first words I got from Mike, the generous man hiding behind a slightly surly and grumpy exterior who was about to teach me how to drive a steam engine.

I was in Alresford, the small town in Hampshire where I grew up, standing in the cab of an Ivatt-class 2MT 2-6-2 tank locomotive (number 41312, for all you nerds out there) in the station of what's known as the Watercress Line. It was a hot day, but that was nothing compared to the heat coming from the furnace in front of me. I mentioned this to Andy the fireman, also with us, and he laughed. 'It's barely lit! You wait till we're moving.' I had decided that the only way to get a hint of the passion so many people had for steam trains was to experience what they were actually like to drive and get 'on the footplate' myself.

There is a widely accepted lineage of the steam age that includes the familiar names of Newcomen, Watt and Trevithick, which we'll come to in a minute, but prior to them the ancestral line of steam pioneers is far more complicated than school history books would have you believe. I had worked out by now that, when it comes to 'invention', it's not always a matter of who did something first but of how far back you are prepared to look. For example, in 1633

Edward Somerset, or the 2nd Marquess of Worcester, as he was also known, published a book outlining a design for a steam pump to power a fountain. So he could reasonably hold a claim for being the first to invent the harnessing of steam power. If a fountain sounds like an absurd context for the first use of steam, then scholars of Alexandria in the first century AD will regale you with an even earlier appearance of a steam engine – invented by a man called Heron – to power the world's first automatic door. It was called the Aeolipile.

The widely accepted story of the origins of the steam engine and the railway age itself is still something of a quagmire of fascination, invention, greed, power and, ultimately, a man called George Stephenson, who sounds to me like Anthony H. Wilson, all-round Manchester man and founder of Factory records, in a previous life. But before we get to him, we have to track down Thomas Newcomen and then Richard Trevithick, a man who'd been fighting to bring an end to James Watt's suffocating patent, mentioned briefly in Chapter 1.

Newcomen's engine, built back in 1712, is usually referred to simplistically as a large kettle. It would boil water, and the resultant steam pushed up a piston (a huge plunger) inside a cylinder. This upward movement was then harnessed with a rod at the top of the plunger that led up to a long beam at right angles to it. At the beam's other end a chain was attached down to the pump in the mine below. Once the plunger had been raised by steam, cold water entered the cylinder to condense it, creating a partial vacuum as the air pressure above the piston pushed it back down again. This up-and-down movement created a machine that looked a bit like a huge nodding dog. (The use of outside air pressure to push the piston back down is why Newcomen's machine was labelled the 'atmospheric' engine.) The cold water was then heated to create steam and the pump would be raised and so on and so on. James Watt realized the inefficiency of Newcomen's design in 1765, having spent years pondering how it could be improved. Each time cold water entered Newcomen's engine to condense the steam and bring the piston down, the cylinder had to be reheated before the cycle could begin again. Watt's idea was to build an engine with a separate condenser so the cylinder could remain hot all the time, something that improved its performance by up to 70 per cent. Precisely because it was so inefficient, Newcomen's engine was really of any use only in places with inexhaustible supplies of coal. Watt's design improved the efficiency, reducing the amount of coal it needed, and allowed it to be used in Cornish tin and copper mines far from the coalfields of the north-east.

Trevithick, born in 1771, was working as assistant to William Murdoch – the man responsible for assembling Watt's engines in Cornwall. Trevithick soon saw that Watt's engines worked with steam pressure of about 15 lb. per square inch. By this time the technology of boilers had been improved sufficiently, Trevithick believed, to get the steam to a much higher pressure (he called it 'strong steam'). Yes, this made it dangerous, but a steam engine able to work with a pressure of 100 lb. per square inch meant something very important for the future of the world: steam engines could now be far smaller but still be more powerful than the ones that had come before. For the first time this created the possibility of self-mobility. Trevithick's first plan was to mount one of his new engines on a road-going carriage. He wasn't the first to create a machine that moved under steam power, though. That prize could go to a few people, most notably a Frenchman called Nicolas Cugnot, who invented a steam car in 1769. He had been working on a steam-powered device that could move a cannon for the French army, but an off-road vehicle was something of a stretch when getting an on-road vehicle was a big enough challenge (not to mention creating a road surface capable of coping with the weight of a steam engine in the first place). Cugnot does surely get the credit for having the first car crash, though, when his *fardier à vapeur* lost control and crashed into a wall. He can also take credit for the second-ever car crash too when he – quite impressively, bearing in mind it could only manage 2½ miles per hour – managed to roll it into a ditch. Cugnot and his vehicle were locked up before they caused any more trouble. His car can be seen today in the Conservatoire National des Arts et Métiers in Paris.

Trevithick too was determined to make a steam carriage, and his attempt in 1800 also ended up in a ditch but, unlike Cugnot's, it then exploded for good measure while he was drowning his sorrows in the pub. In 1802 he tried again with a new engine in Shropshire, and this one ran on rails (his heavy steam road carriages carved the primitive roads of the time to bits). The new engine managed to reach 5 miles per hour while pulling 9 tons of wagons but, despite this success, Trevithick found it impossible to persuade the railway owners that the future lay with steam. They preferred horses to pull the wagons because they didn't crack the rails (and were far less likely to explode).

Trevithick's engines still attracted plenty of interest, though. In 1804 he was commissioned to build a high-pressure engine for the Penydarren ironworks in south Wales to power a steam hammer. It proved to be so powerful, running at a pressure of 150 lb. per square inch, that he soon put it on wheels. At a public display in 1804 the engine pulled 10 tons of iron, 5 wagons and 70 men over 9 miles of track at a speed of 5 miles per hour. Trevithick could now lay claim to having designed and built the first successful steam-powered loco-motive to travel on rails. Four years later he organized another public display for a new engine, which he called 'Catch Me Who Can', on a large circular track at the present site of Euston Station in London. By now he was desperate to prove that the future of railways lay with steam, but the display turned out to be something of a PR disaster. Few people turned up, and once again the track couldn't cope with the weight of the engine. Sadly for the high-pressure steam pioneer, this proved to be the last railway locomotive Trevithick ever designed, but his subsequent adventures give a hint of the excitement, opportunities and pitfalls that defined the time. His later attempts to make his fortune included patenting tanks that could be pumped full of air to raise shipwrecks. The tanks worked – they raised a sunken ship in Margate – but a dispute about money resulted in Trevithick cutting the lines to send the wreck back to the depths. After many more failed business ventures he and his business partner were declared bankrupt in 1811, and five years later Trevithick left Britain bound for South America. There he soon fell out with Francisco Uville, the Swiss entrepreneur who had employed him to help drain water from Peruvian silver mines. So he set off into the Andes to try and get work teaching improved mining techniques instead and met a man called James Gerard, who persuaded him to go off to Costa Rica in search of gold. Unbelievably they found some, but they needed mining equipment to get at it. As they were now on the Pacific coast, they decided to walk across land back to the Atlantic coast and get a ship home from there. They had no map and just headed off into the jungle with six guides (one of whom drowned) and two local boys whom they had picked up because their parents thought they'd have a better life in England. (The boys were called José María and Mariano Montealegre. Mariano was to become an engineer, while José became a surgeon. Both returned home years later, and José ended up becoming President of Costa Rica in 1860.)

According to his son in a later memoir, Trevithick got himself into a fight with a local man while on a boat shortly after arrival in Cartagena. He was unceremoniously dumped into the river, where he was almost eaten by an alligator and only survived because a British officer, out hunting wild pigs, was able to shoot it (he also shot Trevithick in the eye by mistake). Trevithick was hauled ashore half dead. On recovering he bumped into Robert Stephenson, son of George (we'll come to him in a minute), who gave him enough money to return home to his wife and children. One imagines they were rather cross with him when he arrived home with nothing more than the clothes on his back, because he hadn't bothered to contact them for three years. They were so cross, in fact, that he was to die alone in 1833, upstairs in a pub in Dartford, while working on a new engine. As he had nothing of value to his name, his workmates paid for his funeral, and he was buried in an unmarked grave in the St Edmunds burial ground on Dartford's East Hill.

George Stephenson was the man with the baton now. Having spent years as an 'enginewright' at the Killingworth colliery in the north-east, Stephenson worked on the 'steam elephants' that had evolved since Trevithick's early designs. So-called because of their huge funnel, like an elephant's trunk, these engines pulled the wagons of coal on rails in the coalyard. Stephenson was a pragmatic man, prepared to pinch any idea or invention that hadn't been patented to further his quest to drive on his own status and the steam age.

Mention his name in steam circles today, and you'll get a range of reactions, anything from spitting anger to hearty appreciation with a little grudging respect somewhere in between. He continued to build engines at Killingworth and, despite the haphazard nature of many of his designs – problems included leaking tanks and boilers, not to mention the occasional explosion – Stephenson began to make a reputation for himself, and in 1821 he was given the job of surveyor for a new railway between Stockton and Darlington.

But the battle to convince the new railway operators that the future lay with steam rather than horsepower had still not been won. So Stephenson set about persuading the directors by inviting them up to Killingworth to see his new engines. He succeeded where Trevithick had failed, but because this railway was being built with the same philosophy as the public turnpike roads of the time, namely that anyone was allowed to use the single-line track with their own horse-drawn wagons in the same way they would use other public highways, the Stockton-to-Darlington would have a combination of steam engines and horse-drawn traffic when it opened on 27 September 1825. You can imagine how chaotic that turned out to be. Stephenson lived up to his subsequent reputation by stealing the limelight on the opening day. A horse procession was supposed to lead the inaugural run along the new line, but he fired up Locomotion No. 1 and literally barged the horses off the track. Hitting speeds of 15 miles per hour, he travelled 26 miles in under three hours. The public and world at large were suitably impressed, but the engine startled onlookers, who feared his huge smoke-belching monster would explode at any moment. While that particular fear was not without foundation, many other worries of the time seem rather ridiculous today. Stories appeared in the press explaining how travelling at such great speeds would make it impossible to breathe, or dry up the udders of cows grazing in fields close to the track. But strict speed restrictions were soon imposed on the line for more practical reasons. Once again the vast engine crippled the primitive rails. There was only one engine at first anyway, while Stephenson worked hard to finish more, so horses would still be relied on to pull the bulk of the traffic.

Back in Alresford, I was wearing a blue boiler suit and heavy steel toe-capped boots I'd bought specially for the day. Standing there in the cab, I felt rather wary, but I also felt a tinge of empathy with the public fears of nearly two centuries earlier. Every one of my senses was being attacked. I could hear, smell, feel and even taste the oil and coal. The sound of steam hissing and the pressure of the pipes gave the impression of immense power that I wasn't convinced had been sufficiently caged. Despite what Andy said, the heat was extraordinary. I looked down into the furnace to see a hellish cauldron of flames at the bottom and a host of small, circular openings towards the top. I soon discovered these were the pipes that generated the steam. The series of small pipes rather than just one large one was one of the many tweaks (which he apparently nicked from someone else) that Stephenson applied to power his engines more efficiently.

There were none of the comforts of modern travel, but for the first time in my life I have to admit I found myself getting rather eager to drive this particular machine. The power was rather unsettling but incredibly exciting. I wondered how on earth anyone had been brave enough to drive the early engines when many of them would buckle under the pressure and literally explode.

I did fireman duty first, which a layman like me had rather overlooked in my excitement to get at the puzzling controls. Andy explained carefully how everything worked, but I forgot most of it immediately. The fireman is responsible not just for shovelling coal but also for maintaining the delicate balance of steam pressure, the heat of the furnace and the injection of water into the boiler. (At the end of the day I concluded that being a fireman was far harder work and much more complicated than being the driver.) Andy pointed out the steam pressure had to be kept between 150 and 190 lb. per square inch. For the first time in my life on hearing such mechanical gobbledygook I realized that I actually understood what that meant. My thoughts sidled away to Richard Trevithick and the daring way he had first attempted to try and harness such frightening power. Suddenly the thought of him crashing his steam car in 1802 didn't seem quite so hapless or funny.

I was then set to work shovelling coal, but even that required more skill than I'd expected. Andy demonstrated that you have to put coal into specific parts of the furnace to keep a steady heat and keep the steam pressure up. It was very hot and invigorating work and huge fun. Once the fire was raging and the pressure was high enough, Andy pointed at the funnel of the engine. 'You're looking for black smoke – that means the fire is going nicely.' I wondered what other kind of smoke you can get, but at that moment the engine began to slow down and Andy opened the doors to the furnace to let a little air in and damp the draught from the chimney. 'You've done a great job. If anything, too good.' The beast really had woken up.

I stood back grinning, with a shovel in one hand and a coal-buffed face. The fire seemed unwilling to be controlled. It was such a fierce means of using the elements. I began to imagine how intense this would have seemed 200-odd years ago. For anyone of a superstitious nature, and that would have meant most people of the time, it all must have seemed terrifying, as though you were trying to contain and harness the raw power of God without his permission, as opposed to the more sedate means of harnessing the power of nature with the water- and windmills that had gone before. The fire began to spit and howl. I'd never really understood how shocking and surprising it would have been at the time till I got into that cab. It felt so, well, *wild*.

Driving that steam train made me realize how cut off we are from the machines we rely on today. Compared to the vehicles we drive, where everything mechanical is hidden away, this machine wore its parts on its sleeve. It struck me that it is not actually possible to drive a steam train unless you have some understanding, however basic, of how it works. Clearly this is not the case with modern cars. Most of us, and I include myself, have difficulty telling the oil dipstick and screenwash reservoir apart. I began to wonder whether it's not that machines have taken us away from human nature but that our advancements and technological leaps have allowed us to remove ourselves completely from the workings of our machines. Now that most of us don't understand them, whatever poetry exists in boilers, spark plugs and engines is lost to us as well.

After the success of the Stockton-to-Darlington, Stephenson soon turned his attention to another potential railway line – one that would travel between the two new powers of Liverpool and Manchester. Once again he got the bit between his teeth in the battle for steam to take the place of horsepower, but first he had to deal with angry canal owners, who fiercely opposed any new connection between the greatest cities of the industrial north. In the sixty years since the opening of the Bridgewater canal over 2,000 miles of man-made navigable waterways had been built in Britain. The vested interests of the canal owners were, not surprisingly, keen for the railway age not to begin at all. They did their best to slow the progress as much as possible and, after the initial surveyor was chucked in prison in 1824 for not being able to pay his debts, Stephenson stepped in to replace him. He engaged in a characteristic combination of pragmatism and dirty tricks to get permission for the new line to be granted, but after a less than convincing performance at a parliamentary committee in front of barristers fighting against the building of the new line, the bill for the Liverpool-to-Manchester was defeated. Stephenson the autodidact, gruff-speaking, self-made man epitomized everything the London élite loathed, and he was roundly humiliated. He was sacked for his failure, and the vested interests of the land and canal-owning gentry celebrated.

A year later the Liverpool and Manchester Railway Company tried to get parliamentary approval once again. This time they had learned from their mistakes by watering down some of their proposals and put up a much more convincing witness to speak on their behalf. This time parliamentary assent was received, but the men responsible for persuading the government of the merits of the line were not so successful in convincing the railway company's directors that they should actually be the ones to build it. As he was the only man who had ever successfully built a major railway line before, Stephenson was employed once again.

During the exhaustive building programme the directors made the vital decision to run trains on the new railway instead of horses. They also decided not to follow the public access policy of the Stockton and Darlington and to run all the trains themselves. This meant they would need engines, and lots of them. In April 1829 they announced a competition to build the steam engines that would run on the new line. Six months later the entries, none of which could weigh more than 4½ tons or cost more than £550, would be expected to run for a total of ten 3-mile trips at a speed of 10 miles per hour. George and his son Robert set to work building an engine bearing the name that has become familiar all over the world. It trounced the competition (although their only real rival later complained that the reason his boiler cracked was nothing to do with his design but because he had bought it from George Stephenson). The engine was, of course, Stephenson's Rocket.

Back in the cab, it was my turn to drive. Mike didn't furnish me with much in terms of an explanation about how you actually 'drive' the engine until it was time to go. I was told to put it into 'forward 60' setting. (On the left-hand side was a long, thin brass plate with a zero in the middle, where the handle was placed, and away from zero in both forward and backward directions the numbers began to increase. This is how you select to go forward or back. The numbers, it turned out, reflected the closest thing you get in a steam train to the gears of a car.) I released the brake and pulled up the regulator (a large red iron bar) to increase the flow of steam and accelerate. There was a slight delay as the heat and water combined to lift and crack, but the tumultuous noise soon transformed itself into raw power that began to drive the 60-ton engine forward. I have to admit that an absolutely insane grin spread across my face as we pulled away. 'Keep it to 25,' chided Mike, which seemed unfair because I wasn't going more than 15 m.p.h. at the time. (He got a bit grumpy with me when we reached 40 m.p.h. half an hour later.

'Anyone can drive it fast. It's keeping it under control that's the art of being an engine driver.') It was astonishing to be in 'control' of such power.

Standing there, I realized that this tangible mechanical technology had inspired and excited my curiosity in a way that had never happened to me before. A sensation in stark contrast to the resigned and accepting ignorance I have always felt about the intricacies of computers or modern cars. The noise was incredible, and I longed to get a greater understanding of how this great beast actually worked. At one point the pressure got too much and the steam began to burst out from the safety valve. The control was surprisingly quick too, once we were under way, and as we climbed a huge hill into Medstead Station (John Betjeman referred to this stretch of the line as the 'Alps'), I had to increase the power to maintain a steady speed. The way the engine hissed and clunked, communicating with each of my senses, gave me a haunting feeling that it could easily slip out of my control.

As I climbed back on to the platform at the end of my final run, I took the opportunity to ask Mike why he had become so fascinated by steam engines. He gave me a characteristic-ally curt but well-meaning reply. 'Well, the steam engine is the only transportation machine not invented for warfare, that's why I like them. They are loved by ordinary people too.' I asked him a few more questions about the Watercress Line and how it kept going. 'Volunteers. Without volunteers this place would have closed down years ago.'

But that was all I could get from Mike, so I climbed on board the next train heading for Ropley and began snatching conversations with volunteers where I could. The first person I collared was an old chap called Ray, who worked on the refreshment counter. I asked him why he'd decided to volunteer on the Watercress Line. 'It's not like work because you choose to be here. I started helping out after my wife died. Been coming ever since.' A look of slightly baffled sadness spread across his face, and I didn't feel comfortable quizzing him further.

Dave, who organizes the volunteer days, was much more forthcoming. 'It's the people! We get such fantastic people working here. And it's not just train enthusiasts either. We get people who want to work in the ticket hall, car park attendants, cooks, some who want to run the information department, publicity office, work in the shops, and then you've got signals and telegraphs, the traffic department, platform staff, porters, station master, ticket inspectors, guards. We've got a gardening department. There's the Wednesday Gang, which is popular with single people looking for a bit of camaraderie. If you don't have a sense of humour, then, well, don't come and volunteer, that's all I can say!' It turned out that the Watercress Line relies on 280 unpaid people to keep it going. I asked him why he volunteered, and he just grinned. 'If I don't get my fix once a week, then I'm useless.'

Later I had a brief conversation with a man in an orange boiler suit called John, whose hands, clothes and face were covered in grease. He looked like my three-year-old son does when he's been painting. It turned out John had been volunteering at the Watercress Line for thirty years. I asked him why he'd devoted so much of his life to it and he grinned. 'Because I've had the kind of fun here that you simply can't buy.' He walked off before I got the chance to grill him further.

I'm aware that this could all sound a little perfect, but there was an undeniable sense of belonging among the volunteers I met that day, despite the fact that a lot of the jobs they were doing involved seriously hard physical work. The signalman in the signal box just looked thrilled to be near so many levers. 'It's all about confidence really,' he said, when I asked him what it took to be a signalman. 'If you think it might not be safe, you just don't do it. There are lots of people around you can ask if you're not sure about something.' Once again there was no sense of wealth and power driving the passion for steam trains, although I did get the impression that Mike rather enjoyed standing above everyone else at the controls of the engine. There was a hierarchy of sorts for any volunteers wanting to become drivers that seemed similar in structure to the path you would have to follow back in the age of steam. You had to put in your years as a fireman and some time before that in the works. But that couldn't take away the general spiritual flavour of the steam train enthusiast that I experienced that day.

The Watercress Line does raise money in some rather exciting ways to keep it going too. I was watching the future dystopian nightmare movie *Children of Men* at the cinema a few years ago and was rather shocked when Clive Owen's lead character fled the urban fascist nightmare of London to go and smoke some weed with his mate, played by Michael Caine – only to arrive at Alresford Station, where people were being kept in cages before being deported to Bexhill-on-Sea. It seemed odd to me that Alresford should be portrayed as some kind of haven when I'd been so desperate to escape from there myself (although I commend the realism in portraying it as a place that attracts people wanting to smoke illegal drugs). It was my teenage loathing of Alresford that later inspired my half of *Crap Towns*. I recently discovered that forty years before me a far, far more impressive figure had taken the town to task for the way the local worthies were conspiring to destroy it. The greatest cricket commentator of all time and the most famous resident of Alresford, John Arlott, enlisted another luminous figure, John Betjeman, to try and stop what he saw as the attempts to trash the town he loved. On being asked by Arlott for his help, Betjeman wrote back, 'I so agree about the disruption of little country towns by blind, sadistic-minded do-gooders that I must do all I can to get back to you,' and he travelled down to speak at a town planning meeting. If only he was still around, Alresford might have been spared the recently opened branch of Tesco.

It was while perusing the Watercress Line bookstall in the sheds at Ropley station later that day that I noticed the rather familiar name of L.T.C. Rolt appear once again in front of me. I thought I'd seen the last of him after coming to the end of his very enjoyable book *Narrow Boat* on the canals, but no, it appeared he wasn't done with me yet. His reappearance soon began to make me very curious about the contradictions inherent in machine enthusiasts that I touched on in Chapter 1.

As we've already discovered, in *Narrow Boat* Rolt uses his months on a canal to bemoan the modern way of life every time he comes across it – at one point writing about the emerging obsession with speed and how it has changed people's quality of life:

> Watching the speeding cars from *Cressy*'s deck as she drifted along at her placid three-miles-an-hour gait, I found myself marvelling at the mania of hurry which has infected our unhappy civilization. It would seem that I was beginning to acquire something of the boatman's philosophy, for when I was a motorist myself I was never so struck by the absurdity of expending such prodigality of power and effort, risk and nervous strain, for the sole sake of

saving an hour or so of time which was seldom or never utilized to any creative purpose.

He then fills page after page lamenting the loss of the old skills and crafts of rural England because of the scourge of industrialization and the new ugly towns created in its wake. He even devotes a few hundred words to grumble about the invention of the can-opener for what he sees as tinned food's effect on the cooking prowess of the humble housewife. God knows what he'd have made of the supermarket ready meal. From all this I'd come to think of him as a genial, if grumpy, old man who loathed 'progress' every time he was unfortunate enough to come across it. I then discovered, from a chap called Chris at *Waterways World* magazine, that Rolt was the ultimate enthusiast, who lived on *Cressy* for twelve years, and *Narrow Boat* is as near to the bible of canal boating as you can get. Rolt co-founded and was the first honorary secretary of the Inland Waterways Association in 1946, and it is that organization which we have to thank for the preservation of so many of Britain's canals some sixty years on.

But, rather surprisingly considering his apparent loathing of where 'progress' had led mankind, Rolt wasn't just a fan of canals and was about to become my guide into the world of the machine enthusiast as a whole. At the bookstall in Ropley station I discovered a glowing biography he'd written about Richard Trevithick. Bearing in mind Rolt's attitude to industrialization, this was rather unexpected; but if that wasn't surprising enough, on the inside covers it emerged that he was also the biographer of most of the other important men of the industrial age — Thomas Newcomen, James Watt, George and Robert Stephenson, Thomas Telford and Isambard Kingdom Brunel — all of whom were largely responsible for creating the chaotic, mechanized world that

Rolt seemed so passionately to hate. Then I learned that in his rather packed lifetime he also managed to find the time to be vice-president of the Newcomen Society, was a member of the Science Museum Advisory Council and the York Railway Museum Committee, and a founder member of the Talyllyn Railway Preservation Society (the first steam line to be preserved) and the Vintage Sports Car Club. My curiosity sufficiently alerted, I then discovered a few other things he had neglected to mention in the beautifully pastoral *Narrow Boat* – most notably the fact that the Second World War began half-way through the sedate and uplifting journey he recalls in his travelogue and, as a newly qualified engineer finding himself moored on the edges of Birmingham, he soon got a job with Rolls-Royce making the Merlin engine that would power the mighty Spitfire.

You're probably wondering why I'm giving over so much space to a dead man most people have never heard of, but, as it turned out, I wasn't alone in being rather baffled about these seemingly conflicting aspects of Rolt's character. In the foreword of the first part of his autobiography (originally published in 1971 as *Landscape with Machines*) he says as much himself:

> This [book] is intended to reflect the two sides of my own nature and the varied interests that have stemmed from them. They have often been at war with each other and have seldom achieved more than an uneasy truce. For this reason I have never found myself a particularly easy person to live with; I ask myself too many awkward questions.

The two sides of his own nature were the sides of a battle between mankind's engineering ingenuity in inventing and creating machines and the love and appreciation of the world and life around him that those same machines seemed inevitably to destroy. Put very simplistically, Rolt appeared to be a man who could have got on famously with someone like Jeremy Clarkson at a car show one day, nattering about Brunel and the Rolls-Royce Merlin engine, and then be equally comfortable with George Monbiot at a farmers' market the next, chatting about electric cars and protecting our environment. I can't think of anyone able to sit so easily in both camps today, or anyone even attempting to. But rather prophetically it seemed to me, Rolt saw connecting these two seemingly intractable positions as the key to the future of civilization itself.

> The battle is the more tragic because the gulf of non-understanding between the two sides seems to be so unbridgeable ... I wonder ruefully whether [this book] should not be printed in two colours or two contrasting typefaces, thus enabling each side to skip the part they prefer to ignore, but that would be to admit defeat in a desperate situation. For where there is no mutual understanding there can be no hope of remedy.

I began to wonder whether my quest should become an attempt to join the seemingly opposite worlds of the machine enthusiast and the environmental campaigner. That would certainly be an interesting challenge to tackle.

A few weeks later, my head now full of grand philosophical plans about where this journey might lead, I headed for the five-day Great Dorset Steam Fair, heralded on its website as the 'world's leading steam and vintage vehicle event' and attracting over 200,000 people every year. This was surely the largest concentration of enthusiasts, steam or otherwise, you can find anywhere in the world.

Among the stands I was looking out for a chap I'd arranged to meet called Danny, with, according to a friend, 'spades for hands' and who had a vintage steam lorry. I'd imagined he would not take too long to find. I was very, very wrong about that.

The annual Great Dorset Steam Fair has been going for forty years, and predictably I'd spotted huge plumes of smoke from the road before I'd seen the fair itself. To a steam novice like me it was all rather daunting – taking up huge fields and disappearing far over the horizon. It was the Glastonbury of steam, although instead of grungy tents there were rows and rows of pristine caravans and mobile homes. I parked near the 'Steam Ploughing' section and then walked past the 'Steam Fairground' and the 'Steam Road Laying' (they actually laid a section of road with a variety of steam contraptions grinding stones that were soon 'steamrolled' flat to make an impromptu road surface) before I came to the 'Steam Threshing', 'Steam Sawing' and the 'Steam Heavy Haulage' areas, where huge engines paraded around smoking and belching for the hundreds of video cameras primed to film them waddle up and down a steep hill. At this point I was almost pulled away by the curiously named 'Wall of Death' and one of the donut stalls (which proved to be almost as numerous as the steam-powered machines). I later got lost amid the military vehicles, the commercial vehicle section, tractor pulling, static tractors and the countryside arena via the Catering Alley and Country and Western Marquee. I bought an expensive organic hot dog, a pint of Speckled Hen and a programme, and finally rang Danny. He seemed surprised and then pleased to hear from me. 'Oh, yeah, hello Dan. OK, meet me in the threshing bit in ten minutes.'

I found him laughing with two oily, boiler-suited men wearing flat caps, but Danny wasn't dressed like an engine driver himself. We shook hands. He had a firm but friendly grip – not the kind taught to business drones in an attempt to intimidate everyone they meet, but from a lifetime of hard use. He began showing me round his steam lorry, a 6-ton Foden C-type that was once used for spreading tar but now with a huge tank on the back bearing the words 'New Forest Cider'. We climbed into the cab, and he began to show me how everything worked. It was much more physically confined than the steam engine I'd driven, but the workings were all still familiar. The regulator was obvious enough, but instead of a brass plate it had a long arm coming up from the floor that you pushed back and forward to engage forward and reverse.

In terms of land-going vehicles, steam lorries were the most technologically advanced steam vehicles ever to be built. Despite being more efficient, not to mention faster, than the newly developed diesel and petrol cars (steam lorries could manage up to 60 m.p.h. while petrol and diesel vehicles of the time could only reach 35 m.p.h.), they were soon forced off the road. You might imagine that steam-powered vehicles were reaching the limits of their capacity and that diesel and petrol vehicles were simply a sign of the future, but the real explanation for their demise is more complicated and reveals the power private interest groups then had over the government, much as they do today. The privately owned railway lobby had complained that road haulage firms were gaining an unfair subsidy because the roads they relied on were paid for by public taxes while railway companies had to meet the costs of updating and building the rails themselves. The government were also concerned about the damage being caused to the public highways by the huge increase in traffic. The third opponent of the growth in steam vehicles was the oil industry, which could see the potential for a monopoly on road transport if only steam haulage could be brought to an end. In 1933 the Minister for Transport, Oliver

Stanley, introduced a raft of policies: he imposed new speed limits, a new licensing system for the heaviest vehicles and a new vehicle duty based on each vehicle's weight (thus reducing the advantage of the steam lorries in every conceivable way). These policies were incredibly contentious at the time because they gave a competitive edge to diesel and petrol vehicles, which relied on imported oil, as opposed to steam vehicles, which relied on domestic coal. It was seen as another snub to an already struggling coal industry. This vast increase in taxation soon drove steam lorries off the roads. Another option would have been to nationalize the railways or strengthen the hands of the coal industry, but this was deemed a far too socialist policy for Ramsay MacDonald's third term. The political backdrop at the time, you see, was rather precarious. After the Wall Street crash of 1929 Britain was in economic turmoil and desperate to reassure the world that it was solvent after a lack of confidence had led to a run on the pound. The 1929 election had created a hung parliament and, desperate to steady the nation and prevent economic collapse, the main political parties entered into a series of coalition governments in an attempt to reassure public and global opinion that whatever problems Britain faced would be dealt with unanimously by the leading political figures of the day. Having lost the support of the Labour Party, Ramsay MacDonald resigned, only to become head of this new coalition government. One imagines the option of nationalizing the railways was rather low down on his agenda if it was on it at all. The 'National Government' remained until 1939, to be replaced by Winston Churchill's 'All-Party Coalition' after the outbreak of the Second World War.

By 1948 the railways had been worked to their barest bones during the war effort and were soon nationalized, at which point they, rather ironically considering their role in the demise of steam vehicles, acquired the derogatory description of a 'subsidized industry' from opponents of nationalization, which it retains to this day. Meanwhile road-building programmes began to be described as 'investment' instead, which is odd when, surely, subsidy and investment are the same thing.

Danny's lorry was still in use up to the 1950s, when it was rescued from the scrapyard, unlike many others. He acquired it in 2001 and set about restoring it to its current condition. I asked him how he came to be a steam lorry enthusiast.

'Well, I've always been into machines, ever since I was small. I used to love those Dinky toys and it just sort of snowballed.' That seemed like something of an understatement as he sat in his enormous lorry by a collection of other engines, which I later discovered he also owned.

'I've always been interested in machinery and, growing up, we always had tractors around. There was a local chap who had one of these lorries and broke its crankshaft. Well, it happened to be a Foden eight-wheeler – like my Dinky toy – and he said, "You like old lorries", and that was how my first Foden came along. I've got quite a few since then, but it was always a dream to have a Foden *steam* lorry.'

Danny has been coming to the Dorset Steam Fair since it started, so I asked what exactly had inspired his love of steam.

'I suppose it's a social thing really.' He laughed. 'I mean, where apart from here would you find so many beer tents, fairgrounds and people you can talk to? We all like the same things really.

'I've been interested in mechanical things all my life. Everyone's got that little bit of flair for something, haven't they? Footballers, golfers, writers, whatever. But you won't find many footballers here. Here you'll find people with a flair for mechanics and engineering. We always used to say we wish we'd been born in the steam age. Then we'd be getting paid for what we're doing now for free. But those men back then were heroes. You imagine driving this in the winter, or that threshing machine, which is when they used to do it. You'd have eleven men in the threshing gang. They were absolute heroes. You think now you're in your John Deere tractor with air-conditioning, the radio on and your Sat Nav. No, it's just something that takes you and that's it. Whether it's cars or trucks or steam lorries. It all depends on your environment and what you can do. What you can have.'

I asked whether it was specifically a mechanical thing.

'Machine enthusiasts have all got some mechanic curiosity somewhere along the line. You've got some who are into it for the glory, but most people aren't. There's no competition because you're not trying to beat anyone. Sometimes people will polish up their engine for a prize, you get a few cups for "best working engine", but you're not *racing*. It's just about having a good time. I mean, if something goes wrong with this, I get a bit frustrated, but you don't have a "bad day" out with a steam engine. Even if something breaks, it's nice to take it apart and fix it up again. That's another big part of it. It gets your curiosity and problem-solving going. Most of this old steam stuff is derelict. So you get to bring it back to life, put the kettle on, have a cup of tea and think, "I brought it back". That's a great feeling, 'cause if something breaks, you can't go and pick the bit you need off the shelf in a shop somewhere – not usually anyway. You have to get a mate with a lathe to make you the piece you need. It's fascinating work.'

Danny's friend Steve, who was keen to explain his love of steam, joined us in the cab. I asked him why he was so attracted to it.

'It's in the blood. I like the whole lot, from restoration, driving them – and the drinking, of course.' They both laughed.

Steve grinned. 'We have a laugh, don't we? But the satisfaction you get from bringing something back to life is brilliant. We play with them, wear them out and then put them back together. I mean, my engine over there was totally derelict. It took me fifteen years to get it working again. As and when finances would allow it really. But, as I always say, as soon as you light the firebox in one of these, you're wearing it out.'

I asked him whether he would define himself as an 'enthusiast'.

'Definitely. There's just something about steam. My great granddad drove a steam engine, so it's in the family. We were all brought up with it. People say it's in the blood, and I believe that. I've got a four-year-old nephew, and he's mad about steam already. If he was here now, he'd be looking at that and saying, "There's no pressure, you need to get some more coal on". If you're interested in it, then there's nothing better.'

My attempts to bring in some wider philosophical ideas about the demise of community and how perhaps they were creating their own replacement, about whether their enthusiasm for machines was a way of replacing their belief in a wider spiritual ideal or whether the lack of meaningful work today was what inspired them to toil away at their engines in their spare time, were greeted with generous dismissal. It was as though they were aware of some far simpler yet more profound logic that I had totally failed to grasp. Danny left me smiling with the words, 'It's just about fun, Dan, that's all really. An excuse to talk to nice people, get your hands dirty and have a few beers.' It's not hard, even for me, to see the attraction in that.

Once again the values of modern life were largely being ignored in the world of steam. The overriding philosophy seemed to be the direct opposite of the 'survival of the fittest' principle that powers the economy and therefore all of our day-to-day lives.

Before heading home I had to satisfy one last piece of curiosity. Well, you can't stumble on something called the 'Wall of Death' without taking a look, can you? A man with a generously proportioned bright red waistcoat was doing his best to generate interest from passers-by, but the queue was already huge. 'Step inside now, step inside, witness the greatest show on earth – we're on BBC1 every single night. It's the Wall of Death!' (At the time of writing they featured in one of the between-programme idents on BBC1.)

As far as I'm aware, there's never been a more compelling marketing pitch than the 'Wall of Death'. So I paid the £2 entry fee – far less than you'd spend on an arcade game for a similar length of playing time – and climbed the makeshift stairs up to the top of what looked like a huge wooden barrel. Down in the base were four motor bikes and one of those motorized caged go-karts. I noticed the ramp that ran all the way around the base, which the bikes would ride up to get on to the wall itself. When the crowd were all in position, the first motor cycle began riding around the bottom of the barrel. The rider wore no helmet and the noise echoed up to us, the engines occasionally backfiring, stinging my ears and then, after a few circuits, he was up, riding round and round in a circular motion on the vertical cylindrical wall. He flew up, almost flying off into our faces, and then back down to the bottom again. This went on for some time and each rider took his turn, the difficulty increasing until one of them rode around the vertical wall while sitting side-saddle, no hands, and then on the handlebars themselves. The finale involved two men and a suitably blonde bombshell all riding round together, one at the bottom, one in the middle and another at the top. The noise and close proximity to the motor bikes were astonishing. I grinned and giggled the entire time. I can't think of a better £2 I've ever spent in my entire life. Appropriate too, as a bike, albeit one without an engine, was the next machine on my list.

4

Adventure

Bicycles

THE HUMBLE BICYCLE is probably the most attainable, and loved, machine on earth. As machines go, it is also as in tune with the planet as it is possible to be. Once again, however, the story of its invention is a mire of claim and counter-claim, although it seemed to begin in a particularly promising fashion when I read a book about the history of the bicycle by a chap called Robert Wilkinson-Latham, published in 1977. Wilkinson-Latham writes of the first appearance of a bicycle (without pedals) in 1791. 'It was driven by the famous French eccentric the Comte de Sivrac, and took the form of a small carved wooden horse fitted with wheels propelled by the movements of the legs alternately in a similar fashion as running.'

The Comte de Sivrac sounded like the ideal person to start me off on my cycling journey (I had immediate visions of bicycles, debauchery and bloomers), but he turned out to be not quite as famous as Wilkinson-Latham claimed. Apart from his regular appearance in books about the history of the bicycle that credit him with the same thing, I couldn't find him mentioned anywhere. There was no listed date of his birth or death – just the repeated claim, originally from a book about the history of the bicycle written by a Frenchman called Louis Baudry de Saunier, published in 1871, that he rode his new machine in the gardens of the Palais Royal in

1791. I was left with no option but to conclude that the Comte was a figment of Saunier's imagination, perhaps the result of national pride (in 1871 France had just been defeated by Germany in the Franco-Prussian War), as the actual inventor of the machine that became a French obsession, which became known colloquially as a 'velocipede', 'dandy horse' or, most crucially, the 'draisine', was a German called Baron Karl von Drais in 1817. There are other controversies about the origins of even earlier bikes too. One involves a sketch attributed to Leonardo da Vinci, which has since been discounted by most people who don't happen to work in the museum where this particular drawing is kept.

The first bike with pedals appears to be much easier to pin down, initially at least. Lots of bicycle histories refer to Scotland in 1839 – ten years after George and Robert Stephenson unveiled the Rocket – to the forge of a blacksmith called Kirkpatrick Macmillan. The story goes that Macmillan had been asked to repair a broken dandy horse, was intrigued by the design and set about building one of his own for getting around the estate of the Duke of Buccleuch, where he worked. Being something of an inventor, he altered the design to include treadles on either side of the front wheel, which were connected by a rod to the back axle, supposedly inspired by the system he had seen on the new steam railway locomotives. When he pushed forward and backwards on the treadles, the back wheel began to turn. He still had to run along with his machine, as you would do with the velocipede, to get it going, but once it was moving the treadles maintained motion in the way that modern pedals do. It turns out that Kirkpatrick Macmillan's claim may not be all it seems either. There is some confusion about a speeding ticket he was supposed to have received while out riding his new machine and an incident where a small child was run over by him on his contraption: the rider was hauled before a judge and fined. The machine in question was described as a 'velocipede', with no mention of the revolutionary treadles, and confusingly both events were reported as being perpetrated by a 'gentleman', which in those days was not how you would have referred to a blacksmith. The uncertainty as to Macmillan's class may sound a tenuous reason for doubting the story, but the structure of society at the time meant this would be an unlikely mistake for a journalist to have made.

Even if Macmillan did invent a bicycle with treadles and have these reported mishaps, he certainly didn't take out a patent for his design, or even a far cheaper notification that would inform him if anyone else attempted to patent something similar, which seems surprising given the appetite for invention at the time. Russian historians would have you believe that the uncertainty surrounding the Scottish bicycle inventor is irrelevant anyway, as back in 1801 a serf called E.M. Artamonov supposedly invented the first bike with pedals. The only mention I could find of an E.M. Artamonov referred to a different person (unless he also invented a time machine), who published a physics paper in the 1970s on the 'Generation of Vlf Pulses'.

But while all this was or was not happening, roads themselves had undergone something of a change, and these alterations would have a huge impact on the success of the first pedal bicycle. New techniques of road construction introduced by Thomas Telford (1757–1834) and John Loudon McAdam (1756–1836) were replacing the simple turnpike toll roads that ran across Britain. Telford and McAdam's roads were constructed in layers, with large stones at the base, medium-size stones next and a final layer of smaller stones on the top. Horse-drawn rollers (or, later, steam-powered ones like the ones I saw at the Dorset Steam Fair) would then roll over and force the stones together into a compact and durable whole. The addition of camber to make the road slope from a high point in the middle down into the drainage ditches on either side helped prevent water from running down into the road's foundations and weakening the entire structure. This created a surface far more refined and comfortable to travel on than the potholed quagmire that had come before. Telford's design included an additional base of bricks at the very bottom, which made his roads stronger but far more expensive to build than McAdam's. (It was McAdam's roads that were later covered with a layer of waterproof tar to create the 'tar-mac' road surface we rely on today.) In the mid-nineteenth century McAdam's road surfaces reached the boulevards of the French capital, where they were put to good use.

In 1863 a Parisian blacksmith called Pierre Micheaux and one of his employees, Pierre Lallement, are known unequivocally to have built pedal bicycles. Which of them did it first, on the other hand, again depends on which book you read. One argument is that Micheaux invented the first one, but Lallement pinched the idea and took out the only patent. The other view is that Lallement did it first and took out a patent, but that Micheaux stole the idea from him. Whatever the truth is, we know that Lallement headed for the USA to try his luck launching the bicycle there. He soon sold his patent, only to die in poverty in Boston in 1891, having failed to make his fortune. How Micheaux could have got away with building and selling a machine that someone else had patented is, conceivably, explained by Lallement's decision to head to America, or the fact that the patent's new owner was busily trying to protect his interests from other inventors there rather than the actions of someone thousands of miles away in France. Micheaux, meanwhile, had begun building and selling pedal bikes to an excited public. In 1863 he sold 143 of his new machines, and it was these bicycles that moved *The Times* to comment on a new 'terror of the streets' in Paris. Micheaux then got the funding he needed to build bikes on a larger scale by joining forces with four men who had become, perhaps, the first real bicycle enthusiasts: George de la Bouglise and the brothers Aimé, Marius and René Olivier. The four of them formed Micheaux and Company, and the first mass-produced pedal bicycles emerged from their factory, which was capable of building five machines a day, in 1868. A bicycle craze soon erupted for the brand new 'velocipede', but it was later in the USA that the name 'boneshaker' appeared, which still sticks to these early bikes today.

Bicycles then evolved into the famous high-bicycle design that is often referred to as a 'penny-farthing' (much to the annoyance of many high-bicycle owners). The leading wheel, to which the pedals were fixed, grew to an enormous size because the early bikes had no gear system and a large wheel simply meant you could ride faster. One revolution of the pedals would turn one revolution of the wheel. The 'safety bicycle', with two similar-sized wheels, invented by John Kemp Starley from Coventry in 1885, used pedals to power the back wheel via the use of a chain instead, which freed the front wheel and made steering much easier. It was Starley's addition of the chain that allowed gears to be introduced for the first time. The 'two-gear' bicycle emerged first, with two different-size cogs, one on either side of the back wheel. To change gear you literally had to stop, take off the back wheel, turn it over and reconnect your chain. From all this you may imagine that long-distance bicycle travel would have had to wait until 1888, when John Dunlop brought a new level of comfort to the bicycle by replacing iron tyres with his new pneumatic ones, or twenty years until Frenchman Paul de Vivie invented the first derailleur gear in 1905. But unbelievably, in 1884, a mere nineteen years after the first bicycles came off the production line in Paris, a man called Thomas Stevens set off on a staggering journey from San Francisco on a black enamelled 50-inch high-bicycle. Looking back today, you could argue that Stevens invented the 'gap year' even if he was actually away for three. He returned in January 1887, having cycled (or 'wheeled', as he described it) 13,500 miles across the globe.

The preface to the subsequent book of his adventure, *Around the World on a Bicycle*, is written by Thomas Wentworth Higginson and recounts a talk Stevens gave on returning home from his adventure, like a modern-day Sinbad the Sailor. Higginson writes how unlike other machines the bicycle had turned out to be:

> We found that modern mechanical invention, instead of disenchanting the universe, had really afforded the means of exploring its marvels the more surely. Instead of going round the world with a rifle, for the purpose of killing something, – or with a bundle of tracts, in order to convert somebody, – this bold youth simply went round the globe to see the people who were on it; and since he always had something to show them as interesting as anything that they could show him, he made his way among all nations.
>
> What he had to show them was not merely a man perched on a lofty wheel, as if riding on a soap bubble; but he was also a perpetual object-lesson in what [Oliver Wendell] Holmes calls 'genuine, solid old Teutonic pluck'. When the soldier rides into danger he has comrades by his side, his country's cause to defend, his uniform to vindicate, and the bugle to cheer him on; but this solitary rider had neither military station, nor an oath of allegiance, nor comrades, nor bugle; and he went among men of unknown languages, alien habits and hostile faith with only his own

tact and courage to help him through. They proved sufficient, for he returned alive.

If that doesn't make you desperate to read about his remarkable journey, I don't know what will. A hint of the incredible
trials Stevens faced is given in the opening pages. After the
first 7 miles of the streets of San Francisco, Stevens writes:

> The wave-like macadam abruptly terminates, and I find
> myself on a common dirt road . . . the country gets some-
> what 'choppy', and the road a succession of short-hills, at
> the bottom of which modest-looking mud-holes patiently
> await an opportunity to make one's acquaintance, or
> scraggy-looking, latitudinous washouts are awaiting their
> chance to commit a murder, or to make the unwary cycler
> who should venture to 'coast', think he had wheeled over
> the tail of an earthquake.

If that was on the outskirts of San Francisco, it's hard to
imagine how he managed to get as far as Tehran while sitting
over four feet up in the air.

After reading about Stevens's journey, I went to meet a
chap called Lionel Ferris, no stranger to long-distance journeys on high-bicycles and a member of the Veteran-Cycle
Club, to see if I could have a go at riding one of these fabled
'soap-bubbles' myself. I got off the tube in west London and
headed up the road, past a few posh nursery schools, and
soon found a tiny purple car stuffed between the pavement
and the steps up to an overgrown and somewhat dishevelled
house. All around were posh residences and expensive flats,
but this particular house had a touch of Roald Dahl about
it. I hadn't seen the number at that point but knew instinctively that it was where I was supposed to be. Chained up to .
a large tree, which I had to squeeze past because of the odd
little car, were three vintage bikes. I jumped up the steps,

eyeing my watch a little nervously because I was twenty minutes late, and pulled the bell to the left of the large red front door. Almost immediately a tall man in a white fisherman's jumper wearing small circular glasses, with white hair over his ears, opened the door. He grinned. 'Ah, I've just told someone on the phone that you're not coming. Come in, come in!'

I apologized profusely and followed him into his front room, navigating through four huge high-bicycles, a sofa bed and a TV to an open-plan kitchen with a huge window that looked down into an untamed garden. I sat down in one of the three chairs, spilled around a wooden table that itself was hidden under piles of letters, postcards, magazines and general day-to-day paperwork, while Lionel left an apologetic phone message to whomever my tardiness was about to disrupt. He came back offering tea, and I got the first proper glimpse of the wide grin buried in his white beard and the first sound of his Basil Brush laugh, 'ha ha ha ha!' (but with a comic book 'tee-hee' instead of a 'boom, boom'), while he made his way to the kettle.

Lionel had been described as rather 'eccentric' by other cyclists I'd met who flirted with the edges of the Veteran-Cycle Club community. It's worthwhile to note that people always describe others as 'eccentric' as if to warn you that, on balance, they shouldn't really be trusted with a pair of scissors. But I like to think that the inherent interestingness in supposedly 'eccentric' people is what prevents them from simply being labelled 'mad'. I certainly found Lionel interesting before I'd even got through his front door.

We got straight to the business of living far away from the mainstream and worked our way on to the subject of bicycles too. Lionel seemed in a reflective but chatty mood and, once he started talking, forgot all about making tea.

'The thing is, Dan, all of my life I've been told to be some-body else. But last year for the international meeting for antique bicycles they gave me a medal. Now because this meeting was in Holland the award was in Dutch, and I've no real idea what the medal was for but I think it was for *being me* – against all the odds for a long period of time in a world, as I say, that's been telling me all my life to be somebody else.'

I asked when he first came across this sense that he didn't really fit in.

'I suppose it goes back to school. Like all sorts of things, we're not taught at school anything useful about living. You're only told about how to earn a living. In someone else's factory or wherever. Speaking as an eleven-plus "fail-ure", we were supposed to be factory fodder. So ever since I read that Shakespeare said "Above all things to thine own self be true", which effectively means be yourself, I've tried to always live up to that.'

I mentioned that at *The Idler* magazine (of which I'm the deputy editor) we refer to school as 'pre-work', and he began to laugh.

'I worked with kids who were bunking school a few years ago – good kids, Dan. But it was while working with them that I realized why those kids were unemployable. They had not learned the basic lesson that from nine to five, Monday to Friday, you must do what you're told and call the guvnor "Sir"!'

I wondered whether the nine-to-five had ever ensnared him.

'Well, there's a story. There's always a story, Dan! I suffer from this thing called ME. I've had it, I suspect, since I was a teenager. But of course, part of being told to be like every-one else was that nobody knew of a thing called ME back then. They just told me I was a lazy bugger and must work harder. And I agree! But I simply can't do nine to five, Monday to Friday. So for a long time I was self-employed, and really the old bicycle was from poverty as much as anything else. We were a poor but aspiring family originally, and the attitude at home was make do and mend. I remember us four as kids fighting with one another to use *the* roller-skate. Not the pair of roller-skates, *the* roller-skate. So if you wanted a bicycle, you either had to make one yourself from scratch or you had to find an abandoned broken one and repair it or you had to steal one, and I did all of those things. It did show initiative. I feel very sad today for the people whose bicycles I nicked, but there wasn't another option. It's about being aspiring middle-class. Now, you admired this house. This house really should have been pulled down, but I bought it as a ruin. Quite truthfully I am unemployable. I registered a dog as a limited company, told the building society that I worked for Dog Ltd and thus got a mortgage to buy this ruined house. This was in 1979. The end of the winter of discontent. Now from what I understand the extreme left tried to start a revolution in this country, but Mrs Thatcher was voted in to crush it and, in the end, thank goodness! But at that time, at the end of the Callaghan government, the rate of inflation was much greater than the rate of interest. So when I borrowed £25,000 for this place, I knew that I would be on to a winner. I mean, it was a ruin. I've done everything, from the roof to the cellar. I learned from an Irishman that the best time to pinch things was while everyone else has their head down in their cars going home after a hard day at work. They're so busy getting home that they don't see what's going on around them! So I spotted a load of roof tiles that had been taken off a roof of a house being demolished down the road. I had the lot! But Mrs

Thatcher soon came in, changed bank rates and at one stage I was paying 21 per cent interest on that £25,000. But I survived it. I filled this place up with tenants and slept in the back garden. It was awful! And then I had to put the dog down so I'd lost my employer! HA HA HA HA! TEE-HEE-HEE!'

I leaned back in the chair with my eyes blown widely open and slightly gasping for breath. Lionel was certainly a passionate character, but I have to say he showed no immediate signs of the ME that he had just mentioned. Sitting with Lionel was rather like listening to an old radio playing a pleasing tune that occasionally decides to hiss and burst up five notches in volume for no apparent reason, shaking the insides of your brain before dropping back down to the level you had been quietly enjoying. I decided to hang on quietly and see where his staccato reminiscences would lead.

'When I was in my teens, the fashion was for quite a small-frame bicycle with a very long seat pillar – you would put the saddle up as far as you could. Now to try and get a bicycle for my long legs I was finding early Victorian bicycles much better. Because the early Victorians rode very tall bicycles, like this one.'

He got up and pulled out one of the vintage bikes from his lounge with a beaming smile on his face. It was a huge but conventional-style bicycle, unlike the enormous high-bicycles in the room.

'Leigh and Francis, 1901. Built for an aristocrat. Now I think that's glorious.'

He held it slightly from his body and went quiet for a very brief moment.

'It's wonderful to ride, it really is. Cost me a thousand pounds, mind you. It's ridiculous, isn't it! Going from broken and stolen bicycles to paying a thousand pounds for a rusted wreck! Even better, well, it makes me laugh, it's Leigh and Francis, who were trying to do what Rolls-Royce had done with cars. Leigh and Francis were ten years before them, mind.'

He showed me the entwined LF emblem on the front of the tubing.

'Lionel Ferris! So I've got a monogrammed bicycle!' He wheeled it back to the lounge and sat back down with a sigh.

'But I was riding round on old high-bikes, this would be about forty years ago, and someone wound down their window one day and said, "Did you know there's a club for bicycles like that?" I didn't know. Now, of course, I understand in England there's a club for EVERYTHING! Every perversion is catered for here! Well then, I first saw the pennies and, of course, I couldn't afford one, but I thought, I'd like one of those. Now this one . . .'

He got up again and began pulling out one of the four high-bicycles that were leaning up against the kitchen wall.

'. . . I got from a builder's skip. Well, I paid a thousand pounds to the guy that took it out of the skip; don't think my life's that easy! But I think this one is just utter magic, it's a glorious beast. This is 1881, the handles will be about 1886 or '87 I hope you've noticed how wonderful they are for just leaning on?' He stood astride it (I have to say, rather suggestively) and folded his arms on the saddle. 'They come in different sizes, and you get one that's the right size to lean on.'

Knowing my book was a search to discover why men are obsessed with machines, he then asked what I'd come up with so far. I got as far as mentioning the nature/machine paradox that had stumped L.T.C. Rolt, and a huge grin emerged on his face. The name was becoming something of a password.

'Good old Tommy Rolt! Now Tommy wrote about the bridge-builders. The people who could build bridges. I don't mean civil engineers, but people who could build connections between individual people with their different approaches to life and join them together. It's about a balanced life, Dan! Now on a bicycle you need a balanced life, but I would also argue, at least for myself, that the two gyroscopes on the damn bicycle at each end help me retain my balance and my sanity! I'd go further than that! My poor old mum died recently. She was ninety, that's just how it is. But I used to have to help her in her wheelchair to the hospital, down by the canal, for various appointments. Now, as we went into the hospital by the back gate one day we found about a dozen cyclists, and I felt that ten of those were nutters and two of them were social workers. As we were coming out a few hours later, they were coming back in, and we got talking, and it did transpire that this was right. Ten nutters and two psychiatrists, and these people were being given occupational therapy of riding a bicycle along the canal bank. Now it does *me* good. I can't say it for anyone else, but quite frankly a prescription for a bicycle ride is a damn sight more use to me than a prescription for many other kinds of stabilizer! I mean, look at me, I rode that to the far end of the Czech Republic, that one that I got out of a skip, all the way across Germany, ferry to Hamburg, right to Berlin, ride on to Dresden, ride on to Prague and through the whole length of the Czech Republic to Brno, where our international meeting was. Where, truthfully, the road sign pointer said Vienna 50 clicks, but by that stage the bicycle was breaking up, and so was I! I have range, but I have to go slow, and if you let me go slow at my speed, then I can do great things. But I'm not fast enough for industry, and I'm not fast enough for the dynamism of an office. I've also got an appalling memory, another symptom of ME. So I'm never quite sure where I'm going or where I've come from or where I am, but if you're riding great distances, then you navigate by compass anyway! You just point the compass east and ride.'

I looked at him incredulously and blurted out, 'What, so when you rode from here to within fifty miles of Vienna, you didn't even have a map?'

Lionel started to laugh hysterically and slapped his knee as though I'd, finally, well and truly fallen into his lair. His voice went up another notch in volume.

'One of the reasons I got the medal last year was because a chap I've got staying here with me at the moment, who is re-establishing himself, got married in Dresden ten days before the international meeting, which was in Holland. Now Germany is more or less square, and Dresden is as far as you can go into one corner while Holland is in the other. So I was in this wedding in Dresden. Now, you can't carry many maps on a bicycle anyway, and you certainly can't carry a huge pile of inch-to-a-mile maps, which is what you want, and I had seen motor-car maps, and it was more or less a straight line where I wanted to go. So I was discussing this at the wedding, and they said, "You can't ride across there, Lionel, there's mountains in the way!" Now, motor-car maps don't show contour lines. So what they said was "Ride three days along the River Elbe going back towards the North Sea. Three days along there you'll find the Metternin canal, and it goes right across the middle of Germany, and if you ride along that for a week you'll find the River Rhine, which goes into Holland." Now it's not quite as easy as that, because there aren't towpaths all along the canal, so you have to leave the river, go inland and get confused, but I rode all the way across Germany with a page torn out of an atlas of the world! I don't remember whether it said "Germany" or "Western

Europe". But on a bike you can just point it in a direction! Too often, particularly as I got to the Low Countries, I found I couldn't go in the direction I wanted because I couldn't find a road and in the end realized there was a river in front of me. But maps of the world don't tell you where bridges are, so one evening I found a beautiful meadow, a hayfield, that went down to the River Maas, and I just lay in the hay for the night. All the way through I'd learned you just have to *simplify!* You just unroll your bedroll and lie down. I lay there for the night, watching ships go up and down, and I swam out to the middle of the river and looked upstream and downstream in the morning to see if I could find a bridge, but I couldn't see one, so I just rode and then I found a ferry boat – of course, ferry boats aren't mentioned on world maps either – and that took me into Holland. So you just have to busk it, you know? The lesson I've learned from life is that you have to find your own way. It's beautiful, and it's not only astonishing, it's cheap! It's unbelievable, Dan!'

I wondered aloud whether he gave much thought to the actual mechanics of the bicycle, and he began to push himself up from his seat, as his voice got louder still.

'The point of high-bicycles is that they are PURE! I talk of the Church of the Holy Bicycle. I see it as the one true religion. The one religion where you will get to heaven, not by buying indulgences, not by endowing a great church, these are PURE! There's nothing there that you can do without!'

I mentioned Thomas Stevens and his epic journey. Lionel actually stood up and began shouting.

'As it says in the Bible, "Let your light shine before men that they see your good works and glorify your father in heaven!" Sorry, I was a church choirboy.' He laughed, sat down and I gasped again. 'Yes, he went out on a grand adventure with just his penny. That's all you need! Two speeds is enough. Riding it and pushing it. You don't need thirty gears! On my bicycle you are a little bit eye-catching too. People come up and talk to you. If you are open to people, then you get involved with people. It's the way. But it takes a long time to realize this, and I'm old. It's this instinct in us. Why do we like wheels and things that move? Wanting to go fast! Well, you see, I got there in the end, but I'm old. I used to love old cars. There's a radiator for an old Lagonda there.' He pointed to it, leaning on the wall behind me. 'I used to thunder up and down the A1 in that when I was an apprentice. I've still got the car. It doesn't go, needless to say. If I can find somewhere to park it, I'll get the damn thing going again.'

I asked whether it was all machines that fascinated him then, or just bikes.

'Well, it's been a long journey, Dan. It's been a long journey. I was apprenticed, again through cheating, with De Havilland, the aircraft engineers, at Hatfield for five years. I was riding from Ealing here to Hatfield every day! Well, that was the tragedy of it. I burned myself out. And the long and short of it is that's when I lost my engineering career. Quite truthfully, when I got that Lagonda, my life was in a mess. One of my mates was getting married in Norway, and he told me that in the shipyards they were crying out for engineers like me. So the crackpot scheme was to drive the Lagonda to the wedding in Norway, go down to the shipyard to get a job and have another go at life. Now the first bit worked. We got the Lag from Hatfield, drove to Dover, crossed the Channel, turned left and didn't stop until it got very cold. In a 1930 Lagonda that I bought behind a pub for £250! (Ha ha ha ha, tee-hee-hee-hee!)' He slapped his leg.

'But needless to say, the shipyard didn't want me, I had totally the wrong qualifications, but I got myself a job in a little workshop. You know, you meet people! Well, they took me into this workshop. Norway, where I was, half-way up the North Sea coast, it's mountains. Very little flat land and then down into the fjord, and that's where the little workshop was, right next to the fjord. It was lovely. Of course, the big old car showed I was an engineer and I got a job there. The peace, the stress off me, enabled me to get my head back together. But that's another set of stories. The point is that the motor car dominated my life for a while in my younger years, as it does, I suspect, for all young men.'

I mentioned that cars had never really done it for me and that I was starting to think of this love of engineering and machines as a language that I'd rather lost out on. Lionel raised both his hands in the air and bellowed with watering eyes.

'It is a language! It's an art form! I want to make a T-shirt, because I think it's a totally right statement, that an engineer is an artist, because you've got to be able to imagine this thing before you create it. And a scientist, otherwise it will break. But he's also got to be a philosopher, because good engineering design has to have an intellectual integrity. High-bicycles have an intellectual integrity because they are self-refining! Cars aren't. You can make a crap car, but if you put a big engine in it, it will still go. But with a bicycle you've got to get it right or your legs will hurt. You can't cheat, and that's why it's pure in a religious sense. God sees what you do, even if the world admires you.'

I mentioned that it sounded like he was pedalling around on a metaphor for how to live. He smiled and actually remained quiet for a relatively long time before replying very calmly. 'I think I am, yes. I think that you are right.' He looked at me slightly differently, perhaps wondering whether he should say what had just dropped into his mind.

'But if you ask why it is that men love machinery,' I nodded fiercely, 'well, I would suggest that men are the most beautiful creatures on this planet. Noble, but also the most ugly, doing the most horrible things. Women have learned to cope with the horror in men by being manipulative and by being deceitful – for self-preservation. Now men have learned that violence is wrong, and most don't do it, but women have not yet learned that manipulation and deceitfulness are wrong. But violence is honest. You can see it coming. And in that respect a machine is not deceitful.' He sat back. Finally content with silence.

Startled, I pointed out the obvious contentiousness of the statement that all women are manipulative and deceitful, and he replied, 'Yes, but is it wrong?' I flailed about for a response but, seeing my shock, he sought to reassure me, saying with a gentle smile, 'Well, I've given you *an* answer as to why men love machines.'

I sought to clarify it again. 'So you think men love machines because they are seeking a relationship that is incapable of being deceitful?'

'It may well be, yes.'

Putting aside whether or not women are by nature manipulative and deceitful – which, to put it rather mildly, is something of a can of worms – I began to wonder whether the traumas in Lionel's life were caused by failed relationships. But discounting his lack of faith in the female sex, I had some sympathy with the view that men love machines because it's a relationship with which they feel at ease, a relationship they can trust. The world of machines is one they can retreat into that seems to operate under predictable rules, unlike the universe we live in, which is so intimidating and baffling.

This idea lingered in my head for quite a while. Personally I find the eternal and colossal questions about the universe, space, time and the rather trifling scale of my own minuscule life within than reality rather unnerving, to put it mildly. No one seems to talk about the ultimate existential reality of life very often, though, so it made sense to me that solace from these vast questions might be found in a mechanical world with rational and predictable laws.

Lionel was certainly an 'enthusiast'. I don't think I've ever met anyone more enthusiastic about anything in my life. He wasn't joking about the Church of the Holy Bicycle either. He was thrilled when I explained the origin of the word 'enthusiast' and immediately turned to his two-volume edition of the *Oxford English Dictionary*, which he 'always keeps to hand, it's marvellous!', to check to see if I was right. He also took notes on our chat, I like to think to remind him of something I might have said that was of interest to him. But it soon transpired that we'd done enough talking. 'High-bicycles are for riding, not for talking about!'

We went outside, after he had taken the precaution of telling me how to fall if I felt I was going to, and how much the bike would cost to fix if I broke it, and then he ran along behind it before jumping up and riding ahead to show me how it's done. A walking bus of schoolchildren looked on delighted as he moved away in an astonishingly dignified fashion. You can see why they were so popular in the late nineteenth century, giving a literal leg-up to any man of status, who could now ride along in a sedate and venerable way.

Not for the last time on this journey I began to wonder what the hell I was doing as I attempted to mount the enormous high-bicycle a few minutes later on a more secluded path. Lionel tried to reassure me. 'Now I'm going to hold it and will tell you when I've let go.' I put my left foot on a small wedge by the small back wheel before pushing myself up into the saddle on another wedge with my right foot further up the frame. 'Now tuck in the front of your jumper so it doesn't catch on the saddle when you try to get off.' Lionel then explained that high-bicycles do not free-wheel, and every time I pushed down on one of the pedals it would push the wheel slightly to the other side. 'So you can't really ride straight, you have to slightly wobble.' It was all getting rather complicated. 'Right, now pedal.' It was horribly unstable. Suddenly aware of my immense weight, I began to wonder whether Lionel had the strength to keep me from toppling over, but he kept telling me to pedal and so we wobbled together further on down the hill. It was at that point I began begging him not to let go because I had absolutely no sense of control. He completely ignored me and began to say over and over again, 'I'm letting go, I'm letting go!' I shouted desperately 'NO DON'T, DON'T LET GO! PLEASE DON'T LET GO! FOR GOD'S SAKE DON'T LET GO!' as I careered towards a tree. I was about to hit the kerb and instinctively decided to dive over the handle-bars. All of a sudden I felt the bike halt as I plummeted face-first towards the earth. The bike had no reliable brake to speak of, and I remember thinking that Lionel was probably more concerned about his thousand-pound bike than me. Sure enough, once he knew I was going over, he had decided to hold on to it. I continued moving forward and down before landing on my face at the base of a beech tree with a painful crunch. I heard Lionel shouting gleefully, 'It's all right!'

I wondered how he could be so confident that the searing pain in my left hand and the stones grating my chin weren't signs of permanent damage, only to hear him shout again cheerfully as I peered up from the mud, 'It's all right, Dan! It's all right! You haven't damaged it!'

A few weeks later, still nursing a bruised cheek, I was in Newport on the Isle of Wight, standing outside a shop called White Mountain. The most recent breed of bicycle enthusiast to emerge and, I imagined, the furthest from a veteran bicycle enthusiast in terms of age and approach is surely the mountain biker.

The shop was covered with caged windows and looked like an enormous black beetle squatting at the end of a row of brick houses. I wasn't even inside yet, but already it felt like the kind of shop that requires a language someone like me has no hope of learning. It's as though every utterance I might make at the counter will be met with howling derision as I inadvertently reveal my total idiocy and lack of cool.

As it happened, that particular bit of paranoia turned out to be misplaced – as all paranoia about the unknown tends to be, I suppose. I walked through the door and saw a large repair area on my right. To the left, in every available space, were hundreds of mountain bikes with other accessories tucked away in glass cabinets or hanging on rungs on the wall. I introduced myself to Russ Newnham, the co-owner, behind the counter, and he began to smile. 'If you want to know about biking, then you've come to the right place.' Russ soon proved to be far friendlier than his broad ear-ring, comprehensive tattoos and punk hair had made him first appear too.

We started talking about how every child has a fascination with bicycles, but his interest had carried on into adulthood, with him now co-owning a specialist shop dedicated to his favourite machine. I was surprised when he immediately began to explain that mountain bikes helped him enter what sounded like a quite profound and more exciting reality than the daily nine-to-five.

'It's just that, however stupid it sounds, you can just get on your bike and forget about everything else in your life. When you get into the style of riding I was into when I was younger, street riding, where you just want to master something, you can spend four or five hours just trying to do one trick. Which sounds stupid to most people, but when you pull it off, that sense of achievement you get is amazing.'

A few years ago we ran an interview in a magazine I worked on with a man who was obsessed with pinball machines. He described a kind of 'fugue state', where you are so entranced by the machine that time seems to bend and you almost forget who you are as you get sucked deeply into what you're doing. I mentioned this to Russ, and he began to grin.

'That's exactly it. Exactly! You're completely oblivious to everything else going on around you. Downhill is another style of riding we do. It's crazy. France is the best place to go. It's a Mecca for biking. Up in the mountains they're all set up for it. You get on a chair-lift designed for you and your bike. Once you're at the top, there are loads of different runs all the way down that spit you out by two or three chair-lifts that will all take you up to different places. Last time I went for seven days with a bunch of mates, and we did a different track every run, and we did about 30 miles a day, which works out as about eight runs. We probably only did half the courses that are up there in that time. It's not just downhill runs either. There's a whole bike park up there. Dirt bike jumps, there are foam pits and air bags put out for you to jump into so you can practise your tricks for a couple of Euros a pop. The tracks go off in ribbons with high-speed fly-offs and jumps, they've got mattresses strapped to the trees, warning signs and catchment nets as well for sheer drops. There are expert and novice arrows with different ways to go down. It's a bit like ski runs. You can't ride some, because they're pretty mad. But there we do twenty-minute downhill runs going anything between 30 and 50 miles an hour. It's hectic. There's so much thinking. By the time you get to the bottom you're completely knackered even if you've done no pedalling. You think, "My God, that was just insane!"'

Russ was another bicycle enthusiast whose passion for bikes literally erupted out of him, but not in an evangelical way, like Lionel – more out of sheer excitement and a desire to open his mind to a completely new, more adventurous, way of looking at the world around him and the experience of life itself.

'It's incredibly complicated too. There are loads of different ways of tackling the obstacles – you don't just complete the course - and you've always got to look ahead to see what's coming next. We've got full-face helmets on, full body armour, goggles, you can't hear anything. You've got limited vision, and on the open path stuff we're doing 58, 59 miles an hour off-road, and the noise at that speed and blurred vision – it's just a different world. Absolute craziness. You feel pretty alive with it all, you know?'

The expression on his face as he talked was intoxicating. I found myself grinning broadly too.

I asked him to try and explain more about what the buzz he described felt like. He spent a few moments looking around the shop in thought before replying, as if the answer was to be found in one of the racks on the walls, and then pulled the words from the air around him.

'It's the adrenaline and the danger, definitely danger . . . but you've also got this thing in mountain biking called your "limit".' With those words he stared at me, insinuating that this was the absolute crux of his passion.

'Your "limit" is when you're riding quite quick, but it's all fine, you're in control. It's when you ride over your limit that you get the adrenaline buzz and it gets scary. You can ride a bit faster than you'd normally feel comfortable with but still manage to go down a hill. Going over that line is terrifying, and that's when you get your adrenaline, because at any moment you can come off and know you're going to get hurt badly. You get to the bottom, knowing you've ridden over your limit and you still stayed on, then you get the buzz. And it's amazing. I don't ride within my limit any more because it's boring. To ride knowing you're always fine is a waste of time. What's the point of going out? I like the feeling of knowing that I couldn't have gone any faster. If I go round a corner wrong and put too much brake on, I get pissed off. I'm really hard on myself. You just want to complete that course as fast as you can and go over your limit. If you're going down the hill out of control, scaring yourself and bor- derline crashing – then that's how you're meant to ride. That's why you're there. If you go down in your comfort zone, then you just feel empty. There's no buzz. You've got to open the throttle and scare yourself to make it a good session. That's exactly what we do it for.'

I asked if he got that unusual or exciting experience – that sense of adventure – from anything else, such as fast cars.

'I do scare myself in my car occasionally. I've got quite a fast one, but it's not the same, because you just think "you idiot", because that's death in a car and it's not really skill. You could easily kill someone else in a car too. On a bike it's fine – at worst I'm just going to break my arm.'

I started laughing, but he had a completely serious, straight face and shrugged his shoulders.

'It doesn't really bother me. Biking is just the only thing I get seriously off on. Even when people do a downhill run on a bike for the first time, you can see them getting into it. They go so slowly. To me it would feel like about 1 mile an hour. I'd be looking around at the view and stuff, but they'll be scaring themselves because they've never done it before, and they'll get to the bottom and be buzzing just as much as I'd be if I'd gone down beyond my limit. That's when you think, "Excellent! That's why you're on a bike! To get that buzz!" It's great at that point to see someone finally understand it. You feel so glad they can now see why I ride this stupid little bike, which is probably what they were thinking before.'

The perception that biking is a bit childish seemed to frustrate him.

'When you're in the industry like I am, the people you see all the time are complete bike junkies. Everyone I know is into it, so it's kind of the norm for me, but speak to anyone outside it and they're like, "Oh yeah, you're into bikes, aren't you", and they start looking for someone else to talk to. And you think, yeah I am, but it's so much more than what you think it is!'

Finally I asked him what percentage of his character was reflected in and by his love of mountain biking. 'I'd say almost all of it,' he replied matter-of-factly.

I left, exhausted by the pace and intensity of the experience Russ had just described. This extreme sport approach to access intense experiences had always seemed utterly pointless to me, but the way Russ spoke about it made much more sense. I began to wonder whether it was this level of intensity with which machine enthusiasts seemed to live their lives, a real passion for the experience of living, that lay at the heart of their fascination with machines. Not always in the high-octane way described by Russ, but any real and intense engagement with what it actually means to be alive: the opposite of the kind of experience you get from working in a tedious job, obsessively shopping or spending every night in front of the TV.

For Ben and Cath on the canals that intense experience of life came from having the time to observe and reflect on it properly. For Brian the lawn-mower enthusiast it was about preserving examples of a kind of engineering intensity that epitomized quality and perfection in a throwaway world. For Danny and Steve it was through friendship and bringing old and tired machines back to life. For Lionel it was about the extraordinary adventures and experiences you could access through a machine, and for Russ, it seemed, his love of machines took him into a different way of thinking – an adrenaline-fuelled passion to push what he was physically capable of. Very disparate interests in their own ways but all were fully engaged with the world they saw around them, and none seemed to feel the need to hide who and what they were. The confidence they all radiated was astonishing. They all shared a kind of courage to live that I found intensely exciting. I felt I was making progress. It was time to pick up speed.

5

Freedom

Motor cycles

'THE THING WITH riding a motor cycle', my Death Metal friend Jamie told me sincerely while we walked around the edges of a classic bike show at Kempton Park racecourse, 'is that the first time you ride, and every time after, you just can't believe you're allowed to do it.' I looked back at him with a look of gruzzlement on my face. ('Gruzzlement' is a word I have invented to describe the slightly uneasy, baffled smile I adopt when someone starts talking to me about machines.) Around us, in the tepid sunshine, men with denim jackets were panning through the bits of jagged metal on the look-out for a piece of rusted gold. We'd only been there for half an hour, but I'd already concluded that bikers were by far the most intimidating enthusiasts I'd come across so far. The most distant stalls included the odd bit of Nazi paraphernalia, and there were limitless pictures of skulls and greasy-haired men with piercings and ghastly tattoos. Then I turned to my long-haired friend Jamie, also wearing leather, with his own pierced nose and a fair collection of tattoos, and began to wonder whether anyone ever found him intimidating, which, having known him for a decade, would be quite absurd. Jamie is lovely. Perhaps the bikers' attempt to shock was all part of some elaborate theatre.

Unsurprisingly perhaps, the invention of the motor cycle is entangled with that of the bicycle. As we learned in the previous chapter, the safety bicycle, so named because its wheels, unlike those of the high-bicycle, were the same size, was invented by John Kemp Starley in 1885. The safety bicycle's enormous popularity soon inspired an idea in inventors across the world. What if a bicycle could be powered by some other means than pedals?

Over in America steam-powered motor bikes were rumoured to have existed as far back as the 1860s, but it wasn't until 1894 that it became possible for anyone actually to buy a motor cycle that looked anything like one we would recognize today. It was called the Hildebrand and Wolfmüller and was powered by a two-cylinder, four-stroke engine. Another name for a four-stroke engine is the 'internal combustion engine', and the story of how it was invented is, inevitably, rather complicated too.

The 'internal combustion engine' was part of that terrifying language I'd spent my whole life convinced I lacked the aptitude to learn, but I'd decided it was about time I got my brain dirty. Rather amazingly, it didn't turn out to be hard to understand at all (at a very basic level, you understand). It all comes down to 'Suck, Squash, Bang, Blow'. There, now I sound like one of them, don't I?

While the 'internal combustion engine' had been mentioned with great reverence in all the machine enthusiast circles I'd orbited so far, I was intrigued that I'd never heard anyone talk about the 'external combustion engine', but it turned out that I had. It's just referred to by another name: the steam engine. In a steam engine the combustion part takes place when the coal is burned in a firebox, which is separated from the cylinder of the engine (where the water that becomes steam powers the piston). As you might guess from the name, in the internal combustion engine the combustion part takes place inside the cylinder. So far, so simple.

While a steam engine burns lots of coal and huge draughts of oxygen to heat water and generate steam, the internal combustion engine compresses a small amount of air and fuel before igniting it. The carbon that erupts from the ignited mix of air and fuel (petrol in modern vehicles) in the form of a gas then does the same job (moves the moving part of the engine) as the steam in a steam engine. Once the heated gas has cooled, it becomes the exhaust that goes out into the atmosphere. This makes it far more efficient and powerful than an external combustion engine, where a lot of the heat is wasted. The pressure in a steam engine is described in pounds per square inch, and the pressure in the internal combustion engine is described in tons per square inch, which gives you some idea of the huge difference in muscle and efficiency. It also explains why the internal combustion engine was later able to power much larger machines.

Going back to 'Suck, Squash, Bang, Blow', the 'Suck' is where the air and petrol are sucked into the combustion chamber. The 'Squash' relates to how the mix is compressed. The 'Bang' relates to the moment of combustion that creates the power, and the 'Blow' relates to the exhaust. Each of these four events is powered by a stroke of the piston: hence 'four-stroke'. While we're on the subject of engines, a diesel engine differs from a petrol engine most fundamentally in the way that it ignites the mix of air fuel. While a petrol engine uses spark plugs to ignite the mix, in a diesel engine the pressure of the air and fuel is vastly increased and effectively ignites itself. (Imagine frantically pumping a bicycle pump – you'll find the action creates heat using the same principle.)

Back in the seventeenth century Samuel Morland invented a pump that used gunpowder to create a vacuum to suck in water, which is often described as one of the first internal combustion engines. (Interestingly Morland was a spy and also invented the megaphone.) Alessandro Volta made a simple combustion engine in the 1780s, using a spark to ignite a mixture of hydrogen and air to fire a toy gun. From that you might have him down as something of a frivolous eccentric, but Volta gave his name to the 'Voltaic battery', the first electrochemical cell. Other internal combustion engine pioneers include the Swiss inventor François Isaac de Rivaz, who built his engine in 1806. But it was in 1862 that Nicolaus Otto invented the first truly internal combustion engine where the fuel burned inside the piston chamber. It's for this reason that you might hear machine enthusiasts refer to a four-stroke engine as an 'Otto' engine or 'Otto cycle'.

In 1872 two men, Gottlieb Daimler and Wilhelm Maybach, joined Otto's company, and in 1876 they refined his designs and built another four-stroke engine that ran on gas. After that Daimler and Otto fell out, and it wasn't until 1885 in Daimler's workshop that Daimler and Maybach together designed the petrol engine that is reproduced and refined in modern cars and motor bikes. Later that year they produced the prototype *Reitwagen*, which looks a lot like a motor bike but which had two small extra stabilizing wheels at the back. You may think it's a bit strange to build a motor bike with four wheels, but Daimler became rather well known for his four-wheeled vehicles some years later. Nine years after the *Reitwagen*, in 1894, the water-cooled twin cylinder Hildebrand and Wolfmüller hit the streets.

It wasn't an immediate hit in Britain, though. In 1865 the Locomotive Act had been passed to try and control the varied steam- and pedal-powered contraptions that had begun appearing on the nation's roads. For public safety it was written into law that any motorized vehicle had to be preceded by a man holding a red flag (although in truth this law was rarely upheld in later years). After a campaign by Harry Lawson (a bicycle and motor-car designer) the Locomotion Act was repealed in 1896. To celebrate Lawson organized the inaugural London-to-Brighton car run, which continues to this day. Freed from the red flag restriction, British manufacturers soon started to experiment with motorized bicycles of their own.

The best-known motor-cycle makers represented at the classic bike show I visited began to appear a few years later: Triumph (who originally built bicycles) and Norton (manufacturers of bicycle chains) in 1902, Harley-Davidson in 1903, Indian Motorcycles in 1904, AJS in 1909 and BMW in 1923. The Japanese invasion of Honda and Kawasaki didn't begin until the 1960s and 1970s.

Back at Kempton Park the beers were flowing, and I spotted a few Hells Angels in the crowd. Now there's a phrase that strikes fear into the hearts of most people. I whispered a question to Jamie to find out whether the Harley-Davidson motor cycles they were renowned for riding were the ultimate marque that all bikers aspired to. He looked back at me with shock and disdain. 'No! They're awful! Slow, heavy, unreliable. The people that ride them are either Hells Angels or middle-aged investment bankers having a mid-life crisis. No one interested in motor cycles would have one. Mechanically they're shit.' Jamie rode a Triumph Speed Triple, which is far superior apparently.

Despite telling myself that they were surely a diluted version of the figures in the horror stories from the 1960s and '70s, I'm afraid I was far too timid to go up and ask the Angels any questions, but a news report a few months later suggested the notorious image might still be deserved. A man called Gerry Tobin, a Hells Angel from south-east

London, had been shot in the back of the head while riding home from the Bulldog Bash Biker Festival in Warwickshire in August 2007. The men charged with his murder were about to go on trial. Other stories in the press suggested the murder was to do with Gerry passing through the territory of another motor-cycle gang, called the 'Outlaws'. It seemed astonishingly brutal, cowardly and, well, primitive behaviour for twenty-first-century Britain. Pictures of Gerry appeared all over motor-cycle enthusiast internet pages, including the extensive 'Memorial' section of the Hells Angels own website.

I turned to Hunter S. Thompson's book *Hell's Angels* (the Angels themselves drop the apostrophe because, they maintain, there is more than one version of hell) to try and get my head round what originally had turned this particular bunch of machine enthusiasts to become self-confessed outlaws. Motor cycles had become more than a part of their identity. They held on to them so tightly that all other priorities in their lives seemed to vanish completely. Unless, of course, that's one of the many myths created about, or by, them. Myth, as we'll see in a moment, has a huge part to play in the story of the Angels.

Say 'Hells Angels' to anyone today and ask them what first comes to mind, and you'll probably soon hear the words 'Harley-Davidson, dangerous, leather, outlaw, gang, rape, wild', and the list of horror will go on and on. There are many stories about where they came from and the terrible things they get up to but, as with the history of the invention of the machines we've read about so far, most of the stories are apocryphal. The most popular myth is that they originated from a B-17 bomber crew who called themselves the 'Hell's Angels' during the Second World War. The story goes that these brave men got home and, after the excitement and danger they experienced during the war, were unable to settle back into normal life and started to ride around on motor cycles under the same banner, causing havoc. Others, desperate for excitement, joined them, and over the next fifty years the Hells Angels as an outlaw club grew to the global organization that exists today. It's a nice story but untrue according to the Angels themselves, although their numbers do seem to grow in the years following any military conflict, which suggests that they have become a magnet for the traumatized, dispossessed, broken men of war.

It turns out that the emergence of the first outlaw motor-cycle clubs pre-date the Hells Angels, though. We have to go back to the Californian town of Hollister on 4 July 1947, when the original act of revulsion perpetrated by motor-cycle clubs took place, involving one club called the Booze Fighters (from whom the Hells Angels claim to be descended). A report of what happened in an edition of *Life* magazine three weeks later, swiftly followed by articles of a similar tone across the USA, came to represent, and argu-ably to invent, the image most of us have of the motor-cycle outlaw today. The political and media frenzy that followed this report created an almost entirely false but ter-rifying myth that subsequent generations of bikers seem to have decided to live up to, or at least revel in, rather than deny.

The *Life* magazine article in question, titled 'Cyclist's Holiday', appeared on 21 July 1947. It was a report on the latest race meeting held by members of the American Motorcycle Association (AMA). These events took place all across America and were designed to give motor-cycle enthusiasts the chance to watch races and hang out with fellow fans. The picture illustrating the story, of a drunk and bloated man sat astride a motor cycle surrounded by broken beer bottles, gives a sign that things in Hollister had gone slightly awry. The article itself begins:

> On the fourth of July weekend 4,000 members of a motor-cycle club roared into Hollister, California, for a three-day convention. They quickly tired of ordinary motorcycle thrills and turned to more exciting stunts. Racing their vehicles down Main Street and through traffic lights, they rammed into restaurants and bars, breaking furniture and mirrors. Some rested on the curb. Others hardly paused. Police arrested many for drunkenness and indecent exposure but could not restore order. Finally, after two days, the cyclists left with a brazen explanation. 'We like to show off. It's just a lot of fun.' But Hollister's Police Chief took a different view. Wailed he, 'It's just one hell of a mess!'

Life magazine's coverage of the Hollister 'riot' directly inspired the writers of a film called *The Wild One*, which was released six years later, in 1953. The film's young star, Marlon Brando, came to symbolize youthful rebellion two years before James Dean in *Rebel without a Cause*. *The Wild One* tells the story of the day two motor-cycle gangs descend on a small Californian town before causing death and widespread destruction. The similarity to reported events at Hollister was no accident. Stanley Kramer, who produced *The Wild One*, went to the town to interview local people about the day the motor-cycle outlaws rode into town. The film was not, he said afterwards, an attempt to make a documentary of what had occurred, but to convey 'the first big divorcement of youth from society', which highlights the powerful impact the reported events of Hollister had turned out to have.

Ashamed of the coverage their event received, the AMA were moved to distance themselves from the '1 per cent' of motor-cyclists who had caused the trouble, maintaining that

99 per cent of motor-cycle enthusiasts were honest, law-abiding citizens. The '1 per cent' comment turned out to stick, but probably not in the way the AMA had imagined. The more extreme motor-cycle clubs revelled in their new status as homes for notorious troublemakers and proudly proclaimed themselves to be part of that outlaw 1 per cent. Even today most outlaw clubs wear a patch that says '1%er'. It was now official. The moral outrage of 1950s America had found the perfect target, and the motor-cycle outlaw was born.

But events in Hollister that day were not, perhaps, exactly the way *Life* magazine had described, at least not according to eyewitnesses. Motor-cycle historian Jerry Smith later tracked down a man called Gus DeSerpa, who claimed to be present at the time the infamous photograph of the drunken bloated man astride a motor bike surrounded by broken beer bottles was actually taken. DeSerpa recalled that *Life* photographer Barney Peterson had persuaded a drunk onlooker (whether he was even a member of a motor-cycle gang is not clear) to sit on the bike while he collected bottles, which had previously been arranged neatly by the kerb, and scattered them around the motor cycle to make a more shocking picture.

John Dorrance's article 'Forty Hours in Hollister' is widely regarded as the most truthful account of what really happened that day. Dorrance tracked down other residents also present.

> Johnny Lamanto, who was 20 years old and motorcycle crazy in the summer of 1947: 'That movie [*The Wild One*] really downed the motorcycle image. The way they made the picture, 90 percent wasn't the way it happened here. In them days there was mostly respectable clubs. There was no big gangs like this Marlon Brando bunch, where guys come in and park and harass the bars and all that.'

Statistics from the local hospital and police force seem to bear out the fact that what occurred was little more than a bit of drunken posturing. *Life* magazine's surely inflated report of 4,000 wild bikers descending on the town makes the figure of forty arrests over the entire weekend seem incredibly restrained. It turns out that only three people were taken, with serious injuries, to the local hospital in that time too, and all three were from motor-cycle accidents to be expected at a race meet of this kind.

The truth, in other words, is far more mundane than the hysterical media reports suggested. But the next generation of motor-cycle 'outlaws' clearly enjoyed the possibilities the myth had unleashed and began to live up to that image instead. Thanks to the frenzied media coverage, which blossomed from the hugely respected and trusted *Life* magazine in newspapers across the country, the motor cycle became synonymous with a wild, freedom-obsessed bogeyman that 1950s middle America had now been whipped up to fear. In the decades that followed, that bogeyman grew from strength to strength and spread all across the world.

The 1 per cent of outlaws that emerged, including the new Hells Angels, certainly weren't content to glimpse the wild freedom they had read about on the weekends before meekly submitting to the voluntary, perhaps mechanical, enslavement of the worker's nine-to-five. For them the anarchic autonomy they'd seen encapsulated in the image of the motor-cycle outlaw became a way of cutting themselves off from society completely. These motor-cycle clubs soon became a magnet for anyone wanting to opt out and live free of moral or 'American' values. Many became convinced that they were the latest incarnation of the notorious gun fighters of the Wild West a hundred years earlier. Wilder and wilder press coverage of their exploits appeared, leading the Angels to trot out the line that's on their website even today: 'When we do right no-one remembers, when we do wrong no-one forgets'.

In order to be untainted by the hypocrisy of society's values and the total reluctance of that society to deal with the truth of life, as they saw it, whatever they could do to alienate themselves from it was done with relish. They revelled in their abhorrence, and the American public seemed only too happy to oblige with unlimited disgust. But the Angels became proud to be loathed by a society that in their view was mired in political and corporate corruption, had been designed with deliberate inequality in mind, was terrifyingly unequal and brutally policed (law enforcement officers feared the myth of the motor-cycle outlaws just as much as everybody else). This would account for the way Hells Angels later adopted Nazi paraphernalia – not because they were Nazis themselves but simply because of how horrifying and vile Nazi images are to members of 'respectable' society. If there is a perfect way to encapsulate the logic of the Hells Angels of the 1960s and '70s (of myth), then this is surely it; they didn't want to be understood. They wanted the public to be so revolted by how they looked and what they did that they would leave them well alone. The tendency not to wash and to urinate on a new member's jeans during initiation ceremonies (which they were supposedly forbidden from ever washing – perhaps another myth) fed into this idea that, the more repugnant to normal people the Angels were, the freer from society they would ultimately be. More stories appeared in the newspapers that detailed this kind of increased depravity, and the bogeyman grew taller still. The desire to be reviled might also account for their deliberate choice of a motor-cycle brand that was mechanically obsolete almost as soon as it was designed. Not content with this, the Angels made a point of customizing their motorcycles – only then could they legitimately be labelled as 'hogs' – to make them harder and harder to ride. Only someone with 'class' (their term of highest praise) would be able to handle the customized monstrosities they sought to create. Seen in this context, the horror stories that seem to orbit the Hells Angels (and which they rarely deny), including their preference for gang rape, violence, drug use, abuse of women, lack of moral values, wild behaviour and total lack of consideration for 'civilians', become a device as much as a lifestyle choice to maintain their freedom and separation from a world they abhor. The list of their supposed degeneracy is quite astonishing. From the different coloured 'wings' an Angel can apparently win ('red wings' for performing cunnilingus in public on a woman who is menstruating and 'purple wings' for the same act on a corpse) to the practice of motor-cycle gangs having 'mamas' – women who consent to having sex with any member of the gang and even with all of them all at once ('pull a train'), if that is what the gang demand. To whatever degree these reported activities and stories actually happen or happened, they were important propaganda to ensure that 'civilians' gave them a wide berth. It was with this in mind that Hunter S. Thompson began his quest to discover whether the terrifying news reports emerging in the late 1950s and early '60s about the Angels had any basis in reality.

He soon discovered in graphic terms the attraction and alienation of this way of life and how crucial the Hells Angels' motor cycles were to their sense of self. It seems that many members he met simply had nowhere else to go, and their motor cycles and notoriety were all they had left. He wrote:

> Most of the Angels work sporadically at the kind of jobs that will soon be taken by machines . . . it takes an employer who is either desperate or unusually tolerant . . . but to

apply for work as a member of a nationally known 'criminal motorcycle conspiracy' is a handicap that can only be overcome by very special talents, which few Angels possess. Most are unskilled and uneducated, with no social or economic credentials beyond a colourful police record and a fine knowledge of motorcycles . . .

To see a lone Angel screaming through traffic – defying all rules, limits, and patterns – is to understand the motorcycle as an instrument of anarchy, a tool of defiance and even a weapon. A Hell's Angel on foot can look pretty foolish. Their sloppy histrionics and inane conversations can be interesting for a few hours, but beyond the initial strangeness, their everyday scene is as tedious and depressing as a costume ball for demented children. There is something pathetic about a bunch of men gathering every night in the same bar, taking themselves very seriously in their ratty uniforms, with nothing to look forward to but the chance of a fight or a round of head jobs from some drunken charwoman.

But there is nothing pathetic about the sight of an Angel on his bike. The whole – man and machine together – is far more than the sum of its parts. His motorcycle is the one thing in his life he has absolutely mastered. It is his only valid status symbol, his equalizer, and he pampers her in the same way a busty Hollywood starlet pampers her body. Without it, he is no better than a punk on a street corner. And he knows it . . .

Man and machine in harmony, of sorts.

The paradoxical nature of the Hells Angels came through in newspaper reports six months later, when I then read the very last thing I imagined ever reading about the murdered Gerry Tobin. It appears that Gerry was a devout Christian and, despite being widely jested about it in motor-cycle circles, made, in typically Hells Angels fashion, absolutely no

For someone with an allergy to machines, there is only one cure.

Left: The opening of the Sapperton tunnel at the heart of the now-disused Thames and Severn canal. The water is shallow, so you can walk into the tunnel to stand before two miles of subterranean darkness – a truly awesome experience.

Below: Ben and Cath beside their canal boat 'Constance', travelling gently to a happier state of mind.

Steam dreams. Under the tutelage of Mike, who was likeably gruff in a way I imagined a steam engine driver of the 1940s would be, I attempted to drive a steam train. At one stage we reached 40 m.p.h., which made him quite angry. I later learned that there is a strict speed limit of 25 m.p.h. across the network, which perhaps explains why.

Above: The belching monsters of the Great Dorset Steam Fair, the world's largest steam event.

Left: Lionel on one of his beloved high bicycles; my riding style was considerably less graceful than his.

Below: Barry with his motorcycle and sidecar.

Bob in his office, and in his shed beside the Wonder Car he built himself.

In the pit lane with the Mitsubishi team for the Britcar 24-hour race at Silverstone.

Left: Andy explains *spielzeug* to me with the help of his collection of firearms.

Below left and right: Out on the tank driving range

Left: How do the drivers of amphibious tanks stop themselves from being flooded by icy sludge when they go into deep water? By driving much more slowly than I did.

My son Wilf and I wrestle with the controls of various bits of heavy machinery at the refreshingly fun Diggerland.

My first flight in eighteen years, in a ludicrously small aeroplane. I am quite nervous.

Back on earth and on top of the world.

apology for the freedom he demanded to be exactly who he was. If there is a better way of proving that Hells Angels seek freedom to be who they are above everything else, for good or bad, rightly or wrongly, morally or immorally, it is perhaps that a Hells Angel could exist who was a devout Christian. That's assuming all the 'myths' are true and that the Hells Angels are not actually a group of men simply trying to conjure up an image of fear in the public that they all laugh about heartily when they're among themselves.

Back inside the exhibition hall, a world away from the rough stalls on the edges of the bike show and the Hells Angels, I soon spotted a chap who appeared to be in his late seventies drinking tea astride a motor cycle and sidecar with a badge on the bike that said 'Ariel'. I hadn't heard of 'Ariel', but it turned out to have its own remarkable pedigree too: it took its name from a high-bicycle (Ariel being 'the spirit of the air' and so named because you sat so high up) built by James Starley, who was John Starley's uncle. 'Barry' as I soon discovered, had first come across Ariel motorcycles in the RAF. During the Second World War the Ariel factory had been commandeered to make military vehicles. I asked him how he'd become interested in motor cycles, and this soon turned into a forty-five-minute monologue, with me drifting gently along on his hypnotic Cornish burr through the wonderful memories of his life with his favourite type of machine. It turned out that Barry's love of motor cycles also emerged in 1947, but not because of the reported events at Hollister.

'We used to go up on the downs as boys rabbiting, and up there was an old dump. We were out one day in '47, and we pulled out all the pieces of a broken Douglas motor cycle. So we took it all home and put it together. We used to ride it, with grass in the tyres and petrol we'd nicked from harvesters left in the field. This was back when petrol was on ration. I was still going to school at the time. But that Douglas started me off. I've been interested ever since.

'After that I made one from a lawn-mower engine, push-bike wheel and forks and a motor-bike frame. No gearbox, just straight drive from engine to back wheel. But I moved on from that and got a proper one, an Ariel, a few years later. When I got married, I sold the bike and got four wheels, but some years ago now I fancied getting back into it. I knew a chap with some bikes, and he showed me one, and then he produced the logbook, which was 1957, and then he got the MOT out, which was the 23rd March. Now 23 March 1957 is the day I got married. So I thought, "What a coincidence!" I showed my wife and said, "See this, it's magic! I should have this bike!" and she agreed, and then, well, I was off.'

Barry was soon regaling me with tales of the rather hapless adventures he'd had on his Ariel ever since, including the time he entered the Land's End trial, a motor-bike endurance run.

'I enjoyed most of it until it started to get dark . . . I was making my way towards Taunton, and the light was getting dimmer. Being a greenhorn, I'd never done any kind of trial in my life, but this chap let me follow him, which was nice, but we came up to a roundabout and I lost him, and I didn't know which way he'd gone. I ended up shooting down the wrong road. So I stopped and had to get my glasses out to look at my route map in the dark . . .' In the end Barry had to give up half-way round. 'I came to a big hill, which I didn't know at the time, but it was "Beggars Roost", a famous hill they've been using at Land's End for years. So I had a go, but the clutch gave out so much, kept slipping, I couldn't make it up. There was smoke, so I had to retire.'

I asked him whether it was the mechanics of the bike that had kept his interest all this time.

'I can't really explain it. Some people are bored doing nothing, so they've got to do something with their hands to occupy their mind. Something mechanical, maybe. Others can sit and read books. Some people can sit around watching TV all day, but I can't. I'm not that sort. If someone gives me a job on this bike to do, or another bike, I'm happy. I mean, I even volunteered the other week to make a manifold for a model engine on an aircraft because I've got a small lathe, you see? If it's mechanical and metal, then I love playing with it.'

His eyes were watering with enthusiasm, and he had a broad smile across his face. I was desperate to know what exactly it was about mechanics and motor cycles that made him so happy. He rolled his shoulders a bit and stepped towards me, raising his finger. His tea, in a small red plastic cup in his other hand, was now long cold.

'The first thing I'll say about that is it's the absolute freedom. You go where you want to go. You're in charge of that.' He pointed to the bike as though that in itself would tell me all I needed to know. They were words worthy of an Angel. I asked if he would ever give it up, and he shook his head.

'I broke my neck nine year ago. My wife was there, and the surgeon said, "No more motor bikes", and I said, "What about push bikes?" and he said, "No, no push bikes." I've got a plate in my neck, see. Well, I went a bit dim, you know, I thought, "What am I going to do?" Then all my mates, they rallied around and said to my wife, "He'll be all right if he had a sidecar, they don't fall over", so we worked on that and I got this.' He tapped it lovingly.

'My wife accepts that. I got an AJS with a sidecar too. They may be machines but they're *natural* things to me. Lot of people say, "Oh, bikes are too dangerous, they should be banned", but there's nothing wrong with the bike. Half the problem now is that most car drivers have never ridden a bike, so they don't know 'em, and they just don't understand 'em.'

I thanked him for chatting, and he grinned. 'I tell you what, if you stay talking to me for too long, you'll end up an idiot like what I am.'

The sensation of riding a motor cycle seemed to tap into something primeval in men, whether they are wild, young Hells Angels or mild-mannered family men in their seventies. It's as if the male body is sufficiently refined and evolution has decided that it must now emerge from the minds of men, rather than grow from their bodies, to provide a powerful new two-wheeled appendage between his legs. If you think that sounds a little over the top, wait until you've read the next passage by another motor-cycle enthusiast, the writer and all-round hero T.E. Lawrence (Lawrence of Arabia), about the allure of motor cycles, from his book *The Mint*, an account of his time training in the RAF in the 1920s. What follows is part of a piece he wrote about racing a Bristol Fighter aeroplane while on his Brough motor cycle. Reading it, you can feel the dust and pain in your eyes and ears, but it's thrilling, hilarious and stupidly dangerous all at the same time. I couldn't help but grin like a child by the time I got to the end. The name Lawrence gave his Brough was Boanerges, a Greek word that means 'Son of Thunder'.

I have [had] the honour of [riding on] one of England's straightest and fastest roads. The burble of my exhaust unwound like a long cord behind me. Soon my speed snapped it, and I heard only the cry of the wind which my battering head split and fended aside. The cry rose with my speed to a shriek: while the air's coldness streamed like two jets of iced water into my dissolving eyes. I screwed them to slits, and focused my sight two hundred yards ahead of me on the empty mosaic of the tar's gravelled undulations.

Like arrows the tiny flies pricked my cheeks: and sometimes a heavier body, some housefly or beetle, would crash into face or lips like a spent bullet. A glance at the speedometer: seventy-eight. Boanerges is warming up. I pull the throttle right open, on the top of the slope, and we swoop flying across the dip, and up-down up-down the switchback beyond: the weighty machine launching itself like a projectile with a whirr of wheels into the air at the take-off of each rise, to land lurchingly with such a snatch of the driving chain as jerks my spine like a rictus.

Once we so fled across the evening light, with the yellow sun on my left, when a huge shadow roared just overhead. A Bristol Fighter, from Whitewash Villas, our neighbour aerodrome, was banking sharply round. I checked speed an instant to wave: and the slip-stream of my impetus snapped my arm and elbow astern, like a raised flail. The pilot pointed down the road towards Lincoln. I sat hard in the saddle, folded back my ears and went away after him, like a dog after a hare. Quickly we drew abreast, as the impulse of his dive to my level exhausted itself.

The next mile of road was rough. I braced my feet into the rests, thrust with my arms, and clenched my knees on the tank till its rubber grips goggled under my thighs. Over the first pothole Boanerges screamed in surprise, its mudguard bottoming with a yawp upon the tyre. Through the plunges of the next ten seconds I clung on, wedging my gloved hand in the throttle lever so that no bump should close it and spoil our speed. Then the bicycle wrenched sideways into three long ruts: it swayed dizzily, wagging its tail for thirty awful yards. Out came the clutch, the engine raced freely: Boa checked and straightened his head with a shake, as a Brough should.

The bad ground was passed and on the new road our flight became birdlike. My head was blown out with air so that my ears had failed and we seemed to whirl soundlessly between the sun-gilt stubble fields. I dared, on a rise, to slow imperceptibly and glance sideways into the sky. There the Bif was, two hundred yards and more back. Play with the fellow? Why not? I slowed to ninety . . .

It's clinically impossible for any human being not to love that. Joy is tempered, somewhat, by the knowledge that Lawrence died while riding Boanerges in 1935. He took a blind hump in the road at speed not far from his home and didn't see two boys on their bikes on the other side. When he did see them, he swerved and crashed. They wore no helmets in the 1930s, and six days later Lawrence died at the age of forty-six. It was an abrupt end. His love of motor cycles was obvious, though, as was the sense that to him this machine was almost conscious, perhaps because its power and design had enhanced his own sense of being alive, regardless of the risks associated with it and its tempestuous nature. 'A skittish motor-bike with a touch of blood in it', he also wrote, 'is better than all the riding animals on earth, because of its logical extension of our faculties, and the hint, the provocation, to excess conferred by its honeyed untiring smoothness. Because Boa loves me, he gives me five more miles of speed than a stranger would get from him.'

'Its logical extension of our faculties' is an interesting phrase, suggesting that men make and enjoy machines in order to fulfil their dreams of who and what they hope to be.

It was with that in mind that I began to read a famous book about motor cycles written by Robert Pirsig.

Zen and the Art of Motorcycle Maintenance is surely the best-selling book with the word 'Motorcycle' in the title, and it's fair to say that its contents were about to surprise and amaze me. While recounting a journey he took with his son and some friends across America on a motor cycle, Pirsig weaves his passion for motor-cycle mechanics into his theory of how to interpret reality, which he calls the 'metaphysics of quality': a philosophical theory that tries to explain and bridge the gulf between those that love machines and those who don't.

As we've already learned, our old friend L.T.C. Rolt lamented how he had never managed to reconcile the two opposing sides of his character and saw an equally intractable division between people who have a passion for mechanical things and those who see them as responsible for destroying the beauty of the world around them. I was interested to read that Pirsig too believes people fall into these two types of personalities and had wrestled with the same question. He calls these groups 'Romantics', or technophobes (like me) with a more spiritual but not religious take on life, and 'Classicists', who prefer rational thought, how things work – machine enthusiasts.

The narrative thrust of *Zen and the Art of Motorcycle Maintenance* is the journey to understand Pirsig's two person-alities before and after he had a nervous breakdown. One is Classicist, the other Romantic. After being released from hospital (having had extensive electro-convulsive therapy), he tries to find a common relationship between the two per-sonalities that he can use to rebuild his life in the future. Like Rolt, he's looking for a bridge.

Pirsig's view is that you will inevitably interpret everything that you encounter in the world and your life according to whether you are a Romantic or Classicist. So, if you'll excuse such clumsiness, a Romantic like me might panic at the mere mention of the internal combustion engine and think of it purely in terms of pollution, how it led to a carpet of tarmac over the beauty of nature, the thousands killed in wars fighting for control of the global oil supply just to feed it over the last century and so on, while a Classicist will hail it for how it has helped mankind progress, extol the sensation of power it can conjure from a vehicle, yearn to understand its workings and celebrate the genius of whoever was responsible for creating it in the first place.

According to Pirsig, technology itself becomes increasingly vile to a Romantic the more entrenched in their view they become (hence the common urge to go 'back to nature'), while the Classicist will simply never understand why a river and a few trees should stall the progress of a new airport runway. As both Romantics and Classicists become more confident, the wider apart their world-views inevitably become, and a total lack of communication and understanding between the two grows and grows. It was all sounding more and more like my earlier, slightly lazy, analogy of the war of words between the Jeremy Clarksons and George Monbiots of this world. Anyone attempting to build a bridge between those two would need immense patience.

Pirsig suggests that this kind of conflict goes all the way back to the Ancient Greeks, who first began to describe the perception of the world and the experience of life in these two ways. Of course, then there were very few machines, but for the Greeks our current divide was examined in a battle between the Aristotelian view, which was a forerunner of the modern scientific method, and the earlier Platonic view, which has much more in common with the Buddhist self-improvement culture of the East. It comes down to whether, like Aristotle, you rely on your senses and measurable things to make sense of the world around you – rational science and the observation of things that can be physically examined and counted – or whether, like Plato, you rely on your thoughts and immeasurable things – such as inner truth and the desire to find meaning in life. Pirsig condenses these ideas into the battle between Aristotelian, rational 'truth' and Platonic, spiritual 'quality'.

It is the Aristotelian view that won the day for those of us who live in the West, according to Pirsig, and which can be seen in the ordered and specialized scientific world we live in. That is surely beyond question. We live in a self-proclaimed time of reason, when technology has no morality in and of itself, and when 'progress' is almost only ever considered in terms of scientific or financial progress and how that can be used to profit mankind physically or economically.

On the other hand, Pirsig associates the 'Romantic' viewpoint with 'quality', something much harder, indeed *impossible* by definition, to measure or even explain; consequently its value and the attention we pay it have diminished. My no doubt simplistic view of it is that 'quality' shows itself to us in those moments when we manage to cut through all the day-to-day nonsense and put our finger on some wonderful, un-vocalizable thing that best encapsulates the wonder of life itself. You may experience that feeling in a work or art, singing your heart out, climbing to the top of a mountain or in the embrace of someone you love. Clearly you can't explain feelings like that in rational, measurable terms. Creativity and love are famously irrational, after all, but most people would agree that these things are incredibly important for a happy and contented life. So in essence this 'quality' human experience is what we all live for, because without it we would simply become robots.

It is somewhere in between the 'Classicist' and 'Romantic' viewpoints that Pirsig finds his truth about our relationship with technology:

> It's a kind of non-coalescence between reason and feeling. What's wrong with technology is that it's not connected in any real way with matters of the spirit and of the heart. And so it does blind, ugly things quite by accident and gets hated for that. People haven't paid much attention to this before because the big concern has been with food, clothing and shelter for everyone and technology has provided these. But now where these things are assured, the ugliness is being noticed more and more and people are asking if we must always suffer spiritually and aesthetically in order to satisfy material needs. Lately it's become almost a national crisis − anti-pollution drives, anti-technology communes and styles of life . . .

For Pirsig contentment ultimately lies in a combination of the Classicist and Romantic approaches, in creating, if you will, a bridge between 'quality and 'truth'. If you do manage to build this bridge within yourself, Pirsig believes, you will have discovered a new way of understanding the world and your life, where each view supports the other. At that point you will begin to understand that 'quality' and 'truth' are, in reality, the same thing. Or, in Pirsig's words:

> The Buddha, the Godhead, resides quite as comfortably in the circuits of a digital computer or the gears of a cycle transmission as he does at the top of a mountain or in the petals of a flower. To think otherwise is to demean the Buddha − which is to demean oneself.

I found the ideas in *Zen and the Art of Motorcycle Maintenance* fascinating, and where they seemed to lead my thoughts over the course of the next few weeks was rather mind-blowing.

But in terms of my journey to understand men's fascination with machines it gave me an interesting conundrum. Was it the success of the machines men have invented while pursuing the progression of life in rational and scientific terms that had, in turn, damaged their quality of life and ability to think about life in a more human and spiritual way? It would certainly make sense if men had begun to find this overtly rational world, in the words of Lionel Ferris, 'deceitful', and it would perhaps explain the apparent comfort they feel in machines and the laws of mechanics, which they can understand, rather than the reality of human existence and the baffling and seemingly impenetrable laws of the universe, which they can't. But much as I liked the idea that these hardcore machine heads were actually exhibiting a kind of Zen-like wisdom to bring us full circle, I felt I couldn't hold on to that as my answer unless I had experienced a tangible example of it myself.

The other problem with Pirsig's ideas, as I interpreted them, is that people don't tend to be so clearly defined in a 'Classicist' or 'Romantic' way. Life is rarely that simple. Most people aren't Jeremy Clarksons or George Monbiots: they tend to fall somewhere in the middle or shift positions from one day to the next. Perhaps they were more clearly defined in this way in the 1970s. What we now know thanks to neuroscience also casts doubt on whether people actually do perceive the world in either a 'sense-' or 'thought'-driven way. The consensus today seems to be that the brain uses thoughts and senses in a combined method to interpret reality. There is no real split between them. Everything comes from the brain.

Nevertheless, I felt there was a profound truth in Pirsig's ideas somewhere. In the West the world of science does have an almost religious awe about it. Its means of empirical factual observation and statistical information-gathering have permeated all aspects of society: the business world, with its purely economic value system, is clearly a very rational approach that leaves no room at all for human spiritual concerns. League tables, whether for schools or hospitals, use the same evidence-gathering philosophy and form the basis of government policy. In fact, when you look around today, this purely rational evaluation of life is evident all around us, even though it is a blunt and hopeless way of measuring things that can't be assessed in a quantitative way. Exams, for example, don't actually tell you what level of education a child has reached – only how well they have remembered what they have been told to reproduce in an exam situation on a particular day. In fact, if we're only teaching children things that can be quantified and measured and assessed in an exam situation, then soon we're probably not going to bother teaching them things that can't be measured in this way. What would be the point? If you can't measure it to prove you've done it, why bother teaching it in the first place? How to live a happy life, for example, or how to question and think for yourself, deal with a crisis, love, loss and rage. Self-confidence, passion, curiosity – all these are rather vital in terms of what we actually value in life, but none of them can be measured in an exam situation at school. So being a human being drops out of the national curriculum entirely.

If you extrapolate that principle further out into the world, you begin to understand exactly how we have created a society that works best for those who see their life in measurable terms (by collecting quantifiable wealth, bigger houses and more and more possessions) and why those who value immeasurable things (things that can't be compared and counted) are considered to have failed, even if the 'losers' are actually happier than those who are 'successful'.

All the things about being human, in these terms, seem to exist outside the measurable world of reason that informs and dictates the actions of the world we live in. They certainly don't get much of a look-in when it comes to politics or the global economy – effectively where all power lies in the world today. In that case it's hardly surprising that, even if we all do have a deep yearning for a more humane way of life, the structures we have built around us are by definition incapable of interpreting and prioritizing them.

Strangely, these thoughts reminded me of a passage in a children's book I'd been reading to my son the night before: *The Little Prince*, by the French aviator Antoine de Saint-Exupéry, a man we'll come to in more depth later. The narrator is explaining to the children reading the book the very strange way grown-ups interpret the world:

> Grown-ups like numbers. When you tell them about a new friend, they never ask questions about what really matters. They never ask: 'What does his voice sound like?' 'What game does he like best' 'Does he collect butterflies?' They ask 'How old is he?' 'How many brothers does he have?' 'How much does he weigh?' 'How much money does his father make?' Only then do they think they know him. If you tell grown-ups, 'I saw a beautiful red brick house, with geraniums at the windows and doves on the roof . . .' they won't be able to imagine such a house. You have to tell them, 'I saw a house worth a hundred thousand francs.' Then they exclaim, 'What a pretty house!' . . . But, of course, those of us who understand life couldn't care less about numbers!

At the time I wasn't quite sure what all this had to do with men and machines. I discovered later it had quite a lot.

6

Power

Cars

THE 2008 BRITCAR 24-hour race at Silverstone was down to its final thirty minutes, and I was in the pit lane with the Mitsubishi team. I'd managed a few hours' sleep but was flagging badly, even though I'd done nothing but watch. The pit crew's tired but jocular presence was coming to an end too, their eyes as red as the branded suits and caps they wore in the soporific gloom. The driver, James Kaye, had just gone out of radio contact and the team feared the worst: that he had crashed, come off the track or that, after twenty-three and a half hours of continual racing, the car had called it a day half an hour too soon.

Faces gawping in exhaustion and horror reflected back and forth while a man in radio headphones gradually eased himself, eyes closed in pain, down the wall of the pit lane to sit with a grimace on the concrete floor. Not now, surely. Not so close to the end? Behind the wall the growl of defiant machines loomed far away and then screamed manically at us at close range before flinging off around the track.

I had arrived at noon the day before, four hours from the start of the race, and made my way to the pit lane to meet James, a self-confessed car enthusiast, who was the lead driver of the Mitsubishi team. He has been racing cars professionally since the early 1980s and spent over a decade competing in the British Touring Car Championship. Here was a car enthusiast who'd managed to do something all petrol heads dream of doing – get well paid to drive racing cars. The car in which I was about to watch him and three other men (the appropriately named Jay Wheels, along with Andy Barnes and Mark Lemmer) race for a full twenty-four hours was the tenth incarnation of the Mitsubishi Lancer Evo (as in 'evolution'), which as cars go, according to the few car nuts I knew, is really rather good. In his review of the Evo X in the *Sunday Times* the Pope of petrol heads, Jeremy Clarkson, described it as 'monumentally, toweringly, eye-wateringly brilliant', and if that seems a little excitable, he ends with a more sober but no less clear statement that it's 'a constant reminder of what cars can, and should, be like'. I assume he was referring to the *entire* car, but two hours from the start of the race the engine was in bits on the floor of the pit garage while most of the other cars were ready to go. On jacks, the Evo had no wheels either. I saw someone walking around with what looked like the brake, clutch and accelerator pedals. Someone else was putting huge Britcar number 48 stickers on each of the doors, and two mechanics sat on the engine reconnecting the turbo while another's legs poked out from underneath it on the floor. JP, one of the crew, mentioned that in practice the day before the engine had caught fire. Conscious of my lack of knowledge when it comes to anything mechanical, he pointed out helpfully, 'That's not generally a good thing, when the engine catches fire.' It seemed ridiculous to be this close to the start of the race and still not have a fully built car. Paul Brigden, Team Principal and Ralliart General Manager (Ralliart is the motorsport division of Mitsubishi motors), explained that it had looked a lot worse at the start of the week. As it was, the only Evo X of its type outside Japan entering a 24-hour race seemed an incredibly optimistic test run. I put it to him that the mechanics clearly had an enormous job on their hands, and he nodded. 'If they were race mechanics rather than rally mechanics, then they'd have given up ages ago. These guys have been putting in eighteen-hour days to get it ready. Race mechanics like to test everything to the millionth degree, but rally mechanics will get the car ready, get it out on the track and fix any problems that appear once the race is under way. If the car gets to the end, it will be these boys that deserve all the credit.'

Everyone seemed to see the mechanics rather reverently. While they were at work at our feet James Kaye, wearing tracksuit trousers, grey Crocs, a Mitsubishi T-shirt and pair of Oakleys, nodded. 'They're unbelievable. Seriously. What they do is just . . .' He shook his head and trailed off. I asked what these kinds of events were like to drive in, and he grinned. 'Well, it's fun work, put it that way. Although you have to be careful. Some of the guys driving the cars out there today are not what you'd call professional racing drivers. And some of them are in cars a lot faster than this one, so you have to watch out. If you get stuck behind them, you have to try and take them on the corners because they'll out-power you on the straight. But being stuck behind them is a constant nightmare.'

These words came back to me as soon as the race began, with the Evo having made it to the grid with only five minutes to spare. On a monitor I watched the cars set off at a rolling start. Everything seemed to be going well until they got to the part of the track on the other side of the wall that separated the track from the pit lane, where we were watching on the monitor. On the screen I saw the front car, driven by Adam Sharpe, spin off the track. A TVR then spun sideways to avoid him before it was crashed into head-first by a Ginetta G50. In my peripheral vision I saw dust, smoke and bits of car fly up into the air. On the screen the other drivers were trying to evade the pile up, but it was chaos. A few moments later an ambulance appeared with a safety crew to try and pull Andy Neate, the injured driver, out of the TVR. Another driver, presumably because he was considered to have been at fault, was immediately pulled out of the race. It took an agonizing hour for Neate, strapped up to a spine board, to be taken from the track and airlifted to hospital. Everyone around me looked pained and surprised. I suppose it must go with the territory, but it was an astonishingly violent start and put a different perspective on the race. The light-hearted jokes fizzled out, replaced by raised eyebrows and knowing glances. A few voices in the crowd around me began to question the point of racing so desperately to the first corner in a race that's going to last twenty-four hours, but none of them knew exactly what had gone wrong. (Andy Neate suffered severe neck injuries and was kept in an induced coma before surgeons could operate. Exactly a month after the crash he was allowed home to recuperate.)

Happily for the Mitsubishi team, their delivery of the Evo X to the track at the last minute the day before meant they had time for only a few qualifying laps, so James was safely at the back of the grid and had managed to avoid the collision. An hour later we discovered he was on his way back in to the pits.

The invention of the motor car, as far as some people are concerned, pre-dates the invention of the motor cycle, so there are probably a few rueful smiles at the fact that I've put cars after motor cycles in this book. Having looked into it for quite some time, I'm still rather baffled as to which came first, but I have come to realize that the perception of machines all appearing in a clearly delineated order, one after the other and designed by a single person, is too simplistic. As we've already learned, the history of the car can arguably be traced back to Nicolas Cugnot or Richard Trevithick, who were the first to build steam-powered road carriages back in the 1700s, but you can go all the way back to the sail wagon (used by Prince Maurice of Orange) in 1598 if you don't mind the first 'car' being powered by sails. The first four-wheeled vehicle to be powered by the internal combustion engine could, as we've also already learned, have been the *Reitwagen*, but then that could equally have been the first internal combustion-powered motor bike too, depending on whether you think it had two wheels with two stabilizers or was a proper four-wheeled vehicle. Whatever their view, most people would agree when they saw it that the *Reitwagen* doesn't *look* like a conventional car. So in the end I settled on the world's first commercial automobile – Karl Benz's *Motorwagen* – which was built in 1885. But even that isn't beyond dispute, because the *Motorwagen* had only three wheels, and even I know that you only need a motor-cycle licence to drive a Reliant Robin. Perhaps the most compelling reason for choosing Karl Benz's *Motorwagen* is the fact that it was the first vehicle recognizable as a car to be powered by a four-stroke petrol engine, although at the time it was invented petrol was being sold by chemists as a cleaning agent. Karl Benz was a remarkable and tenacious engineer who went through a couple of designs, and the odd bit of financial strife, before the 'Velo' model was mass-produced in 1895, but it was reading about his wife, Bertha, that really caught my attention. Concerned about her husband's lack of marketing nous when it came to publicizing his new machine, she decided to set off on a publicity trip with her children and drove his car 60 miles to visit her parents, without telling him first. The trip took twelve hours each way, and Bertha had no team of mechanics, so she replaced the brake linings and cleaned the fuel pipe herself before cajoling a blacksmith to repair her broken chain. Her exploits certainly made the news and caught the imagination of the German public, whose subsequent pride in their motoring industry, as well as in Bertha, is well deserved. Every year in Germany her trip is re-created, much like the London-to-Brighton vintage car run is celebrated in Britain. I'm sure the knowledge that the world's first endurance run in a car powered by an internal combustion engine was undertaken by a large German woman called Bertha would have been something of a surprise to the entrants of that year's Britcar 24-hour race.

Our friends Daimler and Maybach, meanwhile, who take the credit for having invented the first motor cycle, would soon home in on the production of motor cars too, and their first model went on the market in 1892. Daimler died soon afterwards, in 1900, but Maybach went on to design a new faster and safer car for the Daimler Company, to which Emil Jellinek, the agent responsible for selling the new model across the world, then gave a name that would remain synonymous with Benz up to today. He named the car Mercedes, after his daughter. In 1926 Benz and Daimler's company merged to create the world famous car marque Mercedes-Benz, thus combining the companies started by the two men most people agree have the greatest combined claim for inventing what we think of today as the modern automobile.

Back at Silverstone, James Kaye came into the pits complaining about the smell of petrol. The mechanics were waiting and the back driver's-side window soon had a piece of pipe sticking out of it that I assume acted as a vent for the emanating fumes. James immediately roared off after giving the pit crew the thumbs-up.

To be able to stand in the pit lane was the kind of thing I imagined most car obsessives would have killed for, but rather amazingly, to me at least, no specific pass or ticket was required to get that close to the racing teams. There was no sense of it being a sealed-off back-stage or VIP area. Earlier James had explained that this is deliberate, because people want to be able to see, hear and smell what's going on with the cars. When it comes to endurance races, the drivers may seem the obvious stars, but clearly the cars and the mechanical prowess on display were the main attraction. Apparently a hushed crowd had gathered to glimpse the Evo X when it had been unloaded from the van the day before. These machines had taken on almost mythical status.

The lack of private space from the public must have driven the team itself a bit mad, though, and unsurprisingly there were lots of calls for people to stand out of the way and grim-looking faces as people like me gawped on, a little too close for their comfort. The fact that the teams could work in such circumstances amazed me. Imagine having a crowd of people staring over your shoulder at the most crucial moment in your job. So I took the opportunity to wander around the track to reduce the amount of onlookers in the pits. I decided at first to walk around the entire track, but then I came to a map that informed me that Silverstone is over 3 miles long and, wanting to preserve my energy for the long night ahead, decided to settle for the nearest stand and took a seat among the small but determined crowd. The cars went past every two minutes or so, and within, well, I'd say about five minutes I'd become rather bored. As the race had been under way for a few hours, you could clearly see the different classes of the entries. Some were far faster and more powerful than the others – although all were fast. A car that I recognized as a Morgan (the largest remaining British car manufacturer) seemed to be out-powering everybody, but, sadly for that particular team, this early pace didn't last. Very occasionally someone would spin off or nudge the car in front, but it wasn't particularly exciting to watch. The prospect of sitting there for the next twenty-two hours was not very appealing, so I went to get an ice cream before surveying the various food options to decide where and what I would eat, and at what time. Planning meals was all I could find to do. Culinary decisions made, I went back to the pits.

Each team had a small garage area filled with whatever food and mechanical paraphernalia it required, along with space to work on its car. Huge transportation lorries and containers were parked immediately behind each garage, with mobile homes in turn behind them. The teams representing the car companies themselves were well kitted out, with lots of food and drink on show and with clearly marked areas for the mechanics and team organizers, while the independent teams were racing on much tighter budgets. By the time I got back to Mitsubishi's area James had finished his first three-hour stint, so I took the opportunity to quiz him, while he stood next to a tumble dryer drinking Gatorade, to ask about where his enthusiasm for cars had come from. I found him to be in an astonishingly lucid mood, bearing in mind he had just got out of a racing car and would be tearing around Silverstone on and off for the next twenty hours. I explained the nature of my quest, and he smiled.

'Why do men love cars? Well people say it's just an extension of your penis, and maybe it is, but so what? Maybe it *is* a sex thing. It's a form of self-expression. That's what I think. Like a punk, only doing it through a car. When you get a car, as a youngster, you try and put your character into it. If you go to Japan, or any of the other Far Eastern countries, most of the guys live at home with their mums until very late on. So they have huge amounts of disposable income. They'll spend a fortune on a certain sticker. Or they'll change lights for different days, different wheels. We've got lads at work who live for the next thing they can buy for their car. It's unbelievable – the fast and furious culture, which started in Japan and has now found it's way over here. It's a whole different world.'

I asked whether he thought of himself as an 'enthusiast', and he nodded.

'First and foremost, yes. It was just ingrained in me. I definitely think that. When you're subjected to it from being in a cot or a pram, every weekend being involved in some form of motorized competition, it's inevitable. My parents told me they did production trials for cars with me in the car when I was six months old.

'My father was involved in all forms of motor sport, and it wasn't a case of "What are you going to do when you leave school?" I was always going to be a racing driver. We didn't even discuss it. Everything for me has always been about cars. It's about conditioning yourself. Conditioning your brain to get the best out of a machine, or of a lap or whatever. But it feeds into every aspect of my life. Every door I've opened has been through a love of machines and racing. Everything has been to do with that. Friendships, meeting girls, everything. It's a language to me. I can go anywhere in the world – anywhere – and suss out people who've got an interest in motor sport and they'll know who I am. So it's my calling card.'

We then learned from Paul that the petrol fumes were affecting the other drivers in the team, one of whom had just come in and begun throwing up (it turned out to be a faulty breather valve), so James was told he would have to go out again, much earlier than planned. He didn't seem fazed. I asked him how he was feeling about the night ahead.

'The worst thing about 24-hour races is getting in the car when someone else has pissed in it. People forget that. You have to drink a huge amount to stop yourself dehydrating, and when you're driving a two- or three-hour stint, that means you're going to need to have a piss occasionally.' He tapped the tumble dryer and smiled. 'That's what this is for. Even Lewis Hamilton will piss in his car if he has to.'

I was surprised that the technicians hadn't come up with a better way of dealing with this situation, and JP responded, deadpan.

'Well, you could have a catheter fitted, I suppose, but then if you crashed, your knob would get ripped off.' He and James started laughing.

Before James left to get back in the car, he had a rhetorical question for me.

'What I want to know is why we're not all flying around in jet packs or zooming about in hydrogen-powered cars. That's what you should be asking in your book. The internal combustion engine has been around since God was a boy. The exact same working principle has been around for so long now. The technology that's gone in to refining the internal combustion engine is mammoth, but the initial design is still there. It fascinates me that we aren't all Roger Ramjets by now. Why aren't we all driving electric super-cars? Why is everything else we've got still based on the same mechanical principle? Think about it. The internal combustion engine is not mechanically efficient, is it? It's metal sliding on metal. It uses a fossil fuel that's expensive and takes a lot of processing. It's from the Stone Age. Why haven't we moved on?'

I gave him my best gruzzled expression, but he carried on talking.

'Because most of the car companies are in league with petrol companies, that's why. They are all interlinked. Whichever way you look at it. The big fuel companies can't afford for there to be another form of propulsion. So it just won't happen, and it ain't going to happen for a long time yet.'

A few hours later the skies began to darken, and the track took on a slightly more sinister tone. The noise was now well and truly fixed in my subconscious, and the drivers were getting more comfortable with their roles on the track, which meant they seemed to be driving much faster. The spectators had thinned, and I decided to take a wander around the circuit. I thought back to the 12-hour lawn-mower race and how hapless that had seemed. This appeared far more dangerous and brutal but strikingly similar at the same time. The few spectators that remained sat huddled under blankets higher up in the stand opposite the pit lane, with flasks emanating steam. I bought a pint of lager and took a seat to try and get a glimpse of the action from there. It was getting late, and the cold was stiffening my bones. The pit lane had become an island of lumination in the dark, with a constant reef of light from the cars orbiting around it. I shuddered at the incessant acceleration of growling cars going past, over and over again. I closed my eyes and listened out for the 'pop' that the Evo made every time it powered along the straight and smiled each time I heard it. I had made it to ten o'clock. There were eighteen hours still to go, so I decided to head for my car to try and get some sleep.

I woke up at 2 a.m. to the sound of the engine in the car next to me starting. The occupant was clearly suffering from the cold too and had opted to get his heater going. I'd slept fitfully, shivering, for nearly four hours and decided to head back to the track to see how things were progressing. I walked until I'd found an entirely empty stand called Luffield. I walked and walked but, apart from a few marshals behind the wire fences sitting behind banks of tyres on the edges of the track itself, I couldn't see another soul. The stands were completely empty, and the sheer scale of the track really began to register in the ominous dark.

Everything had become rather surreal as I sat there alone in a vast stand with only the roar of engines and the head-lights of passing racing cars for company. I was wondering what on earth would make anyone sit in such a place alone in the middle of the night just to watch cars going monoton-ously round the track, only to realize that, as there was no one else there apart from me, I could safely say that writing this book appeared to be the reason I was looking for.

The surface attractions of noise, speed, glamour and the excitement of motor racing were clear enough, even though they didn't really do it for me, but I was convinced there must be something else more meaningful behind it all. So far I hadn't felt as though I really understood cars very well at all. James had told me how he had taken the corner at Copse earlier at 130 m.p.h., which sounded insanely fast, but I'm sure it would seem pretty tame when compared to the speed of a Formula 1 car. So you are in the realm of increasing speeds, and then, before you know it, you're spending your time getting excited about numbers. Cars are always described in numbers, aren't they? Numbers that always have to grow, whether it's horsepower, size of the engine or whatever else is under a bonnet of a car that I can't comprehend. But those numbers don't really have any meaning. If you can go from 0 to 60 in 5 seconds or 3.8 seconds, does that really add colour to your life? Is that really progress?

I wondered whether this obsession with minutely increasing engine capacities and acceleration speeds was really just a way of trying to excite car enthusiasts while the car manufacturers went about the serious business of postponing the advent of a new technology to make as much money from the old one as quickly as they still could. It's easy to understand why car manufacturers would want to sit on or hinder the discovery of new technology, whether it's to maintain the associated profits they make from spare parts and servicing, their shady connections with the oil industry or a determination not to have to invest in brand new delivery systems for whatever technology inventors think of next. James Kaye is right that the principles behind the internal combustion engine are rather outdated. When I began to look at exactly how these noisy, dirty engines work, I was astonished at how primitive they seemed, even to an techno-ignoramus like me.

As we learned earlier, the internal combustion engine uses a mixture of fuel and air to create a small but incredibly powerful explosion that moves a piston. This up-and-down movement is then harnessed to drive a part of whatever machine the engine is attached to. In modern cars they call the piston chamber a cylinder, so if you have a four-cylinder engine in your car then you have four cylinders, each with its own piston, inside. One of the major issues is how to get the right amount of fuel and air into each cylinder before each mix is ignited. Karl Benz invented the carburettor for this purpose and a spark plug to ignite the mix once it was in the cylinder, but to improve the engine's efficiency the ignition of each cylinder in a multi-cylinder engine is offset so that they fire one after another (hundreds of times a minute in modern cars). It is this succession of pistons firing that creates the constant 'pfut, pfut, pfut' noise of the engine while it's running. This offsetting is achieved by the camshaft and a series of valves. A camshaft is a long bit of metal with what look like egg shapes (the 'cams') running along it, spaced to fit in with each cylinder. As the camshaft turns, the protruding end of one cam pushes open the respective air and fuel valves that supply one cylinder while the flat edge of the next one keeps the valve in the next cylinder closed while the mix inside it is ignited; and so on along the shaft, depending on how many cylinders the engine has. The camshaft is attached to the engine on its other side by a belt, and the movement generated by the engine is what turns the camshaft.

A 'twin-cam' engine has two camshafts, to increase the amount of cylinders it can have or to reduce the length of the engine. A twin-valve engine has two valves feeding fuel and air into each cylinder (so each one has four valves in all) to increase each cylinder's power-producing potential. Obviously the more technical all this becomes, the more electrical gadgets you need inside the engine to monitor exactly what's going on; but the actual 'metal sliding on metal' that James talked about is the same principle used to power Karl Benz's three-wheeled *Motorwagen*. When you accelerate, you simply allow more air and fuel into the engine to magnify the power of the explosions inside each cylinder, which in turn increases your speed. In our wireless, electrical world, where computer chips are being created that are so small and powerful that one day they will be grafted into living cells, James Kaye's caveman analogy for the internal combustion engine seems indisputable. It's hard to believe that no one has managed to come up with a better way of powering vehicles than the technology of a piston powered through the combustion of air and fuel that Thomas Newcomen came up with nearly three centuries ago.

You would have thought that, at the very least, electric vehicles would be commonplace nowadays. When I drove across the country in a 1958 electric milk float the previous year, I was astonished at how simple the mechanics of electric vehicles are. You have a motor, a large battery, some wheels, a brake and a steering mechanism. It works very well, and there is very little that can go wrong in comparison with modern cars. Apart from the batteries, which had been updated in the late 1970s, our milk float was mechanically the same as it had been fifty years earlier. Servicing electric vehicles is as simple as checking the distilled water levels in your batteries and checking the tyres are properly inflated. But there's not a lot of money to be made from a vehicle that never breaks down, or requires little maintenance, as we discovered from the mechanically superior but ill-fated lawn mowers of Chapter 2. We drove 680-odd miles in our milk float in the course of three weeks without any problems. I can't imagine you could say the same of a conventional car of the same era. We had certain limitations – it took between four and six hours to charge up enough to travel a distance of about 20 miles, depending on hills – but surely battery technology has progressed beyond that range in the last half-century?

As it happens, there are all sorts of conspiracy theories about the potential capacity for electric vehicles today. This is a topic, of course, that invites rumour and speculation, as enthusiasts smitten with new forms of technology are not enormously trusting of the explanations given by big businesses – who have already invested heavily in other, older kinds of propulsion – as to why new technologies are not commercially viable. I heard one about Land Rover, who supposedly made an electric version for the army, to allow the potential for stealth (electric vehicles being comparatively quiet without internal combustion going on) to surprise the enemy. A milk float enthusiast I met once told me this was no myth, because someone he knew who belonged to the Land Rover Members' Club had managed to get their hands on one. But the most curious story that relates to the non appearance of electric vehicles on our roads is the tale of the EV-1 (not to be confused, incidentally, with 'EVI' – a US company that makes electric and hybrid vehicles) which was made by General Motors in the 1990s. Getting the full story about the EV-1 is far from easy. The accusations of the disappointed EV-1 devotees are presented in the film *Who Killed the Electric Car?* (which, like all murder mysteries, is tremendously exciting) but GM have publicly rebutted those accusations, suggesting that the demise of the EV-1 was due to natural (or rather, straightforwardly commercial) causes.

The EV-1 was designed and built in response to the California Air Resources Board's (C.A.R.B.) 'Zero Emissions Vehicle' (ZEV) mandate passed in the state of California in 1990, which was an attempt to curb increasing pollution levels. The ZEV mandate stated that by 1998, 2 per cent of all new cars leased or sold by the seven largest car manufacturers in the state of California would have to be completely emission-free. By 2003 this figure would rise to 10 per cent. It was a challenge that General Motors, and the other six car companies, would have no choice but to meet – so they set about designing a new generation of electric cars.

In 1997, 680 Generation One EV-1s were leased to the public. They were capable of up to 75 miles from every charge, but once the batteries had been updated in 1999, this range was increased to 160 miles. In terms of speed, the EV-1s were restricted mechanically to 80 m.p.h. It took the batteries eight hours to charge fully, but the second-generation battery, designed by Stanford Ovshinsky, could be charged to 80 per cent of capacity within two to three hours, which would make it a practical car for the vast majority of drivers in the world today. I can't think of many people who drive more than 160 miles in an average twenty-four hour period. You also have relatively few problems when it comes to refuelling, because you can fill up overnight at home or with a smaller trickle charger that fits in the boot to plug in wherever you happen to be. The cost of the EV-1, worked out from comparing the leasing costs with conventional petrol cars, was a maximum of $40,000. Factor in the tiny cost of fuel for the life of the car (we worked out that the cost of the electricity our milk float used was one penny per mile), and I think it's easy to see the attraction of a modern electric vehicle. The EV-1 was certainly a long way from the performance we'd managed in our fifty-year-old milk float.

You're probably wondering why you've never heard of the EV-1, if it was capable of the speeds and range that most people would consider perfectly acceptable in any car, electric or otherwise. You may also be wondering how much better they have become in the last decade. Surely they must be capable of going about 300 miles per charge by now? Electricity is much cheaper than petrol, even when the price of a barrel of oil isn't rising astronomically. The EV-1 must have heralded a whole new future? It certainly appeared that way to the EV-1's fans, but according to GM, public demand for the EV-1 then disappeared.

The ZEV mandate was watered down. The C.A.R.B. was accused of breaking a law that prevented individual states from being able to regulate fuel economy and decided they had no option but to give ground. So instead of 2 per cent of their annual car sales having to be from cars with zero emissions, the seven largest car companies were required only to keep up with the demand that existed for zero emission vehicles instead. Despite long waiting lists for EV-1s, General

Motors found that, once prospective buyers had been informed of the EV-1's restrictions when compared to conventional cars, this demand dwindled. The subsequently high unit cost in producing a small number of electric cars to keep up with this demand supported the logic of GM's decision to close the EV-1 programme completely, but it baffled the EV-1's legion of admirers, whose surprise then turned to anger and frustration.

In the last ten years the EV-1 has disappeared. Well, that's not quite true. Of the 2,234 EV-1s that were made, sixty or so still exist in museums and colleges across the USA, but even these were all disabled by General Motors before being bequeathed. From the start EV-1s were available only on a lease (the cost of long-term servicing and maintaining access to spare parts indefinitely was GM's rationale for this decision at the time) and, as the leases expired, EV-1 owners had to see their beloved vehicles towed away.

There are lots of theories as to exactly why General Motors would choose to bring an end to one of their own products in this way, but it was their decision to sell the 60 per cent stake in the second-generation battery they bought from Stanford Ovshinsky to the oil company Chevron Texaco, that particularly angered those hoping the EV-1 would usher in a new epoch of electric transport.

Instead of seeing electric vehicles as the way forward, oil companies seem to have placed their faith in hydrogen-powered cars to propel us around. Hydrogen-powered cars are seen as a red herring by some. So many obstacles to the practical everyday use of hydrogen fuel cells in cars exist – not to mention the cost of creating the delivery systems required to get a network of hydrogen fuel stations on the planet's roads – that you could argue only someone desperate to put off change as far into the future as possible would seriously propose them as a realistic solution in the short-to-medium term. This perhaps explains why research into hydrogen is so popular among oil companies, as it could well be that by the time we're able to use hydrogen to power cars all the oil in the world will be long out of the ground. On the other hand, electric vehicles offer an answer *today* for those people interested in reducing their dependence on expensive foreign oil or looking to reduce their carbon footprint (assuming their electric vehicles are supplied by renewable energy producers).

Critics may think this glosses over the drawbacks of electric cars when compared with cars powered by the internal combustion engine, but if the political will to support electric vehicles existed, then in my view the EV-1 represented an astonishingly good starting point. You would imagine that government-funded research into improving the technology could have quickly reduced the pitfalls that existed at the time. Whatever the reasons for the ultimate failure of the EV-1, it is heartening, at least, to know that electric car technology has developed so much over the past few decades; and you have to hope that electric cars do have a commercial future, if someone has the wit and courage to venture on that future.

Ironically some car manufacturers, particularly Japanese ones, took the Californian ZEV mandate seriously as a sign of the future and pushed forward research programmes into alternatives to petrol and diesel cars. From that research came hybrid cars such as the Prius, which uses a combination of petrol and electricity to make it far more efficient (although the increased carbon footprint in construction largely wipes out this saving at present, this skewering will apparently diminish as the volume of production increases). These are the cars now best placed to benefit from an expensive-energy future and are proving popular with the public concerned about the state of the planet. GM meanwhile has a lot of catching up to do, something that, at the time of writing, is evident in their collapsing share price and the plea they have made for a financial hand-out from the US government to prevent them from going bankrupt in order to preserve American jobs.

Back at Silverstone, dawn took me by surprise. I woke shivering in the stands and immediately went out in search of sustenance, of the fried, dead animal kind. Dew on the seats around me and on the hand-rails as I reached out for stability caused me to slip my way into full consciousness, and I made my way round Brooklands to try and find a bacon baguette and a bottomless vat of tea. Predictably the cars still growled around the track. There were eight hours left to go. I then realized, as I gazed through sleep dust and discovered a croaky throat, that my attitude to the race had completely changed. By sleeping I had cheated slightly but, as with the pointless heroics of the lawn-mower race, I could see the element of human endurance morphing into a kind of beauty once again.

I wondered whether these kinds of overnight trials were an attempt to create discomfort for these men to fight through because life itself has so few sharp edges these days. In days of yore the adrenaline junkies would presumably have got their fix out hunting for food, but our lives are rather mundane and few of us have ever seriously had to fight for our survival. When real danger doesn't exist, perhaps you have to create some for yourself.

As the morning sun crawled into the sky, I crossed over a wooden bridge back to the pit lane and found JP astonishingly full of life (he'd just drunk a few family-size cans of Red Bull before offering me the same).

'There you are. Where have you been?' I murmured something sheepishly about having a few hours' sleep, but it seemed he'd had some himself. 'Me too, dozed off in a VIP suite somewhere.' Then he threw a luminous yellow tabard at me (you're not allowed out on to the pit lane itself, or the wall that separates the pits from the track, without one). 'You can help me tell James his lap times.'

As I caught it, I suddenly felt like I was eight years old again. I put my bag down and pulled on the vest. Looking back, that sense of belonging and temporary camaraderie was a very powerful fun-inducer and it changed my perspective on the attraction of the race enormously.

Out on the wall the sound was even more deafening. JP had a board that he was using to put up lap times and the number of laps left before the driver would need to come in and refuel. James Kaye was doing laps in just over two minutes, so there wasn't much time to do anything other than register the time, update the board and hold it out in a space between the railings before he burst round Brooklands and tore down the straight. JP was timing the laps with his phone, such was the no-frills reality of this kind of motor racing. (Later on I was amazed to spot a familiar chunk of sponge being placed behind James Kaye's back, just as I had seen back at the lawn-mower race.) Each team had a similar small space in the fence to put its signs through, but on either side of us the teams had either pulled out completely or were lying under crumpled machines hoping to bring them back to life.

Hallucinatory tiredness had clearly crept in when JP decided to write swear words on the board with the numbers and few letters he had found in a box. Remembering the schoolboy glee of writing 5318008 on a calculator before holding it upside down (it spells BOOBIES), I suggested this, but he'd already spelt out PENIS by using the P for petrol and NI in the box (presumably for Northern Ireland) before writing PISS with the P, a 1 and two 5s. Word came through over the radio that James Kaye thought we were 'a bunch of cocks'. The whole episode had me laughing harder than I had in a long, long time. It didn't do much for James's lap time, though. Next time round JP did BOOBIES, which brought guffaws from the pit crew. After that we began to capitulate to tiredness and the astonishing heat. JP and I were soon replaced, and things seemed to fall into a kind of exhausted haze as the final hours slowly scraped by.

Then, with barely ten minutes to go, disaster seemed to strike. On the far side of the track the driver always went out of radio contact, so each time they drove round it would be anything up to forty seconds before they became reachable again. Word came through that James was having a problem, and it turned out he'd been out of radio contact for over three minutes. As he'd been doing lap times of around 2 minutes 15 seconds, this was not a happy development. It was as this news emerged that the ashen faces I described at the start of this chapter began to appear. Paul looked sickest of all. Then, finally, James came through on the radio. He'd had a problem 'with his helmet', which solicited huge relieved smiles and laughter among the crew. Surely now it would get to the end?

As the final lap approached, a car in the pits next to us, which hadn't been on the track since about eleven the night before, was carefully wheeled out. Everyone who saw it started laughing. Someone muttered 'Cheeky fuckers' as the driver got in and prepared to pull away. It seems that, as long as you are on the track on the final lap of a 24-hour race, you are considered to have finished, even if you've only done a fraction of the laps the other cars have done. And then, at the behest of Paul, everyone in the pit crew, including wives and children, was told to 'get over on that wall' to cheer the cars home. It wasn't just the Mitsubishi crew. All the way along the pit lane collective amnesia about the yellow tabard rule took hold, and hundreds of people charged over and began to climb up on the fence. A few moments later the winning car came through, to wild celebrations, and a few cars back we spotted the Evo. James thundered along, right by the wall, waving as he went. The last car, followed by a hilarious plume of smoke, then spluttered and coughed its way over the line too. It was the one that had been wheeled out for the final lap. There was so much smoke as it slipped away that you could barely see the huge Welsh dragon emblazoned on its side. After that, everyone began charging towards the podium – in our case not because James would be on it but to find him and the car. You could see how much it meant to the team that they had made it to the end.

There were scenes of relief and pride when they finally got hold of James, while everyone else was focusing on the three teams of drivers on the podium. He looked exhausted but had a broad grin across his face. A few team members rushed up to him but then checked themselves and gave him nothing more than a slightly fierce and emotional shake of the hand. Everyone milled around in relief, seemingly not quite sure what to do with themselves, but someone instigated a team photograph and that seemed to be the required end. They all cheered as pictures were taken and then gradually began to laugh the nervous energy away, completely oblivious to the prize ceremony going on above their heads. I saw quite a few exhausted tears in gruff men's eyes. I caught up with James ten minutes later. He was grinning and still had the strength to hold his daughter on his hip. 'A bit of excitement that!' he whispered and asked me what I'd thought of the race. I told him it had been surreal at times but that I'd loved it. I thanked him and asked how he felt now he'd got to the end. 'Brilliant, but I'm bloody knackered.' His exhausted but appeased expression intrigued me, but, feeling somewhat tired myself, I smiled my gratitude towards the faces I'd spent the last twenty-four hours making polite gestures at, and left.

I didn't feel awake enough to drive home but still had the can of Red Bull in my bag that JP had given me on the pit wall. As an Idler I hate Red Bull. If it's possible to be morally opposed to a drink, then I am morally opposed to Red Bull, but I was so tired that I gulped it down. At home just over an hour and a half later, having driven thrillingly at over 100 m.p.h. for the first time in my entire life, I began to wonder whether my antipathy to cars might be overturned after all.

A few weeks later I went to meet a man called Bob Jones, whose particular fascination is at the far end of the automobile spectrum from high-performance racing cars. He's particularly enamoured with cycle cars – machines that I had never even heard of before I called him to arrange a visit. Bob loves cycle cars so much that he is a co-organizer of something called the 'Festival of Slowth', which in 2008 was held at the home of Lord Raglan (a direct descendant of the Lord Raglan of the Charge of the Light Brigade fame). The 'Festival of Slowth' is a tongue-in-cheek reference to the annual 'Festival of Speed' held every year at Goodwood in Sussex.

Bob turned out to be a friend of Lionel Ferris, something I discovered when I asked about a high-bicycle I spotted in the hallway of Bob's vast and impressive house. Bob's wife, Antonia, an artist, scampered up to say hello before furnishing us with a pot of tea and some astonishingly tasty biscuits. After that she 'had to pop out to the allotment to paint some chickens'. Bob told me, as the front door closed, that she was working hard before an exhibition of her work in a few weeks' time.

We stepped inside Bob's 'office', which looked more like a cross between a museum and a playroom to me. An enormous bookcase that took up all of one wall was filled with books and bound magazines dating back to the earliest days of cycling and motoring. There were framed posters of bizarre contraptions on the other walls and even a working Meccano display model of the Blackpool Tower. Beside that was a glass case filled with all sorts of antique motoring paraphernalia and a picture of an old car, which Bob told me he'd 'had to sell to pay for the roof'. I told him I was very jealous that he had such a space to go and relax in.

'Ah yes, well, it's only very recently that I've managed to spend any time in here at all. When I'm between ninety and a hundred, perhaps I'll take ten years off. I shall probably be dead next week.'

We talked about his love of cycling first and about how I'd been getting on with my quest so far. He seemed intrigued by, but not in agreement with, Lionel's assertion that, when it comes to their fascination with machines, men are looking for a relationship that they can rely on, to make them feel secure. He smiled and shook his head.

'Lionel's a wonderful friend, but that's absolute rubbish. No, you could say that about a dog or a shed, couldn't you? I'm fascinated, whether it be a lawn mower, a car or a bicycle, I'm just interested in the way it was made, what you can do for it and what it can do for you. The thing with these old beautiful machines is you're getting something for nothing. If you sell them, you're almost certain to get what you paid for it, if not make a profit, so you get all the pleasure you've had from it for nothing. Not that you go into it for that reason. Some people who buy Brighton Run cars – a lot of them have just bought them because they've got the money – but some of them will have them because their father bought it sixty years ago, drove it for thirty years and they've been driving it for the last thirty, and it's the last thing they'd ever part with. They mean different things to different people.

'The absolute reality is that I'd love to just get in that old car and drive off and enjoy myself. I've had absolutely fascinating adventures out with the high-bicycle, which is a different machine but the same principle. I went to Australia for the bicentennial on the high-bicycle; I've been to Japan, America. All sorts of fascinating things like that. A year or two before John Pinkerton [a famous vintage bicycle enthusiast] died, he rang me up about how to celebrate the millennium in 2000. I asked him if he was organizing anything for it, and he said, "No, no, you organize big events and buggers just let you down. Let's do something simple." And as it happened, I was reading an old volume of *Cycling* from 1899, and there was a chap who described himself as "one of the old boys", who was probably about forty. He said something like, "I remember the old days when we'd go off on a two-week tour to Ireland, wonderful times, but now we live in an age where we've got a Queen on the throne that's been there longer than anyone can remember, and I can see very soon in every corner of the land these newfangled mechanical contraptions" – cars, you see, from 1896 onwards – "even in the air! I heard two aeronauts in a café the other day saying they felt soon man would be able to circumnavigate the globe in a balloon." Now I'm reading this a hundred years later, and Elizabeth's been on the throne longer than anyone can remember, people are saying that cars are the ruination of the world, and Richard Branson and Per Lindstrom were talking about circumnavigating the globe in a balloon in 2000! So this guy was saying, wouldn't it be nice in the year 1900 to go off on a long adventure on our old high-bicycles? So John said, "Well let's bloody well do it then". So we did. We rode 300-odd miles in five days, but that whole trip was as though we ourselves, and I'm not exaggerating, had been taken back a hundred years. It was just sensational. Partly because we were riding on fairly small roads. We picked a route that could have existed in Victorian times. The sensations we had, because we didn't have any mechanical support, we hadn't planned anywhere in advance, some nights we weren't sure if we'd even get a bed for the night. It was just wonderful.'

On my milk float adventure we had a very similar experience. I came to believe that serendipity and coincidence will always come to your aid if only you can lose the fixation with haste and allow yourself to stop and engage with the world. Our journey had felt like a window into a different kind of life, one vastly different from the system we all live within most of the time. Bob nodded. It had been the same for him. I asked how important his cars and machines were to him, and he smiled and shook his head.

'People sometimes say to me, "Oh Bob, what would you do if you lost your cars!" and I say, well, I'd be all right, it would give me more time for cycling. So they say, "Well what if you couldn't cycle?" Well, I tell them then I'd love to do more long-distance walking. It's something I've always wanted to spend more time on. I love it. "Well," they say, "what if you couldn't walk?" Well, I used to be a very good chess player, and I love chess but I don't get time to play these days. "*Well*," they say, "what if you forgot how to play chess?" And I say, well then, I've got time to read all my books, I love to read, I've got so many I haven't been through properly, and they're "Oh forget it!" You see, I get excitement from lots of things.'

Paradoxically, Bob's enthusiasm didn't seem to be about possessing anything, even though he had collected more fascinating machine-related things than I had ever seen. His was more an enthusiasm in which he lived his life generally: he simply loved where all the things that fascinated him could take him in his own mind.

'It's all about trying to find things in life that are a little bit different,' he told me as he pointed out things on the shelves around his room. Everywhere I looked prompted a story, but perhaps the most pertinent to my quest to discover why men love machines related to his impressive collection of Meccano, including the huge working display model of the Blackpool Tower.

'When I was young, I remember going to Lewis's, the department store, and on the top floor were all these incredible toys that I would never have. My father was a bus driver, so we couldn't afford much, but I have always remembered the Meccano display models. There was one of those there.' He pointed to his Blackpool Tower.

'Meccano is a subject in itself. I read an old article by David Smith the other day about the nuances of Meccano, and it ended by saying that "the Romans' legacy to the world was to leave us Latin. When the English conquered the world, their legacy to the world was Meccano", and there's a picture of the Calcutta Meccano Society with all these people holding up their models. Every old motorist somewhere in his box of bits has got a piece of Meccano in there somewhere. This article expressed the humour that I like to extol but it's about the reality hiding behind the superficial thing that you see. We were an engineering society, you see, and Meccano made all sorts of kits that I hadn't even seen until twenty years ago. I must show you this.'

From under the table he brought out a box containing a delightful Meccano car kit that you could imagine a child of aristocratic parents opening *circa* 1923.

'I've got another one that's not in quite as good condition as this, but it's never been out of the box. You never see these.' Out came another.

'But it goes even deeper than that. Meccano was part of the Hornby train sets, which were really big things at the time. In the early 1930s this kind of thing was a frippery really' – he pointed at the car – 'it would have been very expensive, £2, say, which would have been a week's wages at the time for a man. Probably more than that in the late 1930s. So it was a fairly indulgent thing. Not many people would have been able to buy these cars. But in the late 1930s the government came to Frank Hornby – and he was very famous at the time, like Dyson now or Richard Branson – and they said, "Frank, we've been talking it over and the Germans, you never know what the Germans are up to, and we feel that their boys are more advanced as engineers than our boys are, because Marklin are making things similar to yourselves". They did a Meccano-type set, and in engineering and toymaking, even after losing the First World War and the reparations the Americans had put on them in terms of raw materials, the Germans were still fairly strong. So the government were getting concerned around 1934 that we were perhaps slipping behind. They were worried that the boys who were fourteen at the time would need to be on-side when they were twenty-four, because who knew what was going to happen? So they said to Frank, "Is it possible that you could come up with a plane kit to get boys really involved with plane construction?" So this was done not because he thought of it but because he was approached by the government.'

Bob then brought yet another huge Meccano box out from under the table. I felt like a child at Christmas. He took off the cover and inside was a pristine, original 1930s Meccano Build Your Own Aeroplane set. I looked up, and I swear his eyes were watering with joy just from gazing at it.

'I had to pay a lot of money for this when I eventually found it. There's something nice about it being in the box, isn't there?' He was in a reverie, but he soon collected himself.

'So this is what they asked Frank to make. You could already make a plane out of Meccano. But this is more like a plane and less like Meccano, if you see what I mean. This is a Number 2 set, but the ultimate set was a Number 2 Special.' He leaned down under the table yet again and produced another vast, flat box.

'Not everybody sees this.' He beamed, as though it was true treasure. He took off the lid, and inside all the pieces of a plane were laid out perfectly, all bound with red thread, with a booklet on top, which I began to leaf through, that explained the laws of aerodynamics and had pictures of different aeroplanes to look out for in the sky. 'But what you've got here, you see, is not just the kit. This is coming up to your level here. Now imagine when you were fourteen, and obviously you're fascinated by stuff then, and you would read this booklet and think, "My God, when I'm eighteen if I get the chance I would love to fly". And of course out of this came, during the war, books on aircraft recognition, and very often boys were more advanced at spotting planes in the sky than their parents. But this booklet tells you how to build single-engine aeroplanes, racing monoplanes, low-wing monoplanes, and then of course during the war boys were really encouraged to know that plane. And you know what boys are like, you can imagine them saying, "No, Dad, it's not . . . that's a Messerschmitt!" and running for cover. It gives you a hint as to how an entire generation of boys were inspired by mechanics and engineering though, doesn't it? But car friends of mine roll their eyes when I talk about Meccano. They say, "Things move on, Bob! Things move on!" But it's not that things move on, it's the history of how we got to where we are, and if we're in the crap now then how did we get into the crap?'

Listening to Bob, I found myself grinning in realization that this could be, in part, the answer to my conundrum. Perhaps men do not love machines out of some unexplained mechanic tendency. Male machine obsession has been carefully cultivated over generations because it lies at the heart of a nation's future survival. Superior mechanical knowledge inevitably leads to greater military power, which preserves the nation itself. But while I pondered this, Bob continued.

'I've got an article somewhere from an issue of *Meccano* magazine from about 1974 by a chap that had one of these planes, and it was about his reminiscences of opening it as a boy. He could remember every element of it: how he opened it, how he cut the string, should he do this, should he do that. But things like this are personal to you. Is it enthusiasm? Is it "I've got to have one of these because it's worth so and so!"? I don't think so.' I was peering with delight once again at the intricate contents of the box.

'Now look at that, that's the cord for the wing bracing. Can you see the transfer there too? Look, with Meccano on the wing?'

It *was* true treasure: so lovingly created and a world away from the TV tie-in plastic crap that most kids' toys seem to be made from today.

'But I'm not even really a Meccano enthusiast,' Bob continued – rather unconvincingly, I have to say.

Standing there, I found the contents of the room beginning to morph around me from the unrecognizable mishmash of objects I'd seen when I walked in into individual things, each reflecting some part of Bob's personality. It was like a scatter graph that had erupted out of his head. He had antique prints of aeroplanes up on the wall and then, having stood next to it for half an hour, I realized the armchair I'd rested my bag on was covered in a print of racing cars chasing each other over the cushion, seat and arms. I began to realize that everywhere you looked was a feast for a curious mind.

'Oh yes, that chair.' He seemed thrilled I'd noticed it. 'I like it because the cars have obviously been done by someone who understands how cars work – the proportions are right.'

He then handed me a photocopy of an advert for 'The Wonder Car'.

'My problem is that, if something is there but forgotten, I get a lot of pleasure in treasuring it. It's one of the reasons I like cycle cars. They really were heralded as the "new motoring". They were like, "We've got motoring by the balls now! Everything will change!" But, of course, now no one's bloody heard of them!' He started laughing.

'This is the car I'm building a replica of, the Grahame-White "Wonder Car". Now [Claude] Grahame-White founded the aerodrome at Hendon, do you remember that? Well, one of his concepts was to build the Grahame-White "Wonder Car". It started off as £150. In three months it was down to £105, then it went to £75 and even £50. They were a disaster.' He grinned. 'They just didn't sell. I'm making a replica of it. I didn't do the panelling, but I made all the body in ash. Fortunately one does survive unrestored – it was found twenty-five years ago – which has got the metal frame on. That is what I needed. Everything else could be done from photographs.'

He showed me a silver badge and, focusing in on it completely, passed his finger around its edge.

'What I did was scale up the badge from an original photograph to get the right size and then began cutting it out from a piece of silver. I was so busy working at the day job at the time that I used to get up at 2 a.m. and do a letter before I went to work. I did all the easy bits first. I don't know how many hours I spent filing it.'

After that Bob suggested we go and have a look at some of the cars he had in his shed. The 'shed' was at least twice the width of a normal double garage. On the left I recognized the Wonder Car: a small, spindly, white, open-topped car that was a quarter of the size of a modern car. Behind that was another I couldn't quite see, and to its right was another, slightly larger than the cycle car but dwarfed to its right by the kind of huge vintage car you see on pre-1900 car rallies partially hidden under a huge green sheet. Behind that was another car, with offset seats. It looked like a racing car from the 1930s. Bob pointed to his Wonder Car with pride.

In the presence of a *bona fide* cycle car – albeit a replica – I asked him to explain more about the Festival of Slowth I'd heard about. He began laughing and mumbled something about lobsters.

'Well, the thing is with me is that I like to do things that are a little different. Otherwise people will still come, but

I've got a very small pool of people with cycle cars, perhaps thirty or so in the entire country, so I've got to find a way to fire them up. If you can find something that fires yourself up, then sometimes you can fire other people up too. It's rather like the Victorian trip on the bikes. If you read car magazines of the time, often the articles are ever so dry, but I read that the Cycle Car Club were heading out on their first outing. Most of them lived in London or the Home Counties, and they had decided on an adventure down to Selsey, on the south coast. So I got the next issue out. I've got back issues of all the cycle car magazines from the time. It turned out that one chap had got stuck in tramlines and another had nearly fallen into a canal [curiously the very canal my journey had begun on]. Some people didn't even get to Selsey, but the rest of them stopped at a hotel that had lobster on the menu, so they had a lobster supper and, as people were arriving at midnight or one in the morning, they decided to have lobster again. So they got absolutely pissed out of their brains, someone's car ended up in a tree, people slept on the billiard table and then it said, "The following day we were supposed to be hill climbing but we didn't, we decided to have lobster yet again". In the end they came back and it said it had been "very exciting, excellent feeding – all at moderate expense and we will do this again next year". Well that was in 1913, and of course they couldn't do it the next year because of the Great War.'

The memory of those laughing men fell between us quietly for a moment before Bob continued.

'So I thought, that's what we're going to do. We're going to have a lobster supper. Now I was hoisted on my own petard because me and a pal of mine spent two hours preparing the damn things, but it was an absolutely amazing weekend. But one of the guests there was the chairman of the

Bugatti owners' club, Fitzroy Raglan, who has always raced historic cars, and he had a fantastic time and he said to me at the end, "Bob, it's been wonderful. Now you know we've got a little drive at home. I don't know whether it would be suitable, but if you ever think of doing this sort of thing again, will you bear us in mind and keep us on the list?" So we did it again this year, and his place is just incredible. Two hundred and eighty acres, everything utterly wonderful, gardens manicured, you know. Cannons from Sebastopol either side of his front door! You almost feel privileged just to be involved. I know this house looks impressive, but I'm hanging on by the seat of my trousers! But I know how all this sounds – all these old men in big houses eating lobster, but it's the humour of the thing that is so wonderful.'

It's true that, prior to meeting Bob, owners of vintage cars were filed in my brain as wealthy, barrel-chested gout sufferers of advancing years. The kind of people with protuberances on the ends of their noses caused by too much fine wine and who drive around the south of France with preposterously attractive Italian wives two decades their junior. Bob wasn't like that, though, and nor were the other cycle car enthusiasts he showed me on a DVD of the inaugural Festival of Slowth someone had pulled together in his office a few hours later. It was less Merchant–Ivory and more *Wind in the Willows*, with each one vying for position to reflect the most endearing characteristics of the inimitable Mr Toad. I would say they were all over fifty, and while one or two had yellow waistcoats and flat caps, most shared expansive smiles and tears of laughter as they hurtled about in their apparently calamitous cars.

Bob then moved on to the other vehicles in his garage.

'Next to the Grahame-White is an Austin 7. Now, the first thing I wanted to do when I retired was not build a

bloody conservatory,' he pointed at a half-built conservatory being erected against the kitchen wall, 'but drive all
the way around England, Ireland, Scotland and Wales in
my Austin 7. Since then the *Coast* programme has come on
the box. I just wanted to go round the coast, with a small
tent, to think that before I die it would be nice to get the
feel of my own country. I said to Antonia she could come
with me and paint, but she said, "Oh no", so when I do it,
I shall do it on my own. And perhaps in two stages. But
these cars are so useful for that because you can still get
everything.'

I asked him if he thought of himself as an enthusiast, and
the watery-eyed smile took hold of him again.

'I've got to be!' He laughed. 'People say, "Bob, you're so
eccentric!" But I don't see myself as being eccentric in my
own terms, because I enjoy what I do and I enjoy even more
what I haven't got round yet to enjoying. It doesn't make any
difference to you if I say, "Right. I'm going to take you out
in all of my cars". I mean, you might come round in ten
years' time, if I'm not dead, and I may have finished them all
by then. It's more likely you'll say, "It's still the same as it was
last time Bob!" It's like that with me. I've got friends who
have got something that's put out to the man who does it for
them, but I do get pleasure from being able to do things
myself. I sometimes get frustrated, because there are things
that I've done that aren't up to much, but I'm happy with the
Grahame-White. I'll give myself points for that. I've done
that, and I've done most of it myself and I've got what I
wanted. Of course, I can't cope with modern cars – nobody
can – it's got to go to the dealer. But everything you see in
here, I feel that, if it's not working, I can get it going. It's a
question of time and money. The enthusiasm is always there.
I don't think you can have any genuine interest if you're not

an enthusiast. I just have a fascination in something primitive and wonder how much it can do. Often with cycle cars you see pictures or illustrations of them looking daft with pictures of people in Victorian times being pulled across the channel on water-skis or something. But people really imagined at the time that you could make your own cycle car for £50 from motor-cycle parts and drive your family down to the coast in it. Now of course there were limitations, but British engineering had to be a certain exemplary standard, and that meant cars were very expensive. The cycle cars were the antidote to that. They weren't necessarily made cheaply, but there were loads of people who aspired to own them who could never have afforded a car. There was a magazine called *Cycle Car* that came out in 1912, and they felt the demand was such that they printed 100,000 copies, all of which sold. Only a few of those people had got cycle cars, but it was like the South Sea Bubble in a way. There was a huge fervour and enthusiasm for them. Everybody was captivated by where these things would take us. What it actually did was force people to pull their fingers out and realize there was a market for smaller cars. But then after the war the cycle cars were gone. Completely forgotten.'

He then told me about some of his quirkier friends back in his study, over another cup of tea, and about their sometimes strange relationships with machines. The whole time I was with him he had a look of fascination in his eyes, as though the world was constantly trying to entertain and trigger his curiosity. With enthusiasts it's always in the eyes, which brim with laughter but are never far away from a poignant and tragic story too. I could have stayed there for hours and longed to tuck into a few bottles of red wine and really find out what it was that had pushed and pulled him throughout his life, but sadly I had to go. The room itself intrigued me enormously, though. As I went to leave, I wondered whether inside it were the answers to a whole host of other questions about life that I might one day become curious enough to ask. Perhaps in the glowing fire. The photographs and prints. The old boxes, posters and signs and the figures of men looking out from years and years ago. It was the kind of room I've always longed to have. Somewhere to go to sit, read and fiddle about with thoughts and ideas. Not a place to take refuge in from the real world, but perhaps a portal *into* the real world from the fabricated upside-down priorities most of us seem to live within these days.

My thoughts turned from cycle cars back to Silverstone and the high-performance monsters I'd seen hurtling around the track. They and the cycle cars were related by an enthusiasm for cars, but it seemed to me that both passions revealed a profound shift in attitude. I had started to watch *Top Gear* while on this quest, and although in every episode the three presenters went on a similar kind of adventure to the one described by Bob, in an attempt to create the kind of fascinating story he had recalled about his high-bicycle journeys and the one he hoped to have around Britain in his Austin 7, their adventures never really managed to leave a lasting impression. Except for one episode I saw, when Jeremy Clarkson, Richard Hammond and James May drove through the aftermath of Hurricane Katrina and were so astonished by the reality of the carnage they witnessed that they ended up giving their cars away to locals in a gesture that I was quite unprepared for. No one wanted James May's car though, which maintained his presence as a kind of reliable failure for everyone to feel superior to. Interestingly for my search, it was May that clearly knew the most about cars though. Any real machine enthusiast is clearly far too nerdy for *Top Gear*. But the main principle of the show seemed to be to try and keep up with all the latest infinitesimally small progressions the car manufacturers had managed to produce in their latest models. One week a car would be proclaimed as the best anyone had ever seen, having been driven round a racetrack, and then a week later it would be pipped – only very slightly, mind you – by something else. It seemed enthusiasm for machines had been absurdly commoditized to such a degree that no car could ever hold your loyalty for longer than seven days. Not that the vast majority of the *Top Gear* audience would ever own these expensive supercars given so much screen time anyway. The celebrities on the show certainly could, however, and they tentatively sought Clarkson's approval each week, after plugging their latest book/film/album/TV show. But something seemed to have changed from Bob's passion for the Wonder Car, where he clearly revelled in its incredibly primitive design, to the slightly ridiculous obsession with acceleration speeds and the exact number of horses being flagellated under the bonnets of the most recently released cars. It is undeniably the most watched and talked-about cultural reference to machines that exists in Britain today, but very little of Bob's essentially life-affirming motivation to get out there and experience life, which I'd also seen in some of the other machine enthusiasts, was reflected in this blokey, essentially car catalogue, TV show. I began to wonder whether everyone that professed to love *Top Gear* had a secret, awkward feeling that it was all a bit simple and only the rage it inspired in the George Monbiots of this world gave them the sense that it represented the sharp edge of life or contained anything meaningful that they alone understood.

As I drove away, leaving Bob to work on his Wonder Car, the significance of a throwaway remark he had made as we left his study dawned on me. 'You know, Dan, if you really want to understand why men love machines, then the first thing you've got to try and understand is why you don't.' It was an avenue I hadn't gone down but he was right. It was about time I did.

7

Spielzeug

Diggers, Trucks and Tanks

NEXT UP, I found myself just outside Rochester, on the banks of the Thames at Diggerland. Yes, you read that right. Diggerland. Think Disney World, but instead of Mickey Mouse and Donald Duck there are diggers and JCBs. My three-year-old son Wilf and I had come to learn how to drive a digger. Then I spotted a sign advertising 'Digger Ballet'. Now I'd seen it all – or at least, I would have once I'd seen a digger dance.

The philosophy behind Diggerland appeared primarily to be to stick two fingers up to the makers of the various machine safety videos I had been forced to watch in my rural primary school. Back then, certain death awaited anyone crazy enough to nudge even slightly the control panel of an empty digger, and your head would surely be crushed under some vast unidentified tyre if you so much as dreamed of mucking around with any stray bits of farm machinery, but here at Diggerland five-year-olds were ushered behind the controls and told to 'dig for treasure' in full-size JCBs. Clearly the numerous attractions were all perfectly safe, but they were certainly a little unusual in this over-coddled day and age. Adults are not supposed to be able to muck about in huge digging machinery, let alone kids. One or two of the teenage marshals looked like they might have had a heavy night in smoking weed the night before, but all were patient and helpful, pointing out the ludicrous ease with which you could control the various heavy machines. Another digger had been customized, with seats for about eight people set inside the vast bucket at the front, so the driver could lift them up and spin them around at an alarming speed. I soon learned from park manager Simon McCann that 'Normal digger drivers can't control Spin Dizzy' (the name of this particular attraction). 'It goes against everything you're supposed to do with a piece of construction machinery. We've had a few come down to be marshals, and none of them can operate that one.' Further down were more filthy machines, again being driven by tiny children, bouncing around various tracks. I saw one man fighting with his young son to get at the controls of a dumper truck as they pummelled their way around another course. Simon laughed. 'Yes, I think the dads love it just as much as the kids.' At this point Oasis began blaring out of the speakers and another small boy gritted his teeth while the arm of a JCB flailed around in front of me. 'Surreal' simply doesn't do it justice. It was as though the age of health and safety had never happened.

'What we don't try to do here is educate anyone,' Simon continued, in his astonishingly refreshing way. 'We work on an average of about five minutes per ride, so if you spend two minutes explaining to a kid how the controls work, which they will forget the moment you walk away, they've lost half their ride. But with the kids you can throw them on, and most of the diggers have two controls. Two joysticks, one on each side. Exactly the same as a PlayStation, Xbox, whatever. It's what they do all day anyway. So they get in the cab and think, "Oh yeah, I know how it works", and they're off.'

Still rather stunned at the sight of young children powering around in enormous machines, I asked where the idea for Diggerland had come from.

'Hugh, our chairman, had an open day at HE Services, the head office of his hire plant firm. He had a lot of clients come down and told them to bring their families for a barbecue, and he had lots of machines outside. Pretty soon he had all these kids climbing in and out of machines with huge grins on their faces, and it must have been one of those light-bulb moments. Why don't we do this deliberately?'

Hugh sounded like the Willy Wonka of the construction world. We soon came to a full-scale cardboard cut-out of him, a tall, balding man wearing a silver boiler suit, beside a silver JCB that he'd used to drive from John O'Groats to Land's End for charity. He looked like Evil Knievel would have done if he had pursued a career in middle management.

'There he is.' Simon grinned. 'What we're trying to achieve is to be different from other theme parks. With all the other ones, first, it's a procession of queuing for ever, then you're strapped into a machine, given a ride and then you get out. It's almost an extension of queuing. You don't actually do anything other than get the hell scared out of you. Yes, it's exciting, but there isn't the interaction you get here. I remember being about seven or eight years old, sitting in my mum's car pretending I was driving. All I wanted to do was drive something, which is the experience we try and give kids here. You get behind the wheel of something like that' – he pointed at a JCB – 'and there is a huge sense of power. With a flick of the wrist you can tear the ground apart. Kids just love it. Mind you, so do adults. We get plenty of people who come down on their own and spend the afternoon driving the big machines, before going home with a huge smile on their face.'

As we walked, I noticed two smaller diggers with caged cabs that looked rather battered.

'These are our fighting machines. We use them on our corporate event days. You put a driver in each of them at the controls, and they basically fight with the arms until one of them is knocked over. Sometimes the bouts last fifteen minutes, sometimes thirty seconds. We also do JCB racing, which is quite exciting. They go fast enough so that if you hit a bump you can easily get all four wheels off the ground. It's quite an experience to race one of those. They weigh seven and a half tons each.'

To go back to the first digger we must rejoin the steam age and a patent taken out by William Otis in 1839 for the 'steam shovel'. Originally manoeuvred on rails and built on a converted railway truck, the steam shovel surely had its finest hour with the excavation of the Panama Canal, but it was also largely responsible for the scale of the advancement of railways and mines across the world. Sadly for Otis, he did not live to see the world his steam shovel would carve from the earth: he died in the year of his patent at the age of twenty-six. It was not until the 1930s that modern diesel-powered diggers began to emerge, which led to the modern equivalents that I was now itching to have a go on at Diggerland. Wilf was pulling me over too in his desperation to climb behind the controls, so I made my excuses to Simon and clambered inside a stationary JCB. 'Cooooool' then came repeatedly from Wilf's mouth as he sat on my lap and lunged for the joysticks. I suppressed the urge to say, 'You can't just play on the controls of such a dangerous machine!' because that was the whole point of our being there. Within seconds the digger arm was being waved around haphazardly, to his exuberant delight. Pretty soon he'd got to grips with it and was merrily scraping the huge digger bucket on the ground, pulling it towards the cab and opening and closing the bucket, laughing hysterically all the while. After ten minutes of that we decided to have a go at driving a JCB. Freddie, the digger-driving marshal, explained the ease of driving it – 'We get ten-year-olds who are very good with it very quickly' – and soon we were bumping and grinding our way towards a vast road bridge that spanned the width of the Thames. 'It's an old landfill site,' Freddie explained, 'so it's the perfect use for it. You couldn't do much else here, that's for sure.' Diggerland was certainly getting something right, I decided as we climbed a big hill before sailing at speed down the other side. There were none of the 'DO NOT HAVE ANY FUN!'-type signs most of the country seems to be plagued with, and Simon had told me earlier that injuries were practically non-existent. Apparently the dodgems caused the most accidents.

After that we drove around on some small tractors, got stuck for a while in gloopy mud in what looked like a modi-fied forklift truck with its forks removed, had a race in some go-karts and ended up with a few goes on the dodgems. By the end the two of us were filthy, tired and very, very happy. 'How was that then?' I asked Wilf as we drove home. 'Diggers are cooooool,' he repeated over and over again. 'Let's come back tomorrow with Granddad and Uncle Gaz.' Yes, I thought as we drove away, I think you've hit the nail on the head there.

A few weeks later I was heading to a remote and secret part of the English countryside to meet a truck and military vehicle enthusiast called Ian. Because of the vast array of machines he keeps in a huge complex of sheds behind his house he asked me not to divulge his precise location, which added a wonderful air of mystery to the small country lanes I had to bounce through before I reached his home.

I arrived and was immediately offered tea by Ian, wearing what looked like a very thick, warm boiler suit and Dr

Martens boots, but there were no wannabe army-style dog tags around his neck, bullet belts or the kind of things you might expect from a military vehicle enthusiast. He seemed slightly suspicious of me initially but soon began to open up as we entered the first of his vast sheds. He grinned with pride as we approached an enormous 1957 Peterbilt truck. You probably know what a Peterbilt truck looks like, even if you don't think you do, because it's most famous for appearing in *Duel*, the Steven Spielberg road-rage film from 1971, in which businessman Dennis Weaver is terrorized on a lonely Californian highway. Spielberg said after it was completed that, because you never actually see the driver's face, the truck itself becomes the villain. It is a film about the fear of the unknown, man versus machine, and in this instance, at least, man comes out on top. Standing there, it looked a lot smaller than the one in *Duel*, but it still had a slightly sinister air about it. It was being repainted after its long journey from California in a crate on a huge cargo ship.

Behind that and to our left I could see more trucks, armoured cars, motor bikes, bicycles, an amphibious buggy, a cannon and all manner of general mechanical detritus. It was the kind of place a hapless Texan criminal would consider ideal for using temporarily to imprison *The A-Team*, only for them to burst through the wall in some vast and terrifying iron contraption half an hour later, with Mr T shouting inaudible obscenities while spraying all and sundry with a huge flame-thrower. Everywhere I looked I could see machines. To my untrained eye most seemed to be ex-Second World War vehicles. There was a Red Cross truck of the kind I had as a toy when I was a small boy, an American-style commando green jeep and armoured personnel carriers. It was by far the largest collection of machines I'd ever seen in private hands, and this was only the first of Ian's huge sheds.

I mentioned *The A-Team* and he began to laugh.

'It's safe to say that we're into machinery. It's probably programmes like that that got me into it all to be honest. I used to love that.'

I asked whether he was working on renovating the Peterbilt full-time.

'I've been working on it most afternoons this week. I spend the mornings doing paperwork for export licences for some more stuff from the States. Importing tank parts causes massive issues. There are a few hang-ups with arms dealing.' He laughed. 'Finding the parts involves a bit of investigative research, though. It's a quest really – a jigsaw puzzle, with the pieces scattered all over the world. The thrill of the chase in trying to find this stuff is one of the things about restoration that I love the most. Now let me show you the tank, which is what we need the parts for.'

We walked out of the shed. To our right a huge field was filled with even more heavy contraptions, and I could see smaller shacks at the back. We then dived into another dark space. Ian called out over his shoulder, 'Watch where you tread.'

I followed behind, stepping over chunks of metal, coils of wire, numerous screws and nails and emerged into the light in front of what looked like a huge chunk of scrapped, twisted metal. Ian tapped it, smiling.

'This is a 1941-*ish* Sherman tank. It's had a bit of a hard life.'

That was something of an understatement. I stared at it for a moment, trying to determine its precise tankishness, but there was little I could identify. Finally, like one of those pictures that contain a myriad of images, a tank emerged from the iron mess in front of me. I looked down and could see where the treads should go, but the entire top half seemed utterly ruined. Then I realized there was no gun turret, which is probably why its tankish nature had been obscured.

'It was built in around '41. Used somewhere in the Second World War. We think it was then sent back to the factory in the States in '44 and fully overhauled. Fitted with later model suspension, turret and up-armoured. Then it came back here in late '44 as a brand new tank. Don't know if it then saw service again. If it did, we don't know where. We don't think it did, though, because of these,' he pointed to the sprocket – the bit the tracks go on – which was comparatively undamaged, 'and then, we believe in the '50s it was put out on a firing range by the British army and shot at. For quite a long time.'

The top section was filled with holes of the kind that that birds might select to nest in.

'Those are rocket-propelled grenade holes. It was clearly getting battered, so what they decided to do to make it last longer was fill it with concrete. That was in 1980 or something. They then shot at it quite a lot more, got bored with it and tried to scrap it in 1989 or 1990. A friend of mine saw it on a range in north Yorkshire and went back to find it in 1991 with a view to scrounging some parts off it, but it wasn't there any more. It turned out that the scrap man had come out to take a look at it, seen it was filled with concrete, said "This isn't worth scrapping", and they buried it. So last year we heard a rumour of a buried Sherman tank. Well, a buried tank's a bit like treasure, isn't it? So you go and find it. It was on a disused army range, so we had to get permission from the military to buy it, which was very complicated. It involved solicitors, benevolent funds, all sorts, but we got permission to buy it. Bearing in mind it was still underground and no one had seen it for twenty years – we paid £5,000 for it. We then had to pay the contractor who buried it to unbury it, because he was the only one who knew roughly where it was. Now at this point no one had mentioned to us that it was full of concrete. So it was only when it was winched out of the ground that we found out it had 16 tons of the stuff inside. We've had to gun all the concrete out with road-breaking jackhammers and lots and lots of time. It's what you call hard-core tank restoration.'

I pointed out, as politely as I could, that it would clearly be a great deal of work to restore.

'It looks a bit shit, doesn't it?' Ian agreed. 'But it will look as good as new once we're finished.'

I then asked why on earth anyone would want to put themselves through that kind of graft.

'Well, it's probably the second most desirable tank to own. In the last five years these things have gone up and up in value. Five years ago a restored one of these was worth £35,000. Now they are worth about £150,000. So five years ago this wasn't viable. You couldn't do it because it would cost too much in time and parts to do. Now it is. Everything we do we aim to not lose money on. Because when you've done it and played with it a bit, you might get bored with it. So if you then sell it for £20,000 and it owes you £50,000 you'd be depressed, wouldn't you? If it owes you £50,000 and you sell it for £80,000, then you'd be quite happy. It's very expensive to do tank restoration, you see. We spent £3,500 just on the crane to lift it out of the ground and put it on a low loader. Then we had to pay the guy to dig it out of the ground and a recovery team to winch it out. Because we're not MOD-approved on that site, we couldn't use our own tank recovery vehicle either. So we had to pay someone else to do it, which was annoying because that would have been part of the fun. To dig it up and rescue it yourself.'

It seemed to Ian that it was more about rescuing things and bringing them back to life than about having them for their own sake. I was curious where he put the thoughts and feelings about what tanks are specifically designed for – to kill people – while going about restoring them though. Presumably his Sherman tank was the last thing quite a few people saw before being blown to bits.

'That is an unpleasant side to it, but the only way of looking at it is that they were used to defend us. Tanks were invented in 1914 to combat trench warfare in Normandy because all our guys were getting slaughtered. The army worries me intensely because it's done some terrible things. At the Battle of the Somme they lost 60,000 guys on the first day. Simply by feeding them over. Now anybody with a quarter of a brain would have said, "Hang on a minute. We're not getting anywhere. Stop." But that's the army mentality.'

I was still baffled. Putting aside the potential financial gain on this particular project, because it was clear that Ian wasn't in it for the money, doing all that hard work only to end up selling it on a year or so later seemed a bit odd. But then, as he himself said, perhaps it was the journey of restoring it and not the destination that made it all worthwhile. Seeing my mystified expression, Ian sought to explain.

'Think what sense of achievement we're going to get when everyone has told us we're mad. It does look a lot worse than it is. It's in pretty good condition when you consider its history. It needs a new engine, new wheel stations, which we're bringing in from the States. But the tank to own if you are a tank collector, the one you want to find in a barn, is a Tiger. The main reason is that they are very rare and worth about a million pounds. There are very few in "free hands", as we call it. There's a few in museums, but the second most desirable tank used in the Second World War is a Sherman.'

Ian then gestured for me to follow him out into the field, past a 1950 Chevy ('my runabout work truck') until we reached his '1953 International Tank Recovery Vehicle. Otherwise known as a heavy wrecker.'

It was an absolutely enormous black monster, which made the Peterbilt look like a Mini, and Ian clearly enjoyed the way my mouth dropped while walking up to it.

'This one is six-wheel drive. Has a 10-ton front winch, a 3-ton rear winch and 6- to 10-ton crane in the middle, depending on how you use it. It's quite a useful bit of kit. They were built with the same shape as this till about 1980. When the Americans get hold of a good idea, they tend to keep using it. The ones they're using in Iraq now are still very similar to this. It weighs 16 tons, but it's lovely to drive. It's got power steering, and it accelerates reasonably well. It sounds absolutely awesome. Turbo-charged diesel with no silencer. I don't drive it very often, though. Might take it to one or two shows a year, just to intimidate all the jeep owners.'

Not usually one to pry about such vulgar things as money, I couldn't stop myself asking how much it had cost, imagining tens of thousands of pounds.

'I paid four and a half grand for it. You might think it would be worth more, but it's huge. Where do you keep it? A jeep is worth more than this because it fits in your garage. Anybody that wants an army truck can have a jeep. Not everybody can have one of these. There are an awful lot of trucks that are worth low thousands. Restored Second World War trucks are only worth three or four grand because they're big and thirsty. We used to have lots more than this, but we're trying to thin them out.'

I should point out here that Ian and his father are not just big machine enthusiasts. They have turned their passion into a way of earning money by occasionally renting them out to film companies.

'We used to do a lot of film work, before the government bollocksed the UK film industry, and rented out these trucks a lot. That truck over there spent six months in Ireland making a film called *Reign of Fire* [a futurist dystopian nightmare flick with fire-breathing dragons, starring Matthew McConaughey and Christian Bale]. We had about eight or nine vehicles in the film and another two or three were used as back-up. The heavy wrecker was there because we had two tanks there too.

'Because we do it for a business, the money side of it is a bit of a grey area. Some of our machines are purely hobby vehicles. The wrecker truck is, but that Chevy is for work. But then again, the wrecker will go out on a job when we need it to so that earns money as well. For *Saving Private Ryan* they rang up wanting twenty-five landing craft. Well, I happened to have a real Second World War one at the time that I'd taken a fancy to, and we went to look for some more. I found two, but the trouble is film companies tend to destroy things. They want to make a movie, so to them it's just a prop. They don't care about its history. They quite often blow things up by accident. Things get wrecked. It's a bit of a problem. I've gone off for a cup of tea and come back to find a bloke with a drill standing next to one of our trucks, wants to drill a hole in the door to put a wire through for the camera. Literally no sense of its value at all. On the last Pierce Brosnan Bond film I had six Humvees on hire to them. They wanted to simulate blowing them up. So we said, "OK, well this needs to be done quite carefully." We had a meeting, and the explosion man said, "Why can't we just blow them up?"

I said, "Well, you can, but they're £30,000 each." He says, "Well, is that a problem?" The film hire guy who got us involved is nearly falling off his chair at this point and says "Of course it's a bloody problem!" So they had to simulate blowing them up by putting an explosive device in front of the machines with chunks of foam on it. So the foam goes up in the air, and at the right angle it looks like the Hummers did, but they didn't. In another Bond film we worked on they destroyed twenty-two hovercraft. They're just props, blow them up!' He shook his head.

Inside another shed Ian pointed to the far wall.

'That is the Batman search-light used in every *Batman* film. It went out to Prague earlier this year. It's a Second World War American search-light.' Pointing to the left of it, he continued. 'That is a regular army jeep. There's another one behind it and another one over there. That's a First World War gun that we restored. There's my air force tractor, a 1942 David Brown, which I bought when I was about twelve . . .'

I began to see the vast array of machines as Ian's play-things. I was curious why there were no new vehicles, though. Nothing in the collection had been originally made more recently that the mid-1950s.

'Modern machines are shit. That's why I haven't got any,' Ian retorted defiantly. 'It's a throwaway society today. They're not even welded. They stick cars together with glue, which tends to make repairing them a bit more difficult. It's utterly crap. It's something that makes me not want to own a modern car, that's for sure. It makes you wonder whether we've actually improved anything by building all these machines, though, doesn't it? We lost our way somewhere along the line. Roads have half wiped out the countryside; people get from A to B quicker, but what does that actually achieve? They still seem to have no time and aren't happy with their lives. They are probably the same as they were before they had all these machines to help them.'

The philosopher Bertrand Russell once made a similar point. A hundred and fifty years ago a man might have walked half an hour to go to work. Today that same man would not be able to walk to work, because he might not be able to afford to live as close to work as he used to, or he might not want to, or that job might have disappeared thanks to mechanization. So he will end up getting in a car or a train to get to work instead. His new journey will probably take at least half an hour. So from that you might conclude that transport machines haven't actually saved us any time; they've just increased the distance we can travel.

Something inside Ian suddenly seemed to have woken up and he began to aim a few questions at me. 'But if you ask me why I love these old machines, what I want to know is why other people don't.'

I looked at him quizzically. He seemed pleased that this counterintuitive approach had me stumped. I gestured for him to continue.

'When you said on the phone that you've never been into machines at all, I thought you must be a bit strange. I've got a lodger who is a bit like that. He doesn't have any interest in anything really. So what are your hobbies then?'

It was a fair question. I don't spend lots and lots of time on anything outside my family, friendships and the things I do to earn money, but for me my hobby and the way I earn money are the same thing. I do quite a lot of travel journalism, but of all the places around the world I've visited I've never found anywhere as fascinating and fun to journey through as my own ignorance. Hence the pleasure I get on going on a journey like this in an attempt to understand a view of life I haven't experienced myself. So to me writing and doing things like this book are my hobby, even though it's also how I pay the rent. I explained all this to Ian, but the questions kept coming.

'So you don't have a practical hobby where you've done something to something or with something and you've got something to show for it at the end. Like, you'd go out and take pictures, say?'

I pointed out that the book I'll have written at the end would be something physical I can hold, but he wasn't convinced because to him writing a book was my work. He then asked what my wife did to earn money; Rachel is a part-time teacher. We both only work part-time because, rather like Ben and Cath whom I met back on the Kennet and Avon canal, we value our time far more preciously than money. I write three days a week, and my wife teaches for two.

'So what do you do the other four days of the week?'

I explained that we just, well, live. Look after our son, spend time with family and friends. Go for walks on the beach, muck about in the woods, have adventures in the countryside, that kind of thing. We always try and do something every day that has the potential to be remembered. I suppose we're looking for the 'quality' experience that Pirsig wrote about. We often fail, but it's something we strive for. Having been freelance and part-time for about a decade now, I simply can't understand how anyone finds the time for a full-time job.

Ian seemed impressed with the idea of a life where work isn't the main priority. 'Bloody hell. That's cool. How do you afford it, though?'

The simple reason we can afford not to work very much is because we don't spend very much and we have no debt. If you are in control of your own time, you simply don't care if you don't have much money, because you don't need nearly as much as you think you do when your time belongs to someone else. If you value the spiritual benefits of being in control of your own time, which as we've learned are literally incalculable, more than money, then in my experience you'll find happiness too somewhere along the way. Sadly most people fall into the trap of thinking that they can only be free after they have become rich, but the truth is that if you can live on £10,000 a year, then you are five times freer than someone whose annual outgoings are £50,000.

Ian raised his eyebrows at that, but for some reason he appeared more relaxed and open talking to me afterwards.

'So what you should be asking in your book is not why I love machines or why you love to avoid work as much as is humanly possible,' he laughed, 'but why everyone else seems to like working nine to five and then subjects themselves to the mind-numbing shit that makes everybody depressed and want to kill each other on TV every night. Why don't these people go out and do something sensible? Things like *Big Brother* are so cheap to make, but why the hell does anybody watch it? Now they're on series 4, 5 or 6 or whatever, and they're going out of their way to get total fruitcakes on it. Why do people watch that crap? Because they've got no interests, that's why. They've got nothing better to do with their lives.'

Ian was on a roll.

'I mean, look at what kids have got for entertainment today. Bloody axe-murdering video games, vicious comics and cartoons, and they wonder why these kids are going round stabbing each other. They're showing them *Big Brother* – a house full of fruitcakes – or *EastEnders* – a load of people who swear all the time and want to knife each other, run over each other, sleep with their daughters and all sorts of other weird shit – and you think, I wonder why this country is going down the pan? It's utterly barking, and

I can't get my head round it. So I can see the sense of this other guy [earlier I'd mentioned Lionel Ferris's theory about men seeking a relationship they can trust] wanting to go to his workshop and have a relationship with his machine. You can sort of see where he's coming from, can't you? I've got a list of things to own, and when I've had them, I tick them off the list. You get it as a wreck, save it, improve it if you can, muck about in it for a while and then sell it on. Now even if you don't like machines, that's surely a more sensible way of spending your time than watching crap on television every night.'

I agreed heartily and asked what he would do when he got to the end of his list. He laughed.

'Dunno. Have kids?'

And then pass his enthusiasm on to the next generation?

'I doubt it. I think it will be increasingly difficult to keep these things. Like that big wrecker that you couldn't believe was only worth four and a half grand? Ten years ago it was much easier to keep that somewhere than it is now. All the places where you used to be able to keep things have disappeared, either cleared up by the council or built on. There's a big scrapyard down the road, and now it's 47 acres of development land. All these little places are going. The people who have all the knowledge about these things – there are less of them around now too. There aren't many people of my age into this hobby. There's also the running costs. My first Chevy pick-up, which I bought in 1997, used to cost me £30 to fill it up with diesel. Now it costs me about £90. The engine hasn't got any bigger. If you drive it gently, it does about 20 to the gallon, which gets silly if you go a long way. But they're trying to stamp down on this stuff, aren't they? The cost of fuel is going up, and they're going to tax these big things. But the engineering is going too, and that's

probably the main reason. Thirty years ago you'd have a
Morris Minor, and it would probably be twenty or twenty-
five years old before you thought "I'm going to stop welding
it now and scrap it". The idea now is that the car gets to about
four years and you chuck it, because you can't fix it once all
the electrics are fried. The glue holding the body together is
going. It's utter crap. We go to scrapyards every now and
then, looking to scavenge parts for other things. You see
much newer cars now than you ever did before, and I'm not
that old. Five- or six-year-old cars being scrapped! How is
that progress? Old machines were better built. Built to last. I
can't imagine in fifty years time there will be a Ford Ka in
anyone's garage being renovated. Even if you could find
someone who wanted to restore the damn thing by then, it
will probably have dissolved.'

Ian's thoughts stayed with me for a long time after I got home
that night. I'd always found the argument that newer and
newer technology was by definition 'progress' a rather frus-
trating argument, and now I had an even more powerful
reason to doubt it. It seems if you're looking for a more sustainable way of living, an end to our throwaway society, you
could do worse than reinstate the principles behind proper,
old-fashioned engineering that all the enthusiasts I had met
so admired. We live in a throwaway society simply because
the things we buy today are so badly made.

Ian's love of machines was also, I felt, an instance of someone taking comfort from the world of machinery not because
it followed rules he could comprehend instead of raising the
big questions of life, which were far harder to get to grips
with, but essentially because the priorities of modern life are
incredibly passive and fundamentally rather inhuman and
pointless. When he talked about hunting down these old

machines and their parts, pouring his heart into rebuilding them and making them work again, having fun with what he had put back together and then selling them on so he could repeat the process, you could see how richly he was engaging in the experience of life itself. It was a quest that gave him a chance to put something tangible into the world that pushed him to learn new things that clearly gave him enormous pleasure, despite its being hard work. But he wasn't so tied to it when it was finished that he then obsessed over it for ever more. He just sold it and moved on to the next thing. Compare that with most people's mode of life, where they are constantly chasing the dream of life fraudulently created by the marketers and advertisers by pursuing rational, financial wealth in a job they probably wouldn't do for a second if they weren't getting paid for it – all in the hope that one day they will be able to retire and become masters of their own time for a while before they die and finally have the kind of rich life experiences that the enthusiasts I'd met, such as Ian and Bob Jones, manage to have without all that pointless rainbow-chasing first.

As I drove home, Ian's questions about my own specific outlet for enthusiasm, or lack of it, seemed to feed into Bob Jones's point that in order to understand why men love machines I would also have to try and understand why I had never come to love them myself. I decided to look at how and when mankind's impulse to create a mechanical world had emerged.

Pondering this when I got home, I picked up a book by Lewis Mumford a friend had recommended that had been sitting rather dauntingly on my bookshelf. Mumford wrote extensively about the relationship between men and machines in a book called *Technics and Civilization*, which was first published in 1931. Interestingly, bearing in mind the global financial meltdown going on as the backdrop to my own journey to understand man's relationship with machines, this meant that Mumford was writing during and after the great Wall Street crash of 1929.

He begins by explaining that mankind's relationship with machines can be examined in three phases that overlap as each merges in and out of the other: the 'eotechnic phase', when man had a more basic, craft-like relationship with tools and primitive machines, from 1000 to 1800; the 'paleotechnic phase', which encapsulated the Industrial Revolution, from 1700 to 1900; and the 'neotechnic phase', which went from 1900 up to Mumford's present in 1930 and off into his future, which is our past and present.

Fascinatingly, according to Mumford, the machine age began not with James Watt's steam engine, as is often suggested, but in the eotechnic phase, with the humble clock. It is that machine which truly and vastly altered our relationship with the world we live in and is surely the first machine that the human race became obsessed by. The clock was what irrevocably disconnected us from existential thoughts about life and focused our attention on the quantifiable, scientific laws that govern our senses instead. The clock is the regimented, structured prism through which we all experience life today and which sets us on a path of specialization in the way it divides and subdivides our perception of the world around us into units of regimented time. Mumford examines how this first mechanical or scientific invention then helped create the intellectual framework that preceded and allowed the world of mechanization to emerge.

By what means was the new mechanical picture put together? And how did it come to provide such an excellent soil for the propagation of inventions and the spread of machines?

The method of physical sciences rested fundamentally upon a few simple principles. First: the elimination of qualities [that word again], and the reduction of the complex to the simple by paying attention only to those specific aspects of events which could be weighed, measured, or counted . . . In short, what the physical sciences call the world is not the total object of common human experience: it is just those aspects of this experience that lend themselves to accurate factual observation . . .

This echoes the view we've already come across, that the scientific, rational approach to understand the physical world around us has led us to devalue thoughts about the ultimate existential reality of being alive, which simply can't be quantified in scientific terms. Of all the quandaries that face us, in Mumford's view, science is only able to deal with the relatively simple, surface ones: the 'how' of life, rather than the 'why'.

Having come across this idea earlier, I had found myself spotting it everywhere. If things can't be measured, then they are simply ignored by those seeking 'success', and to the rational world 'success' means money and power. Sadness cannot be measured scientifically, and nor can fulfilment, happiness, love, curiosity, laughter, true learning or grief; and because they cannot be measured, we live in a world where these things do not matter to the large structures that rule our lives. They all matter to us as individuals far more than everything else, but they are considered outside the scope of the main institutions that control us. It's baffling when you start to think about life in these terms. How did we get to the stage where all the things that we value most that we experience as human beings have been relegated to the world of irrelevance?

Mumford's argument is that the new clock-watching,

science-based framework was responsible for irrevocably altering our perception of the world.

> The qualitative was reduced to the subjective: the subjective was dismissed as unreal, and the unseen and immeasurable non-existent . . . Much could be accomplished by the new science and the new technics because much that was associated with life and work in the past – art, poetry, organic rhythm, fantasy – was deliberately eliminated. As the outer world of perception grew in importance, the inner world of feeling became more and more impotent . . .

So it was as our dependence on the rational point of view increased that we began to kill off the perceived value of thinking about life in other terms. There is a tendency at this point to think that a world where non-rational things are valued must mean one where unscientific things that are laughed at as absurd today – such as magic, séances, astrology, mind-reading and so on – are suddenly considered 'real'. But I'm not talking about what the world of science would deem irrational. I'm talking about the universal truths of human experience that science is unable to plot on a graph. Mumford argues that it was by demystifying his perception of life in this way that mankind helped create a barren world that was ripe for mechanization.

> Mechanical invention, even more than science, was the answer to a dwindling faith and a faltering life impulse. The meandering energies of men, which had flowed over into meadow and garden, had crept into grotto and cave, during the Renascence, were turned by invention into a confined head of water above a turbine: they could sparkle and ripple and cool and revive and delight no more: they were harnessed for a narrow and definite purpose: to move wheels and multiply society's capacity for work. To live was to work: *what other life indeed do machines know?* Faith had at

last found a new object, not the moving of mountains, but the moving of engines and machines. Power: the application of power to motion, and the application of motion to production, and of production to money-making, and so the further increase of power – this was the worthiest object that a mechanical habit of mind and a mechanical mode of action put before men.

The Industrial Revolution, or the 'paleotechnic phase', had begun, something Mumford describes as 'an upthrust into barbarism'.

In the eighteenth century, Mechanical Societies sprang into existence, to propagate the creed with greater zeal; they preached the gospel of work, justification by faith in mechanical science, and salvation by the machine . . . The impersonal procedure of science, the hard-headed contrivances of mechanics, the rationale calculus of the utilitarians – these interests captured emotion, all the more because the golden paradise of financial success lay beyond.

He then details exhaustively the misery of the lives of those who allowed the figures of the Industrial Revolution, whom we largely revere today, to accumulate so much wealth and become so admired. The factories were essentially slave camps, where people worked sixteen-hour days, and people often lived and died within sight of the effective prison where they worked. Women and children toiled alongside the men, allowing the factory owners to drive down wages further and further. The early days of the Industrial Revolution were a mechanized hell on earth to those who made it possible, but their sacrifice brought vast wealth to those in control. Mumford explains that these towering figures known to us as 'industrialists' made machines of men but also of themselves, describing the luminaries we are all told about with gushing praise in school as people without taste, imagination, intellect, moral scruples, general culture, or even elementary bowels of compassion, who rose to the surface precisely because they fitted an environment that had no place and no use for any of these humane attributes. Only anti-social qualities had survival value. Only people who valued machines more than men were capable under these conditions of governing men to their own profit and advantage.

Mumford calls this the rise of the 'Economic Man', the kind of people heralded as 'masters of the universe' today.

These new economic men sacrificed their digestion, the interests of parenthood, their sexual life, their health, most of the normal pleasures and delights of civilized existence to the untrammelled pursuit of power and money. Nothing retarded them . . . except finally the realization that they had more money than they could use, and more power than they could intelligently exercise. Then came belated repentance: Robert Owen founds a utopian co-operative colony, Nobel, the explosives manufacturer, a peace foundation, Carnegie free libraries, Rockefeller medical institutes . . . These successful neurotics looked upon the arts as unmanly forms of escape from work and business enterprise: but what was their one-sided, maniacal concentration upon work but a much more disastrous escape from life itself?

This brings us to two other concepts that also fit into the two ways of looking at the world that we were introduced to earlier: the contrasting ideas of 'materialism' and 'idealism'. Materialists process the world in terms of what is 'real', in the sense of having form and being observable, which goes some way to explaining why the rational, mechanical approach to life that Mumford outlines has led to a proliferation of materialist desires today. We calculate our worth by the only means available to us – in the things that can be measured – which is why, the more stuff we have, the bigger our homes, the more cars we own and the more money we have in the bank, the more successful we believe ourselves to be. On the other side sits idealism, which is a way of processing the world according to ideas and ideals, as opposed to physical things. Hence the battle we have today between the 'real' world of the materialists and the apparently 'unreal'-istic world of the 'idealist'. Being an idealist is considered hopelessly naïve in our materialistic age because 'ideals' cannot be measured whereas the number of coats, cars or houses you have clearly can. This is why materialists often feel irritated by the behaviour of idealists and shout at them to stop dreaming and 'join the real world'.

Another example of the way the materialists have outgunned the idealists is the way the idealists themselves now latch on to machines. Even those among us who are led more by a spiritual, perhaps artistic, impulse than the rational, mechanic or materialist one have given some machines the status of sacred cows. These are the machines that everyone agrees have brought nothing but universal good: the printing press, for example. The printing press is only ever written about with glowing praise for the way it has transformed the world and aided communication, education and so on. But the printing press has not been a machine of universal good at all. In that sense it is rather like the invention of the first record player, the phonograph, which allowed people to listen to music on records in their own homes. Most people would consider that as advancement, a 100 per cent gain, but it did have another unintended and far more damaging effect on a whole range of human experience. If you can play a record when you want to listen to music, then there's less reason to learn to play an instrument yourself. With the invention of the phonograph the number of people playing instruments dwindled. It also helped turn music into a mechanical profession fit only for 'experts'. What's the point of learning the guitar when you'll never be as good as Slash from Guns n' Roses? You might as well give up and leave it to the 'professionals' – those who do it for 'work' – and listen to them play instead. You might think that recorded music has the 'quality' I mentioned earlier, but which kind of musical experience really has 'quality': listening to a record or being moved with happiness to sing your heart out with joy yourself? You could argue that watching live music has 'quality' perhaps, but recorded music has far less of this intangible magic than the feeling of music erupting from the spring of your own soul. Today the idea of people breaking into song throughout the day sounds absurd. Can you imagine how embarrassing that would be in your office? But we are all still moved by this impulse occasionally. That's surely why people sing in the shower so gleefully. Electrical appliances and speakers are too dangerous to have near water, so we have had no choice but to sing ourselves for our own entertainment when we're getting clean, and it feels amazing! Sadly the world of machines has come up with a way of removing this active joy too, with the creation of the waterproof radio.

There were similar drawbacks with the printing press. Before books stories were told orally, around a fire, and acted out in a communal form of entertainment. Listen to a 'professional' storyteller today, and they will tell you that they do not have a book because their stories are in their head and their heart. We began to need books to tell us stories when we lost the tales of our own souls. My son's nursery had a visit from a storyteller recently and, despite other people reading stories from books in a lovely and animated way beforehand, the life-affirming, active and fully engaged way the children reacted to the storyteller himself was like watching widescreen HD compared to a television with terrible reception. It was not just a story but a kind of theatre, in which everyone was actively involved. Wilf refused to sit to listen; he was so enthralled he wanted to stand up and jump about. The storyteller also changed the story as he went according to ideas the children in the audience threw at him. Storytelling was truly interactive hundreds of years before the supposed interactive 'revolution' of today. Storytelling really is a lost art and, like it or not, that loss came about because of the printing press. (This absence explains why the picture book emerged, because for a story to be reduced to only half of its component parts by giving people the rather empty words, without the action to go with it, was considered to only be half the experience.)

Clearly you can take this argument to absurd extremes. I'm not saying we shouldn't have books, or record players, or that science hasn't brought incalculably huge benefits to human life, simply that we shouldn't allow new technology to eradicate all of what came before. Clearly technology and machines have been good for human life, but they have undeniably increased our passivity and reduced our access to a range of experiences and our joy, for want of a better word, in many ways too. This increase in our passivity actually seems almost to be the goal of materialism. The richer you are, the less you do for yourself. You have servants, cleaners, cooks and drivers even. You go to absurdly expensive hotels and health clubs where you're waited on hand and foot. But surely this increased passivity takes you further and further away from the real quality experiences that bring meaning and delight to your life? Wouldn't we all be better off pursuing the immeasurable and irrational delights of being human rather than the rational and unfulfilling goal of greater measurable wealth?

It is the topsy-turvy system of values of life today that largely explains why I have never really 'got on' with machines. For me mankind's obsession with technology has often been a portal into the worst side of men. I become enraged when mechanical advancement is always described as 'progress'. I'm afraid that, when it comes to the question of whether men have used machines for their benefit or whether machines have enslaved men, I predominantly think the latter is the case. We certainly appear to have become enslaved if you visit Waterloo Station, or any station, on a Monday morning and watch the herds of monochrome people, dressed as though going to their own funerals, heading for the same office they visit five days a week for forty-eight weeks of the year throughout the best years of their adult lives – all hunched over, wearing headphones, wistfully listening to someone else lucky enough to be allowed to follow the human impulse of breaking into song. A sad echo, perhaps, of a time when people didn't need someone else's voice to sing for them because they would have sung on the way to work themselves.

The wonderful and unexpected thing about this journey, though, was that all the machine enthusiasts I'd met seemed to feel exactly the same way as me. They had all spoken of why they didn't 'fit in' or 'understand' the priorities of the modern 'throwaway' world and saw in their machines the essence of different, nobler priorities. It was as though the engineers who produced these vintage mechanical monsters had left some kind of code in the way their pistons, wheels, iron and tyres had been constructed that spoke to the enthusiasts of a purer vision and a purer age. In the light of what we've just read from Lewis Mumford this may sound rather odd – to blame a purely scientific view of life for creating machines that have effectively brought us a mechanical, fundamentally inhuman, mode of life, only then to find hope in the form of the men most obsessed with the machines that started us off down this road in the first place – but Mumford offers a tantalizing explanation for that too. He describes how once the initial astonishing cruelty of the industrialization of the paleotechnic phase had taken hold (in the miserable factories and mills of the late eighteenth and early nineteenth century) engineers, designers and inventors began to learn greater mechanical skills and soon began to recognize the wonder of the 'mechanics' of the natural world. It was then that a subtle shift in the philosophy of machine design began to emerge.

> Machines, which had assumed their own characteristic shapes in developing independent of organic forms, were now forced to recognize the superior economy of nature; on actual tests the blunt heads of many species of fish and the long tapering tail, proved, against naïve intuition, to be the most economic shape of moving through air or water . . . while the aesthetics of the machine is more independent of subjective factors than the aesthetics of painting, there is a point in the background at which they both nevertheless meet: for our emotional responses and our standards of efficiency and beauty are derivable largely in both cases from our reactions to the world of life, where correct adaptations of form have so frequently survived.

It is this change that best explains why Mumford saw hope in machines, despite their inhuman origins. To him the early, brutal days of machines, which always seem to be uncritically praised, were simply man's attempt to learn new skills that he will surely perfect and begin to control to his own advantage in the future, if a combined rational and human perspective is pursued. But, as we have seen, technological progress is being hamstrung today by organizations keen to make as much measurable wealth from the old technology as they can. It is sobering to reflect that the 'near future' Mumford predicted approaching in 1930 after the global financial meltdown following the Wall Street crash included renewable green electric power instead of dirty, difficult-to-access oil and gas and widespread efficient, quiet, electric transport. Nearly eighty years later we're still waiting, but, needless to say, the economic turmoil haunts us still.

To explain the emergence of the new kind of mechanical philosophy Mumford finds a vital link between theory and practice, which enabled this more combined scientific and artistic approach to be possible, in a new kind of man that emerged in the mid-nineteenth century: the engineer. The best engineers had a wide-ranging appreciation for all aspects of life. Chief among them was perhaps the most famous of all Britain's engineering pioneers: the railway, steam train and steam ship pioneer Isambard Kingdom Brunel. On discovering this, I was reminded of a lecture about Brunel that I'd come across, given by L.T.C. Rolt in 1958. But, Rolt pointed out, Brunel's combined appreciation of life and engineering and that of others like him who follow up to this day would largely be drowned out as specialization within the scientific community, and purely measurable, 'rational' objectives, took hold.

> It was only in Brunel's lifetime that the professions of mechanical and civil engineer became distinct with the foundation of the Institution of Mechanical Engineers. This marked the beginning of a process of division and subdivision, of ever increasing specialization which has continued down to our own day. The fact was, of course,

that the accumulation of technical and scientific knowledge was so rapid and so great that specialization of this
kind was inevitable. The sum of knowledge soon became
too vast for any one intellect however brilliant to contain
and the phase of our Industrial Revolution when men like
Brunel could range so freely over the whole field was very
soon over . . .

Materially, the process of specialization has yielded
astounding technical results since Brunel's day as we all
know. Spiritually, however, there are grave dangers inherent in it and the further it is pursued the greater do these
dangers become. Let me try to explain what I mean by this.
Brunel was not only a great engineer but a great man; indeed
one could say that he was a great engineer because he was a
great man and it was his imaginative power and his wide
ranging, liberal intellect which made him great. By contrast,
we have reached a stage now where many specialized depart-
ments of scientific knowledge have become so complex that
their mastery by the student demands the utmost concentration. There is therefore a grave risk that in the effort to
acquire mastery in the particular narrow field he has chosen
to pursue, his wider, more liberal education in the human-
ities and in the arts will be grossly neglected simply because
there is no room for it. If this happens he may become a great
expert in his chosen field but he can never become a great
man. Science is a wonderful thing, but science alone is not
synonymous with civilization, it is only a part of it, and a
man who is only educated to command a small part of that
part is not a whole man and is not civilized. To put it quite
bluntly, in the race for scientific supremacy which now
seems to be going on between the nations it would be fatally
easy to produce a generation of scientific barbarians. That
would be fatal and catastrophic in its results.

The idea that this new more enlightened approach to
engineering, in the form of engineers such as Brunel, had

become the bridge between the spiritual and rational human impulse to create something capable of inspiring both ways of interpreting the world offered an explanation for why the enthusiasts I had met had found spiritual 'quality' values in their machines that Pirsig had seen in the mechanics of a motor cycle. It also hinted at how Lionel Ferris, Russ Newnham, Bob Jones and the other enthusiasts I'd met had accessed such mind-blowing spiritual life experiences through their machines. It also gave a clue as to why certain machines inspired devotion more than others. Some had this 'quality' in the purity of their engineering while others, which were developed from a different, purely rational motivation, did not. That is why an Austin 7 and the high-bicycle had inspired enthusiasm, but a Ford Ka probably never would. The extra 'thing' that gave these particular machines this added dimension was what I would have to try and pin down next, because whatever that was would surely give a compelling answer as to why men love machines.

On that note of intriguing hope I went to visit an enthusiast called Andy, who ran military experience days on an old dairy farm. He had agreed to let me loose with the controls of a 432 armoured personnel carrier and a Russian Gvozdilka tank.

I clambered out of my car on a cold wintry morning and came face to face with Andy in full army fatigues. He looked like a diminutive Robert Plant – with a wild, golden, curly mane of hair. A warm handshake and a friendly smile led to the offer of tea in his house, a green mobile home covered in camouflage netting, which had a huge gold tank parked next to it.

It was warm, with a trace of bloated gas in the air, as I followed him inside and shared a seat with a serene white cat. We exchanged slightly awkward pleasantries for a few moments while he made me a cup of tea, and I soon spotted a machine gun on a shelf, a huge collection of military books and some bullets on the sideboard. On the far wall were two frames; inside each was a photograph of a man with military medals underneath. I later learned that one was of Andy with his military medals, including one that looked like a tank. The other was of his father with his service medals underneath. I have to say that the AK-47 made me feel slightly uneasy, but Andy was calm and friendly enough for me to let it pass.

Like the other enthusiasts I had met, Andy seemed absolutely fascinated by what I was up to. The consensus among them so far seemed to be that, because I was approaching the subject from a totally ignorant point of view, I might have a better chance of working it out than someone immersed in one specific type of machine.

Very quickly I managed to get beyond the trappings of enthusiasm around him that led to others on the site referring to him as a 'nerd' – albeit in a very respectful way. It was a mark of Andy's generous and warm personality that he let these taunts pass with a joke. As with many other enthusiasts I had met, Andy's particular enthusiasm stemmed from his relationship with his father.

'You could go all the way back to the 1930s. My family come from a small village in Lincolnshire. They were undertakers, and my father drove a hearse. Now the amazing thing about that generation before the Second World War that people don't always take on board is that very few people had ever driven a car in those days. So when he got called up in 1941 and they found out he could drive, he got put straight into the 51st Royal Tank Regiment as a Churchill tank driver. He was a very practical man, my father. He was a joiner by trade, and I think the magic got into me from him because from the age of four I took on board all his stories. When I was nineteen, I went and joined the 1st Royal Tank Regiment, but I soon discovered it was no place for a tank enthusiast. Most people who join up are like me, from poor areas; there's no other work available and so you join the army to see the world. I met very few enthusiasts in the tanks. So I left after some years, by which time I had also got into small arms, and I went on to become a battalion sniper in Northern Ireland. I was with NATO for a while and then I was a mercenary in the Chad army and a few other dodgy places. But after twelve years I left the military world and drove bands round Europe for twenty-odd years. I worked for twelve of them with Elton John. But touring enabled me to spend time travelling to places: battlefields and museums that you wouldn't normally be able to go to. I was in Russia a lot and went to Kursk, which is where the biggest tank battle in the world was fought. I've been to the Red Army Museum in Moscow. I went to Volgograd – Stalingrad – so the travelling through work I did after my army days definitely assisted my interest.'

Now I've met some interesting people in my life so far, but no one has come close to covering so many disparate areas in an opening conversation as Andy had just outlined – tank driver, peacekeeper, mercenary, tour manager – and now he was living in a static caravan next to an enormous gold tank. I'm not sure whether it's to do with precise military training, but there was a kind of clinical poetry in the way Andy spoke too. Nothing he said was superfluous. He didn't ramble. I was also reminded of a quote from Samuel Johnson that I hadn't fully appreciated before. 'Every man feels meanly of himself for not having being a soldier.' I immediately became intimidated: not by Andy, who had a very relaxed, friendly and generous demeanour, but by what I imagined his eyes had seen and how sheltered my own life experiences must have been in comparison. I'd only just arrived but was already convinced I was about to have an incredibly interesting day.

The subject then turned to the nature of my quest. What exactly is it about machines that men find so fascinating? Having listened carefully to my discoveries so far, Andy began to reveal a theory of his own.

'Have you ever heard of the German word *Spielzeug*?'

I shook my head.

'I speak German fluently. I lived there for many years. They use a word, *Spielzeug*, which translated literally is "plaything" or "play piece". Now a toy is obviously a *Spielzeug*, but you can also use it in another way. For example, this is a *Spielzeug*.'

He reached over behind his sofa and handed me what looked like the tip of an explosive.

'This is a nose cap of a 120mm Russian howitzer. I found it in the bottom of one of our Russian tanks. I took it out and I've cleaned it up. It's the fuse cap, right? Now feel it. It's a *Spielzeug*. It feels good in your hands, but you're not sure why. Another good example of a *Spielzeug* is a weapon. It's just the way it's made, the way it fits together and the way it feels. You don't have to want to murder someone to appreciate the feel of a weapon in your hand.'

He handed me the AK-47 from the shelf. I took it uneasily at first, as though it was a soiled nappy. I'd never held a machine gun before.

'This is a real gun. An AK-47. Deactivated, obviously, because gun laws in this country are very strict.' He smiled broadly.

'It's very famous. But again, a lot of it is in the machining. Perhaps it's the shape, but it's the way it feels in your hand. It reminds me of that Beatles song "Happiness is a Warm Gun". It's just a feeling. It's solid, and it's well made. Now if you come with me, I'll give you some more examples.'

This was a very interesting and unexpected tack. We walked out of his home, across a car park and into an office that overlooked a couple of barns filled with tanks. It took Andy a moment to get hold of some keys, and a few minutes later I found myself standing in front of a wall with literally dozens of guns displayed on it. There were machine guns on the floor behind me, more guns on tables to my left and what looked like a huge anti-tank gun to my right. I was standing in an armoury. Guns are not something I've ever given much thought to before, other than loathing. Andy took a small pistol that I recognized off the wall and handed it to me.

'Now feel that. This is a Walther PPK, a very famous gun.'

I took it from him and immediately understood what he was getting at. It felt astonishingly good in my hand, but I wasn't sure why. Perhaps because of the weight, the design or the way it seemed to fit so comfortably. I felt slightly hypnotized for a moment, just enjoying the feeling of holding it, but then, just as I was getting to like it, Andy took it away and quickly handed me another one.

'Now feel this one. This is Japanese. Tell me if it feels the same.'

It didn't. It felt nothing like it. It was horrible, like eating a soggy sprout after a cream slice.

'It's badly made. You can tell just by holding it, feeling it. Even if you have your eyes closed and you don't have any appreciation for the construction of guns, you can still sense the difference between the two.'

I know it sounds odd, but he was absolutely right. I can almost feel your eyebrows rising but honestly, really and truly, I could.

'So what's that all about then?' He looked at me, grinning, before pulling a rifle off the wall.

'This is another famous weapon: the Enfield. First issued to British troops in 1895. Used in both world wars, and as a sniper in Northern Ireland I was using one in the 1970s. It was still in use up to 1985, I believe. So that is a very long-standing weapon. Again, feel it. You can sense its quality, can't you?'

Again I could. It felt, well, more than what it was as a piece of machinery: greater than the sum of its parts.

'The Luger is another very sought-after weapon,' Andy continued, apparently pleased his meticulous demonstration was getting through. 'In German it's called the *null acht*, which is "08", the year it came out: 1908. It was actually the First World War standard firearm, not the Second, as people often think.' He took the Luger and handed me another one. 'This is the broom-handled Mauser.' It had a strange square section by the trigger. 'This is before they settled on the magazine being in the grip. This one came out in 1902. So a lot of these weapons are quite old. If you think of the other things that would have been designed and made at the time, these are impressive pieces of equipment. Now, another *Spielzeug* is this.'

He leaned over and gave me an Action Man grenade. I actually let out a gasp as it fell into my hand.

'It's the archetypal pineapple one. This is known as a Number 36, or a Mills bomb. Mills, the man who designed it, designed golf clubs. Now this came out for a reason, which I will explain. When trench warfare came in, we needed all sorts of things that we hadn't needed before because trench warfare was new. So we developed several types of grenade. One such grenade was this one, made by the London Gun Company.'

He handed me what looked like a thick green stick with a heavy gold tip at one end.

'Now this is the original "throw away and use once" grenade. But look at how nicely it was made. It's turned out of brass. This weighted bit at the end is to make it land on its nose. In those days they were experimenting with lots of different designs, and what you have here is quite a heavy piece of brass with a point on it. Now that's in a tube surrounded by the explosives. A pin goes through the hole in the back to keep it safe. When you want to use it, you pull the pin out so only the spring prevents the detonator from going forwards. You throw it. It lands on its head, the inertia of the heavy brass centrepiece continues, the striker hits and it detonates. Great. However, in the trenches they were finding that they would occasionally hit the tip on the other side of the trench as they pulled their arm back to throw it and many exploded in hand. So they thought, "How are we going to deal with this?" In 1915 Mills came up with your Action Man grenade. The army was still using this when I was in during the '70s. It's very heavy, and people are always surprised that you can throw it far, but the truth is when it's live you have an amazing ability to throw it a very long way indeed.' He laughed.

'It's a very simple principle. When you pull the pin out, it is completely safe, because as long as you've got it in your hand it's not going to go off. Not until after you throw it does it strike the cushion and light and a four-second fuse then detonates the grenade. So this became the principal grenade of all time. But again it's fabulously made. It's a nice shape, and it's got the chocolate squares. The principle is it's like a bar of chocolate because everyone gets a square.' We both laughed, but I soon checked myself in, well, horror. 'But again that is a *Spielzeug*,' Andy continued, unflinchingly.

Holding it in my hand, despite my loathing of weaponry, I had to admit he was right. It just felt, well, inexplicably pleasing.

I explained to Andy that I was feeling really torn between the tangible, indefinable quality he was talking about and the implications of what such a weapon could actually do.

'I think you could stand in here and take all of this on board without thinking of those implications. I think some people come in here to listen to me give these kinds of talks and think, "Oh my God, he's a nutter, look at him", but I wouldn't shoot an animal. I'm a pacifist.' He looked at me intently, directly challenging the violent nature he could see I imagined lay somewhere within him. 'I am. But look, what you've got to remember is that you separate things from what they do all the time; it just seems different when it comes to weapons. I'm actually a steam train enthusiast as well as a tank enthusiast, and one of the similarities with steam trains and tanks is that they are devices that are designed entirely from a practical point of view. Yet somehow they come out at the end with more than what the components have combined to make. They haven't designed a steam locomotive thinking, "Oh, it will be nice if we have that there". It's designed totally on practical lines. Yet it's produced something that people look at and say, "Wow, isn't that beautiful?" "Isn't she lovely?" To me tanks are the same. All tanks are designed purely to be what they are. They don't design tanks with curves because it looks nice. But to me they feel the same way you felt holding that PPK. That "thing" is what you're trying to pin down, isn't it?'

I nodded but wasn't quite sure I grasped what he was saying. For me it couldn't be about design, because that would make it dependent on appearance, and appearances are not usually what they seem. He continued from another angle.

'Think about cars instead. We separate cars from what they were designed for all the time. How many car enthusiasts talk to you about going from A to B, which is what a car is designed for? It's not about what it was built for. It's the same with steam locomotives. They are for pulling a lot of people along on a railway line from one town to another. Steam enthusiasts don't mention that when you ask them why they love steam trains, do they? But again, we're not talking about what they were built for. We're talking about something that's appeared out of them. As if by magic. Guns are no different. It's not what they were built for, to kill people, that inspires that "thing" or whatever you want to call it. It's only produced to do what it does. Nothing about what you're looking at has been produced to look good to the eye, but somehow it has managed it. In its solidness. In its smooth lines and in the way it feels. Even though guns aren't your thing and you know nothing about them or how they are made, you can still sense it.'

I was speechless and could feel something falling into place. Andy elaborated further.

'A friend of mine, many years ago, used to renovate grandfather clocks. He was fascinated because they were handmade in the 1700 and 1800s, and you could say these things almost had a soul because somebody had poured so much of themselves into making them. You could almost feel it. Whereas a mass-produced Timex wouldn't inspire the same sort of feeling. Well, it's the same thing, isn't it? Perhaps that "something else", that extra "thing", is what these machines you're looking at all share.'

We were back to Pirsig's indefinable 'quality', which we can all feel but none of us can explain but which makes life meaningful. I have to admit that the last place I thought this would be explained to me so powerfully and explicitly would be in an armoury. But I knew exactly what Andy was getting at. This immeasurable feeling really *was* tangible. I have the urge to describe it here as spiritual, but that seems a bit far-fetched because of what the world 'spiritual' means in our heads, but the feeling of holding a weapon certainly wasn't rational. I had no desire to fire it, just to hold it, for a reason I couldn't explain.

I was truly astonished. It was the first time I'd 'felt' something alluring about a machine and could see from Andy's explanation that this feeling could be what the other enthusiasts I'd met had felt about their machines too. I was slightly concerned that I had felt it in a gun, but Andy pointed out that 99 per cent of the people who came to his armoury talks felt exactly the same thing. 'There's just something about guns. But again, that feeling does not mean you want to go off and kill someone. The feeling is quite separate from what a gun is actually for.'

He then explained it further in something entirely unrelated.

'You can access that feeling in all sorts of ways. I get something similar from bells as well. When I was very young, five or six, my father took me to St James's Church in Grimsby. It's a beautiful church. But the reason he took me there is because that day they were renovating the bells. They had a big peal of eight bells, and they put them all on the floor. They fascinated me, and when I got home I went straight to our *Encyclopaedia Britannica* and read up about church bells. One of the things in this article was about the biggest bell ever made. It's in the Kremlin gardens in Moscow. Bearing in mind this was the early 1960s and the height of the Cold War, there was no possibility of me going and seeing that bell. But in 1987 I was in Moscow, still in the old Soviet days, and I went straight to those gardens and had my photo taken next to it. Weird perhaps, but it felt amazing, and the fact that I saw it still means a huge amount to me.'

This last story lit up something inside me like a firework. It was the memory of an experience that had always stuck in my brain as being hugely important in my life, as though I'd briefly managed to put my finger on some fundamental human truth, but until that moment had never been able to fully understand why. It was the search for the same 'quality' feeling that had moved Andy in that garden outside the Kremlin. It wasn't exactly the same as what I had felt while holding the Walther PPK, but it was undeniably related.

When I was eighteen, I went to university to study Russian. It proved a disaster, and after the first lecture I knew I'd made a terrible mistake. The university was kind enough to allow me to transfer to a history course instead, but I didn't last long on that one either and dropped out completely a few weeks later. I did have one lesson on the history of art before I left, though, about two portraits of the Duke and Duchess of Urbino, by Piero della Francesca. The lecturer didn't have very good examples of the paintings for us to look at while she explained all about them, because the overhead projector was broken, so she held up a blurry photocopy of each picture instead. I remember at the time thinking how, well, crap and unfulfilling it was to learn about art in this way, and I resolved there and then to have the kind of life where I got to actually experience things myself rather than listen to someone else's interpretation and treat that second-hand knowledge as my own. Like Lionel's experience of school being where you learn to earn a living rather than actually to live, this feeling tapped into a deep sense within myself that I wanted my life to be about real, first-hand experience, rather than a passive absorption of someone else's. Two years later I had got enough money together, after I had worked in particularly uninspiring and demeaning crap jobs, to go off Interrailing round Europe with my mate Henry. Top of my itinerary was Florence and in particular the Uffizi gallery, where I stood a week or so later with watering eyes in front of the portraits of the Duke and Duchess of Urbino by Piero della Francesca, lit by the warm light of an early September day through a window that looked out on to the heart of the Renaissance itself. I'm not sure about the merits of those particular paintings, but I felt that my desire to see them and my action to get there years after that lesson had somehow managed to bring the very art of life out from inside of me. The experience of dropping out of university, working my soul away in a crap job for years and then travelling to Florence in order to see the paintings, I'd wager, told me more about 'art' and myself than I would have got had I stayed on that university course soaking up other people's opinions. I certainly treasure the memory a great deal more than I think I would treasure a degree.

It's one of the most prominent examples of what I think of as the core values that guide my life, but I have never quite been able to explain it, even to myself, until that afternoon in a room full of guns with Andy. Standing there with him, I realized that our lives are surely a pilgrimage between these kinds of real desires and experiences as opposed to the fabricated wants and hollow fulfilment of the nine-to-five and the wares of all those advertising and marketing men. It's about the deep yearning in us all to feel what it means to be human, to replenish our souls and enrich the deepest and most meaningful parts of ourselves by actively seeking an inspiring and meaningful way to live. I still can't tell you exactly what that feeling is, in the same way that I can't explain all the other feelings that make me feel happiest about being alive but those feelings mean more to me than any other thing in my life that I can quantifiably explain.

Andy and I then walked outside, towards what looked like an enormous, abandoned battlefield with a crushed car forlornly leaking glass over to one side. I was now wearing full army gear and black wellington boots, but with my own black coat and white scarf on top. Andy stopped in front of me and pointed to the carnage.

'It looks like Passchendaele, doesn't it?'

I didn't get the reference.

'A very famous area of lowlands in Belgium where we fought in the First World War. It was just like this: impenetrable mud. Hell to fight in.'

He paused for a moment, sucking on a cheroot, before stomping off towards an armoured personnel carrier, with me tentatively hopping between mud and grass behind.

An officer in the Royal Engineers, Ernest Swinton, was the first man to propose what we think of as a modern tank to the British army. As Ian, the military vehicle enthusiast I had met earlier, explained, tanks were devised as a means of coping with the apparent endless slaughter of the trenches during the First World War. The central three elements of the first tank designs that still form the foundation of their construction today are mobility, armour and firepower. With a machine capable of those three things the possibility of moving between the trenches at the Somme became realistic for the first time. Once the German line had been penetrated, the original plan was for the cavalry then to charge behind the tank through the opening before routing the enemy from behind. That bit about the cavalry is not a joke, by the way, and reveals starkly how warfare was in the process of evolving from a bloody but traditional method into an unimaginably brutal and mechanical future.

Having seen tractors with caterpillar treads in America, Swinton suggested a similar method for a 'landship' to cross rough terrain. His plan caught the attention of the then First Lord of the Admiralty, Winston Churchill, who ordered the formation of a 'landship committee' that included William Tritton (whose company built the first tanks), two naval lieutenants and Swinton himself. The No.1 Lincoln machine emerged first, in September 1915, and was quickly nicknamed 'Little Willie', but was replaced in February 1916 by 'Big Willie' (also confusingly referred to as 'Mother' and HMLS *Centipede*). On 13 September 1916 forty-nine tanks left from Avonmouth for France and were placed on trains to take them to the Somme. Two days later they began to grind their way across no man's land. A German correspondent wrote of the sight of the tanks from the German positions.

One stared and stared as if one had lost the power of one's limbs. The monsters approached slowly, hobbling, rolling and rocking, but they approached. Nothing impeded them; a supernatural force seemed to impel them on. Someone in the trenches said, 'The devil is coming', and the word passed along the line like wildfire.

The back door of the armoured personnel carrier was open, and Andy clambered inside, so I followed and sat on one of the filthy seats in the back. He turned the engine on and came back to sit with me while it warmed up to explain what would happen next.

'A bit of history first. When tanks were first designed, they needed four people to drive them. The principle of steering a track vehicle is that, if both tracks go at the same speed, then you go along in a straight line. If you want to go left, you stop the left-hand track and the right-hand track continues and you slew to the left, and vice versa. Now in the early days they literally had to have a person operating a clutch and a brake on each one, who responded to the driver's hand signals, which was really complicated. So the next step was to design a gearbox that could do that for them. Merrick Brown designed something called a regenerative epicyclic gearbox, and that is what our Centurion tanks back in the shed have. Old tanks worked on the principle that when you turned left and stopped the left track you lost a lot of power. So what a regenerative gearbox does is transfer the loss of power from one track to the other. So as one track loses power, the other gains power. Depending on what gear you're in, it will turn on a certain radius. A low gear will slew right round, and in a high gear it won't do so much. You have to be in the right gear to do the right turn. The other thing about the epicyclic gearbox is, if you pull a steering lever in neutral, it will do what's called a neutral turn. One track goes forwards, and one goes backwards. That means it can pivot on its axis, which means it is very manoeuvrable.

'The 432s, one of which we're in now, have automatic gearboxes. The idea of that to me when I was driving tanks for the army would have been totally bizarre, but what that means is these are much easier to drive.'

He grinned knowingly. I mentioned I hoped it had power steering, and his face fell behind a vague smile.

'Well, you steer with levers, Dan. A tank doesn't have a steering wheel.' I cursed my stupidity. Again.

He gestured for me to get up and look through a hatch while he drove us to where I would be allowed to get at the controls. It was fiercely cold as we growled our way through the field, and Andy got up to quite a speed as we made our way to a large track. He got out and gestured for me to get in the front. There was mud and filth everywhere. Thankfully

I'd been provided with overalls, and at least the scarf my wife had knitted for me would keep my neck warm.

Driving an automatic armoured personnel carrier turned out to be rather simple. There are two levers. One operates the left track and the other the right. Pull the left one alone and you slew left and vice versa. Pull both the levers back and you slow down, push them forwards and you speed up. Simple. Within moments I was tearing round the track. Well, it felt to me like we were tearing around but I was probably going tediously slowly. As if to confirm this at one point Andy tapped me on the shoulder and shouted over the noise of the engine, 'You don't have to avoid obstacles, remember you're in an APC.' I began to get more confident, bouncing through the vast icy puddles, which would have come up to my waist if I had tried to walk through them, up and over banks, sliding left and right. It was all excellent fun indeed. A few times I feared the surge of water would reach the tiny hole through which my head and shoulders were peering as we entered the huge troughs of water, but each time there was plenty of room to spare. We pulled up beside the Russian Grozdilka twenty minutes later, and I felt rather smug. It was good fun and easy enough to control. So far, so good. Apart perhaps from the power steering comment, I didn't think I had humiliated myself, yet. Andy pulled out a ladder that he dropped down the front to help us climb out. He left the engine running, and we made our way towards the next machine through thick mud that clung desperately to our feet.

'Imagine your feet rotting in this in the trenches,' he called out, and I immediately thought of *Blackadder Goes Forth*.

'I think you'll enjoy this more, because lots of people do. Although it's a bloody nightmare to steer, if you ask me.' He climbed inside to get the engine going, before explaining more about this particular model.

'With Russian tanks like this one, most of them have the capability of going through deep water. This is because they were designed during the Cold War and, when you look at a map of Europe, if a Third World War had happened, the only obstacles that they faced to halt their progress were rivers. So these were devised with the capability of swimming or getting across water. They wanted to come up to a river and be able to deploy across it in formation rather than trust bridges that, first, might be blown by a retreating enemy, second, if they are standing would be a target, and third, would be a bottleneck at the very best. So a lot of these vehicles have various methods of allowing them to continue in formation across river obstacles. Several battle tanks have been equipped with the snorkel, so they can go under the water along the riverbank and then out. All Soviet battle tanks can do that.'

The Grozdilka was not automatic, which meant it had a ludicrously enormous gear stick to the right of the driver's seat. Andy pulled it into place, while I stamped as hard as I could on the clutch. This one had a pedal for acceleration but two levers for steering. Andy elected to sit on top of the tank to my right while holding on to the barrel of the enormous gun. As with the 432, my head poked out of a small hole only just big enough for me to climb through. The levers were a little more difficult to control. You had to pull them all the way back to steer the way you wanted to go but then push them forwards to reset them afterwards, otherwise you'd end up continuing to turn. This meant I had much less control and may perhaps account for what happened next. The other thing to remember when driving a tank that has an acceleration pedal is that you shouldn't put your whole foot on to it; otherwise, when you get bumped about, you'll find yourself accidentally stamping on the throttle at the precise moment when caution is probably the best policy. It went OK for my first lap of the field, but on the second Andy was keen for me to go through the deeper water hazard to experience the Grozdilka's water-going capabilities. Sadly, just as we approached the water, very tentatively, I hit something of a bump and by mistake stamped on the acceleration pedal, forcing us to power forward into the water much faster than Andy or I had intended. I tried to relax as the wave of icy, filthy, orange water surged towards my face, but this time the water didn't stop pleasingly a few feet away. Just before it happened, I remember thinking that there was absolutely nothing I could do. The water flew into my eyes and mouth and all over my head. The immediate intake of breath that follows being soaked in icy water meant that I nearly choked too. Water and mud poured down into my lungs and my lap. As I spluttered, the remains of the icy filth that had got stuck behind me dropped another splurge behind the back of my head. I tried to stand up but smashed my shoulder on the roof of the tank. I noticed Andy hopping up in a very agile way, while laughing hysterically at my increasingly bedraggled state. I felt pretty pleased that none of the icy water that had covered me from head to toe had got into my neck though, but then remembered my nice hand-knitted white scarf. It is now, well, diarrhoea brown.

Andy was trying very hard not to laugh too much as I tried to compose myself, assuring him I was fine and that it was hilarious, while clawing icy mud out of my mouth and my eyes at the same time. It's very hard to maintain composure while performing a full body retch. I have never been so wet and dirty and uncomfortable while fully clothed in my life. The wind then began battering my wet face and forehead as I carried on driving, and the cold, stinging pain it brought with it suddenly made me realize that I could now go home and get warm and dry. A soldier driving a tank would clearly not have the same luxury, so a combination of that, the horror of the cold and my soaked and filthy frame gave me a feeling of intense but bedraggled humility as I drove on and on.

Back in Andy's house half an hour later, having tried to clean myself up as best I could – which meant turning one of his pink towels dark brown – he handed me a cup of tea, chuckling. 'You really look like you've been camoed up for a mission.' My hair was now plastered rock solid with mud so that I looked as though I'd stolen the haircut of a Lego man. Aware of my soaking wet arse and legs, I offered to hover around rather than sit down anywhere and soil Andy's sofa, but he soon laid a towel down for me to sit on and seemed a little more relaxed himself. He began to describe his annoyance at how some enthusiasts seem to miss the point, getting too caught up in exact reproductions of specific vehicles rather than his more practical appreciation of tank design.

We were now both in full philosophizing mode, although we looked absurd: Andy wearing a T-shirt and just some underpants (his army gear, having become as filthy as mine, was now drying by the fire) with a Bond-villain-style white cat on his lap while I sat on the edge of his sofa with soaking wet legs, covered in filth, dirt all over my face and a helmet of slicked, centre-parted hair.

'But you see this slightly odd engagement with the world everywhere you look nowadays,' he continued. 'People are not tactile any more, apart from with a computer. The modern generation don't draw satisfaction from the same solid engineering. They get it from a virtual version of reality. That works for them because that's all they know. I've had a few young lads, eight-ish, coming into the armoury and shouting "An uzi!", because on these games they play now they have all this weaponry. So they are getting knowledge, but in a different way. They've never seen or held a real one, though. No one can ever believe how heavy it all is in real life. That is quite an interesting aspect of it. I don't like those games at all. They're not realistic, for one thing. It's all rote. But doing all that kind of stuff is supposed to be about adrenaline and danger. So if there is no real danger, what's the point? That sense of being alive is just not there. I've been in situations on active service, and I know what it's like to feel alive, because you think it might be your last day. You're never going to get that in a computer game.'

Andy then told me more about how his experiences in Northern Ireland had affected his life. In one day his unit had lost eighteen men, more than Britain's entire losses during the first Gulf war. It had brought into focus the different way you have to live in that kind of environment. Andy didn't mention it specifically in any detail, but at home a few days later I did some research. There was only one day in the bloody history of the troubles in Northern Ireland when eighteen British soldiers were killed in a twenty-four-hour period: the IRA ambush at Narrow Water Castle in Warrenpoint on 27 August 1979. The IRA detonated an explosive as a convoy of a Land Rover and two 4-ton army trucks passed by. Six British soldiers died instantly. On the opposite side of the road from the impact was a gate lodge, where an incident command point was set up by the army to assess the situation. The IRA had correctly guessed that this was where the command point would be placed and had hidden a second bomb in milk pails. When this second device was detonated, a further twelve soldiers were killed. At the time the bombing was rather overshadowed by the assassination of Lord Mountbatten, which took place on the same day.

'If you've been in a situation where you've relied on your wits to stay alive, it changes everything,' Andy explained in a very calm and relaxed way. 'Ireland in the '70s was a rough old experience. From that day to this I notice everything. I notice if a window is open. If I walk from here to the office, I'll spot anything amiss. That car's moved over a foot. The detail is like Technicolor. I'm looking through a magnifying glass at everything around me. I don't miss anything, whereas civilians who haven't been in that situation walk about and they don't see anything at all.'

It occurred to me that a soldier is as close to being a machine as a man can be forced to be. It's hard for someone like me to image the severity of the training required to make a person ignore their powerful sense of self-preservation when bullets and bombs are going off around them. If I ever find myself in that kind of situation, I know I would simply try and run away. Military training clearly dominates a soldier's life completely. This was demonstrated to me on New Year's Eve 2000 in quite an absurd fashion while playing a game with a group of friends. The people I hang around with are all very similar to me. The majority are white, middle-class, reasonably well-educated men and women who were in their mid-twenties that evening. Most of them went to art school, and I'm the only one of them who didn't finish university. Rather bizarrely, one of them graduated from an art degree and went to Sandhurst to train as an officer for the British army. He is one of those people whose life choices make him stand out in a humble but radical way. He was on leave that New Year's Eve and, although I can't remember the game we were playing, it involved writing down the names of four songs. We wrote the names of our songs, all choosing very well-known pop songs, including a few by Metallica from me. His list was rather different though. With no trace of irony at all he had written down 'Land of Hope and Glory', 'Jerusalem', 'Rule Britannia' and 'God Save the Queen'. We all took the mickey out of him mercilessly, but he seemed genuinely baffled by our taunts. That proves nothing, but it shows how far army culture had permeated his character in a relatively short space of time when compared with his non-military friends. (Having served in Iraq and Afghanistan, he has since left the army and is training with a charity to clear land-mines in Sri Lanka.) But this mechanization of men clearly changed the way the world appeared to them afterwards. Andy explained that when you go into the army you go through lots of training to acclimatize yourself to what might be required of you and what you might see, but when you leave there is no official training programme to help bring you back to normal life. I wondered whether his experiences of soldiering had fuelled his enthusiasm for machines.

'I think there may be truth in the idea that the machine aspect fills a rather worrying space in modern life. I suppose I'm quite a loner in a way. I'm not very fond of the human race at all, to be honest. I don't mind my own company. I don't get lonely. If no one wants to come here for a week, I'm happy. I'll do things. I'll read books, keep myself busy, whatever. I don't need to have this sort of contact with people. Yet at the same time I am quite extrovert, and I do get on with people. But that may have something to do with it. Maybe a lot of things in our human contacts are not as sure as they used to be. In the old days, when women had no rights, it was not possible for a woman to divorce her husband and leave with the kids. With equality has come the destruction of the family unit because now women can say, "I think you're a boring old twat and I'm going". That's not happened to men before. So I think men are bigger victims of equality than they realize. I think a lot of men would have a problem accepting the fact that it has made their lives as men more difficult. It's made women's lives more difficult too, because now women have got to prove they can be men as well as remaining women. So maybe we have all got this uneasiness about where we are in the world, and perhaps solace is found in physical objects. You could say it about cats too.' He looked down and stroked his carefully. 'I love my cat. I know that cat is not going to pack its bags and leave me.'

The tone of his voice was now sombre but inquisitive.

'Machines are self-levelling as well. You can switch off, go to bed, or you can do something different the next day. Maybe it's a very convenient obsession – one that you can take or leave. I could go away and not see a tank for a year, and it's not a problem. But with a wife it would be. Maybe objects are coming into our lives to replace human relationships? Men often lose contact with their kids too, don't forget. They get to see them every other weekend if they're lucky. So you haven't even got that that's solid any more, but the motor bike at the back of the garage is there. That's not going to leave. No one's going to run off with that.'

The subject of how men feel about their current role in life is a large one, but I think Andy is correct to say that men of a certain age (90 per cent of the enthusiasts I'd met were over fifty) have had a great deal of adjusting to do from the society they were born into. But any mention of the existence of this adjustment is usually dealt with abruptly through accusations of sexism, the implication being that by finding their new role difficult these men are displaying that they are sexist, whether they know it or not. Since the broader ideas behind feminism have been largely accepted in the West, women have played an increasing role in parts of society they had not inhabited before. To my generation equality is simply a self-evident necessity, and I think things would be a lot better if the question of equality centred on men becoming more like women rather than the situation we have today where, in order to be equal, women seem to think they must become more like men. There is no doubt in my mind, though, that men have found the change in their role much more difficult than they have let on. Of course, I'm dealing in huge generalizations, but only to reaffirm that I feel Andy's wider point is valid and that this sense of unease about their role in the world could increase a sense of powerlessness that might push men further into the realm of inanimate things they do feel able to control.

I was enjoying my time with Andy immensely and sat back as his stream of consciousness spilled out further.

'You wonder where we're going, though, because machines, which are tangible, have been replaced by something that isn't. I mean, I am a very practical person but this thing [pointing at the computer] – it works, it doesn't work. I don't know why. Switch it off, and it might work when you switch it on next time. You can't deal with that in the way that if my gas fire stops working I can take it apart and find out what's wrong with it and fix it. I have a problem with that change. And of course, today we always throw everything away. We don't fix things any more so we don't know how things work, which makes me worry about the future. It's like Twat Nav – that's what I call Sat Nav. What happened to using maps? We're turning into a race of non-thinking people because of technology. It's like people using a level crossing and waiting for the Green Man on a high street when there's no traffic.

'This doesn't sound related, but in a way it is. I was talking the other day about my time as a mercenary in Africa while all the stuff in Darfur was still going on. This guy was saying to me "Oh it's terrible. These poor people." And I said, "Hang on a minute. These poor people that they keep portraying on TV actually have a government. They are not just running around aimlessly. They have a government. It's just that their government chooses to spend its money on weapons. Also the whole thing is tribal. You've got this bunch hitting on this bunch, and in a few years time they'll be hitting on them, and it has always been like that and it probably always will be like that. It's tribal. Without that conflict we would never have had the slave trade." And then he said, "But that's terrible! How terrible for them!" and I said, "Well actually, no. Because when they're not having a crisis, they are happier than we are!" I've seen whole villages of people ecstatic, dancing, happy! I've never, ever seen that here.'

The thought made us both laugh out loud. It's hard to imagine something like that ever happening in Britain.

'They've got a well, they've got a few fields, and they are happy. This is our big mistake.' He pointed his finger. 'We think every country should want to be like us. We assume the Iraqis would rather live like us than the way they do. But maybe these people we think we need to save are getting more things right than we are. Who knows? I'll tell you one thing, though. That whole, entire village that I saw dancing and partying? They had far fewer machines than we do.'

8

Poetry

Aeroplanes

I T WAS THE final day of my quest, and I was at Goodwood airfield in Sussex, known as RAF Westhampnett when Douglas Bader, and many of the other famous 'few', flew Spitfires from here during the Battle of Britain. Standing in front of the statue of Bader, my thoughts turned to Russ, the mountain biker I'd met back on the Isle of Wight. Considering I hadn't been in an aeroplane for eighteen years because of a combination of fear and care for the planet (OK, if I'm honest it was 90 per cent fear), having a flying lesson in a small four-seater plane was about as far beyond my 'limit' as it was possible for me to go. It wasn't just beyond my limit. It was beyond the limits of my limit's limit.

If you were to ask anyone who knows me, they will tell you that I am about as afraid of flying as it is possible for anyone to be. I can't even go to an airport because I get *the fear*. So why had I decided to put myself through it now? Well, because I was writing this book, I suppose. There's no way I'd have even considered doing it otherwise. But, as much as I might hate the prospect, it seemed the only possible way to bring my journey to a close. I have spent my entire adult life being baffled by machines and, when it comes to aeroplanes, that bafflement manifests itself as pure, cold-blooded fear. I'd begun to see that fear as the perfect metaphor for my unease about machines as a whole. If I was

going to understand machines, then I simply had to experience the most iconic one the human race has ever invented.
Mankind has dreamed of flight since he first saw a bird and,
short of building a time machine, human beings will never
achieve anything as monumental as the moment two men
learned to tame the skies. It was the fragment of time when
the dreams of an entire species were finally realized, and it
bequeathed to all the generations to come an expectation
that the impossible could be done. So there was no way to
avoid it. It was the perfect end, the only end, and I was
determined not to back out of it now.

I knew I really was going to do it too. For some reason the
fear that had plagued me seemed to have slipped from my
irrational mind into a more scientific part of my brain that I
hadn't realized existed before. There the fear seemed disabled
somehow, as though a new rational consciousness had managed to weaken the hold it had over me. I'd never thought of
my brain as having a rational section and an irrational section
in the past – a scientific one and a spiritual one, if you
will – but the idea of it just seemed to dawn on me that
afternoon.

The honest truth is that it was a very poignant moment for
me too, because I was about to tackle something that has
crippled my entire adult life. Everyone is afraid of something,
whether it's spiders or leaving the security of a job you hate
to do something you've always wanted to do. I know some
people that won't take their children to London in case
there's a terrorist attack. Fear comes in many guises these
days. We all have some kind of dark horror in our hearts that
nudges us when we feel most alone.

I'm sad to say that fear and I have spent a lot of miserable
years together. I used to have a terribly debilitating psychological illness called agoraphobia – the fear of being in an

environment where you have no control. An agoraphobic's life is ruled by the prospect of terrifying panic attacks, which can occur whenever you are in a place that is unknown or feels isolated or intimidating. Standing in a crowd was impossibly difficult, as was public transport or any situation, for that matter, where there was no possibility of immediate escape. When such panic strikes, nowhere feels safe apart from your own home, so that is where you run. When it was at its worst, in my early twenties, I was unable for weeks at a time to leave the flat in north London where I lived. Clearly I was psychologically up the creek, but, despite my precarious mental state, I still managed to get a job in an office that happened to be two doors up the road from my flat. It was unpaid for the first year, which allowed me the flexibility to be as mad as I liked. The pub that my workmates and I spent every night after work in was two doors down on the other side, so I was able to remain in sight of my home every time I had the strength to walk out of my front door. The only way to keep that kind of problem a secret is to develop a thicket of lies and deceit around you to keep the horrible truth of recognition at bay. I constantly had to fudge invitations anywhere other than within a 100-yard radius of my flat. Occasionally I would develop the courage to get on a train and go and visit my parents, but only if I got a train early in the morning before the city had time to wake up. I could never get the tube or buses to the station so I got taxis whenever I went anywhere, which wasn't often and explains why I could afford it. Those train journeys were a living hell, though. Every stop was Panic Central. The odd bar job in very local pubs and student loans kept me financially afloat throughout, after I had enrolled in a second university course, which I could never cope with the bus journey to attend.

The cruelty of silence about mental illness is almost as hard to bear as the problem itself. You don't want the people closest to you to see it because you feel ashamed. They don't want to see it because it makes them feel awkward, so you gradually slip away. They get sick and tired of you being weird. They take it personally and stop ringing. You're glad they've stopped ringing because, when people stop caring about you, then you no longer have to lie to them any more. You want to be abandoned, because it's much easier to disappear completely if no one is left to try and pull you back into the light. After years of suffering in this way I realized that I simply couldn't take it any more. The fear of getting help and having to admit to myself that I was precariously ill was finally less daunting than the knowledge that even in this terrible state I was still deteriorating. I rang the Samaritans and asked for help. I got some from a calm lady near Mornington Crescent and, as I began to talk through my fears and gradually to recover, I learned that I had been very lucky. It seems that many people with agoraphobia retreat so far into themselves before getting help that they often vanish completely. It's not a period of my life I ever wish to revisit and, in case you're wondering where on earth this suddenly intense couple of paragraphs have come from, I'm only mentioning it here because in some of my darkest moments of self-loathing and panic I would try and imagine a future for myself where I was no longer defined by this cruel and debilitating fear. Invariably through tears, in what I thought of at the time as a futile and unrealistic daydream of hope, I would allow myself to imagine my life without this curse. The best idea of recovery I could muster was one particular daydream where, far off into the future, I saw myself training to become a pilot, flying a small plane over patchwork fields in a luminous sky. It was a ludicrous aspiration for someone who struggled to walk out of their front door and couldn't even get on to a bus without having a panic attack, but I think I chose being a pilot because I knew that if I ever conquered my fear of flying – by far my biggest fear of all – I would finally be free of fear in my heart completely. If I ever developed the courage to fly a plane, then I would finally have become comfortable with myself. I'd have grown into someone far removed from the small person I was back then.

In the decade since those dark and lonely days I have ticked off all my fears (including public speaking and getting on the London Underground) except this final one. It jeers at me around the dinner table at Christmas when people that love me chide me gently that planes are safer than cars. It digs me in the ribs every time I meet anyone new. 'Oh, you don't fly? You only have holidays in Europe? That's *so* sad!' Even though my life is now entirely normal in every other respect, all this time my fear of flying has sat in its own stubborn little box, refusing to budge. I think subconsciously I've always felt that, if I put all my fear into that one particular box, then it would be contained and not spread into other parts of my life ever again. Of course, that isn't what happened. To have a crippling fear – something that prevents you doing things others take for granted – is to have a festering wound that can suddenly infect all your other perceptions of life whenever things get hard.

This will, I hope, go some way towards explaining why a small lump began to develop in my throat, standing there at the Goodwood aerodrome that afternoon, because I knew, thanks to this quest, that I was about to become the future I had once wistfully dreamed of so long ago. I may still be afraid of flying, but I'm no longer afraid of becoming that sick, lonely boy left to cry about his shambolic weakness in a north London flat ever again. I have developed the confidence and self-respect now, thanks to a caring family, a wonderful wife and son, to help that poor sad boy who is unable to form the mental strength he needs to open his front door. Together we would finally shout defiantly at all the ghosts looming out in the dark. I knew that afternoon I was going to take him by the hand from that dark place and free him from all those painful memories. Together we would make that daydream from long ago the metaphorical cuddle of reassurance we'd both always pined for on our own. I think the thought, the dream of it, had only been able to offer hope back then because deep down I knew one day things would be different. One day I would be different, and that day had finally come.

Now, at the end of my journey, something huge and tangible had shifted inside me. Somehow I felt able to take on this vast blockage that has lain in front of me for my entire adult life. There is no doubt in my mind that the things I had done and the people I had met had changed my perception of the world to the point that I was finally able to let something incredibly heavy inside me fall away. I'm not sure why. Perhaps my greater understanding of machines had put these fears to rest. Maybe I had gone some way to reconciling the two parts of my own nature by allowing myself to look in what I'd always thought of as the Pandora's box at the heart of what machines have come to represent. I certainly felt as though I saw the world around me differently, but never for a moment did I expect this journey to affect me in such a profound and practical way. I allowed myself to wonder whether this is the kind of thing we all need to do: investigate and seek to understand the people we see around us who appear so utterly different from us in their worldview and by doing so come to a greater understanding about the dark corners of ourselves. Perhaps it's about learning to build a bridge between the perceptions we use to formulate our expectations of life. Most of us are skewed too dominantly in one direction and simply need to rebalance. Or perhaps we just need the space to confront our fears and learn to deal with them in our own time and in our own way. I was curious what kind of person would emerge from the plane when I landed, though. Of all the machines I'd learned about, it couldn't be aeroplanes that I would fall in love with, could it?

When it comes to the story of flight, you have to start with the science. Most people seem to have a basic grasp of how aeroplanes work, but I didn't have a clue. Clearly the most pressing problem when it comes to something heavy getting up into the air is how to counter the effects of gravity. This is done in an aeroplane through 'lift'. Obviously when a wing moves through the air, it causes air to flow over the wing and air to move under it. Because the angle of a wing is raised slightly at the front, the air that goes over the wing moves faster than the air that flows beneath it. (The point in the wing where the air separates is just below the leading edge.) The faster air that moves over the wing puts less pressure on the surface of the topside of the wing than the pressure of the slower air passing on the underside. This difference in pressure is what creates the upward movement that's referred to as 'lift'. The heavier the wings (and the plane they are attached to), the faster they must travel through the air in order to generate the required difference in pressure to get enough lift and counter the effects of gravity. However, if the wing is light enough and the wind is strong enough, you don't need to generate extra speed to gain lift and this is why, on a breezy day, you'll see people standing beneath kites floating happily in the sky. But if the wind drops below the required speed to create lift, the kite will soon fall to the ground with a bump. (For anyone thinking of the obvious question, 'If the wing shape is so important how do planes fly upside down, then?', the answer is that a wing of pretty much any shape will generate lift if it travels quickly enough. The traditional wing shape is simply the most efficient means of generating lift in a plane that rarely needs to fly upside down.)

I mention kites because it was experiments with kites that enabled the Wright brothers to begin to unravel the mystery of how to make a self-propelled flying machine. From their bicycle shop in Dayton, Ohio, Orville and Wilbur adopted a different approach to other aspiring aeronauts of the time, who concentrated their efforts on simply getting up in the air in a self-propelled machine rather than painstakingly researching how you might control a machine in the unlikely event that you managed to get one up into the air. As far as the Wright brothers were concerned, current wing and engine technology existed at the time that would probably be sufficient to get men airborne, but no one had yet come up with a means of being in control once you were up in the air. So in 1899 they built a box kite with control sticks that enabled them to pull down, or warp, the tops of the kite on each side. In their experiments they soon worked out that this was a good way to turn left and right. Experiments with kites led to experiments with gliders, and in 1900 the first of these took to the air at Kitty Hawk, North Carolina – chosen because, according to the local weather station, it was the closest place to Dayton that had the required average wind speed that their gliding experiments would need. Over the course of the next three years their experiments grew bolder and more refined. Back at home they built a small wind tunnel in their bicycle shop to test existing theories on what wing shape would achieve the greatest lift and soon made more accurate measurements than were considered correct at the time. Then they concluded that the pilot should lie flat on the bottom wing to reduce drag (which reduces lift) and soon discovered the addition of a tail would give greater stability and counteract 'yaw'. The warping of one wing to turn the glider caused the other wing to lose lift, which in turn made the glider move left or right as it went forward through the air. (Imagine running up to an ice rink and jumping on to the ice. Assuming you don't fall over you will skid across the ice in the direction that you jumped, but you'll probably soon find you're not actually facing the way you're moving, having skewed your body slightly to one side. 'Yaw' is when a plane moves, or slides, through the air but not in the direction it's facing.) In 1902 the combination of these features gave the Wright brothers proper control of a glider for the first time. Eventually they worked out what's become known as 'three-axis control': how to control a plane's 'pitch', 'roll' and 'yaw'. Pitch is the up-and-down movement of the plane to lose and gain altitude. Roll is the movement of the plane left and right by rolling it in either direction, and yaw, as we've learned, is the movement of the plane left or right while moving forward in a straight line. Now their gliders were flying well with a man lying flat at the controls, the Wrights were ready to think about attaching a small engine.

I walked into the flying school reception very slowly and took a few moments to survey the scene. Behind a counter were two young men wearing white shirts with epaulettes on their shoulders that signalled their status as flying instructors. I allowed myself a sigh of relief. My single main fear was that my instructor would be incredibly old and die of a heart attack while we were up there, leaving me to land and inevitably crash to my death soon afterwards. I steeled myself and went up to tell them I had arrived. They were both very friendly. I remember thinking at the time that they smiled at me in the way people sometimes do on the very rare occasions I'm mistaken for being rich. Flying is an expensive hobby, that's for sure. I then had to sign a form effectively saying that, in the event of my sudden and painful death, my family wouldn't be able to sue anyone. It was while signing it that it occurred to me that what I was about to do was probably a hundred times more dangerous than getting in a passenger plane.

'Your instructor will be Peter, but he's airborne at the moment. Take a seat in the café, and I'll bring him over and introduce you when he's landed.' I smiled and walked out on to the balcony, which looked out across the airfield. I sprayed my mouth liberally with Rescue Remedy (according to the packet, it 'comforts and reassures'). I wondered whether this was the best approach to conquer my fear of flying after all. I could have just got myself hypnotized, or gone on one of the many courses offered by the airlines, but I had decided that I wanted to conquer my fear without tricking my brain. I couldn't bear the prospect of the psychological equivalent of the way Mr T's flying phobia was handled in *The A-Team*. I wanted to engage with and inspire myself out of being afraid. I had a great respect for my fear. It wasn't born of ignorance and I didn't want to hoodwink it. I'd flown a great deal when I was younger but hated the sensation and the process, for reasons I couldn't quite put my finger on at the time. The last time I landed, after an uneventful flight to London from New York, I'd promised myself that I would never set foot in a passenger plane ever again. Fear, in my mind, is the opposite of love. So it wasn't just a case of getting rid of my fear of flying; I had to try and find a way to *love* flying instead. I had reasoned it was surely impossible to fall in love with the experience of flying while being a passive passenger on a charter plane.

A chap in his late fifties came up ten minutes later and introduced himself as Peter. I suppressed the urge to inquire immediately about his health and gulped. I told him as calmly as I could that this would be my first flight in eighteen years, and he smiled and laughed it off before telling me, rather unhelpfully considering my state of mind, 'You'll either love it or hate it.' We walked out towards the plane with me taking the first of many deep breaths. He told me to climb in while he carried out the necessary checks before we headed for the runway. I stepped up on to the blue wing and clambered over to the left of the two tight seats. I'm not sure what I'd expected, but the plane suddenly seemed ludicrously small. It was a four-seater, but it had four seats in the sense that a sports car does. Any back passengers certainly wouldn't have much leg-room. The icy sensation I then felt informed me of the arrival of a companion who had haunted me for so long. ('Shit. What are you doing? This is tiny! You'd better run away.') But for some reason I managed to wave it off and told myself sternly 'I'm going to do it, whatever happens', like a twelve-year-old about to do a reading in a school assembly.

Peter then got into the plane and began taking me through the plan of what would happen over the next forty-five minutes. We would taxi to the runway, make final checks with the control tower, take off and climb to 2,000 feet, where he would run through the controls before handing them over to me. He would take me through the basics: gaining and losing altitude, turning left and right and how to correct yaw.

Apparently I would then be amazed that our time was up, and he would bring us in to land. It all sounded very easy indeed. ('Shit. Shit. Shit.')

Safety information out of the way, he then talked me through pitch, roll and yaw and pointed out the various information panels to keep an eye on while we were airborne. I think at this point he could see I had become rather pale, and he sought to reassure me. 'I've been flying since I was seventeen. You're in good hands.' Then he smiled generously. 'Now, put on your headphones and we'll talk through them – the engine is too loud otherwise.'

I put the headphones on and began to feel marginally more relaxed, but the fear was still at the forefront of my mind. The sight of Peter going through the rituals did stimulate a powerful sense of curiosity inside my head, though.

'Right then, let's go.' The plane began inching forwards.

Adding an engine to their glider proved harder than Wilbur and Orville had imagined. First they had to design and test a new wooden propeller and then get Charlie Taylor, their bicycle shop mechanic, to build a petrol engine out of aluminium in order to minimize weight. Inquiries about existing propellers and engines had proved unfruitful, so they were left with no choice but to design and build their own from scratch. It seems astonishing to me that they were totally unfazed by this kind of problem. In the age of 'experts' today, where we each have our place, this wide-ranging kind of 'can-do' attitude is almost unimaginable. On 17 December 1903 they made their first powered flights at Kitty Hawk. The addition of the engine, and a few other tweaks, affected the performance of their powered glider only marginally, and their tireless glider flight trials now rewarded them far more than they could have hoped. They were airborne for only a few seconds on the first three attempts, and on the fourth the nose dropped shortly after take-off, but this time Wilbur managed to correct it and stayed in the air for fifty-nine seconds. He had covered a distance of 852 feet (260 metres) in a self-propelled flying machine. They had finally done it. Telegrams were sent to the press that night, but, astonishingly, their achievement was completely ignored.

Baffled at the lack of interest, they decided to carry on with their experiments and reveal themselves to the press and the public when they were ready, and not before. Now that they had their own powered plane they were less dependent on the whims of the wind, and so a year later they set up camp closer to home at Huffman Prairie, a few miles north of Dayton. Methodical experimentation to perfect the construction of their plane, along with their own flying skills, meant that by the end of 1904 they were both accomplished flyers. Wilbur held the brothers' single flight time record, having stayed airborne for thirty-eight minutes, until his fuel ran out. The sky had been conquered, but still no one seemed to want to know. The lack of interest in their flying machine has been put down to Wilbur and Orville's fear that someone else might come and steal their ideas before they had patented their designs and worked out how to make a living from them, which led them to understate their achievements in the presence of others and refuse to let anyone photograph their experiments. Add to that a widespread snobbery that two relatively uneducated bike-shop owners could have come up with something that had eluded the greatest scientists of the age – indeed, worse than that, to many in the scientific community of the time human flight was theoretically impossible – and the widespread disbelief becomes slightly more plausible. More surprising, perhaps, is the fact that the US military showed absolutely no interest in even establishing the authenticity of their claims, which explains why, despite repeated attempts to persuade their own government that they had built a flying machine, the Wright brothers began negotiations with the British and French to sell them prototypes of their new invention instead. The crux of any potential contract was an exhibition to prove that their machine could actually fly, and so Wilbur headed for France, with a dismantled plane in a crate, to build and display their aeroplane at Le Mans, south-west of Paris. Orville, meanwhile, went to Washington in a final attempt to persuade his own government that men could indeed fly.

Scorn awaited Wilbur's claims in France until, on 8 August 1908, he took off and flew effortlessly around a horse-racing track for 1 minute and 45 seconds. It wasn't much of a flight by his standards, but the French public were astonished. In the weeks that followed people swarmed to watch the exhibition flights continue as Wilbur performed increasingly agile manoeuvres. Finally the press, and then the world, were forced to take notice. It had taken a trip half-way across the globe, but the Wright brothers' fame and fortune had finally been assured.

While I jabbered away nervously, Peter smiled at me kindly and we pulled to a stop at the end of the airfield. It didn't look like a runway, just an empty lush green field, but at the end was a hedge and, beyond that, the road I'd driven in on. 'If at any point you want to get hold of something, hold this.' Peter pointed to the top of the control panel sternly. 'Don't grab at anything else.' I nodded. He spoke over the radio to confirm we were about to take off. He got clearance from the control tower and looked at me, grinning. 'Ready?' He didn't wait for an answer before nodding and saying loudly, 'Let's get airborne!' The engine ripped from a slow tick into

a growl, and we lurched forward. I tried to sit back while
breathing slowly, but Peter was urging us on excitedly with
a huge grin across his face. The acceleration tautened my
stomach in a way I hate, but there was no going back now.

'What speed do we need to get lift?' I asked as we rattled
along. 'Oh, about 65 m.p.h.,' he said nonchalantly. We were
now only a few hundred metres from the hedge. 'So when
do we actually get up into . . .', and at that moment, at what .
seemed a relatively slow speed, the front of the plane left the
ground and Peter began to pull back on the controls. I heard
myself say 'Oh fuck' as the back lifted and we began to climb
up into the sky. Peter chuckled. I grabbed the top of the
information panel in panic. 'Jesus Christ!' The plane climbed
at a fairly relaxed angle, but the sight of the land below me
slipping away began to disentangle me from a world of fear
into one of sheer astonishment.

'It's OK, climbing nicely now, easy does it.' Peter was the
calmest man in the world. Thank God. The plane drew us
higher and higher. I looked down as the town I live in slowly
fell away beneath me. Millimetres of fuselage were all that
separated me from a fall I had spent eighteen years imagining. There was no way of running away now. I was scared,
very scared, but my God I felt excited too. This must have
been the moment of realization that Russ had talked about.
The surge of adrenaline as you force yourself beyond what
you think you are capable of. I was terrified, but I still managed to let out a short giggle. Then the speed seemed to fall
away as the noise of the engine lightened. I panicked again
but, gawping for reassurance at the airspeed indicator, could
see we were still flying at 80 knots. I couldn't believe we
were up and very slowly let go of the information panel and
sat back in my seat. 'You OK?' Peter asked, laughing. 'Oh
God,' I spluttered, as we levelled off. He looked around and

sighed in delight. 'We're now cruising at 1,400 feet. I think we'll stay here, we don't need to go any higher. What a beautiful day. It's perfect up here. Now, in a minute you're going to take hold of the controls.' I thought back to the awful feeling I'd had in the saddle of Lionel's high-bicycle. I really didn't think I wanted to pilot an aeroplane, but I was up there now and it seemed rude to refuse. I reached out tentatively and took hold of the steering column. Peter spent a few minutes talking me through the movements before reassuring me once again, and then he let go, turned towards me and smiled. 'You're in control'. My hands were solid with nerves but, despite my fears, the plane was remarkably smooth. After a few seconds I dared to glance to my left out of the window and saw the horizon winking in the sun beyond the sea. The term 'cruising' was very appropriate. Instead of seeing us floating magically in the air, I began to realize that our speed had turned the air into waves, and we were being lightly buffeted, as though in a small boat on a calm sea. It was simply too magical to be frightened any more. I exhaled slowly in relief. An enormous grin began to spread across my face. I was in control of an aeroplane. I was actually flying.

An eight-year old boy had just moved a few kilometres outside Le Mans when Wilbur Wright began injecting into the French public a love of aviation that is no less fierce on that side of the channel today. It's impossible to know whether he actually witnessed these momentous flights, but there is no doubt that across France boys of his age would have been wowed by the magic and wonder of Wilbur's first exhibition of propelled flight. But that boy would have to wait until he was twelve, having taken to hanging around his local aerodrome for weeks on end, before he persuaded a local pilot to take him up for his first flight. That boy would grow up to be the most famous of all literary aviators: Saint-Ex, or Antoine de Saint-Exupéry, as he is properly known, the author of the children's classic *The Little Prince*.

Saint-Ex had become a hero of mine long before I thought of ever getting in the cockpit of an aeroplane, because of his mesmerizing books and a life philosophy that, once I'd discovered it, bloomed into my own. He was born into the French aristocracy, but into a family that had barely enough money to live in the way that was expected. This gave his life a fascinating duality. On the one hand his title of 'Comte de Saint-Exupéry' endeared him to the highest echelons of the Parisian élite, but without the funds to live that life he had no choice but to place a foot firmly in both worlds. He soon showed a Hemingway-esque taste for adventure, which included schooling in Switzerland and then Paris during the First World War, where he climbed to the rooftops when the Germans bombed Paris to watch the explosions when everyone else was heading underground. He then tried his hand as a navy recruit only to drop out and, very briefly, study architecture. Then he turned his attention to learning to fly, at his mother's expense, but gave that up on the verge of a military commission to please his fiancée after the first of many crashes. He briefly became a truck salesman, where part of his training involved learning how the trucks were made in the workshop, allowing him to discover a passion for mechanical engineering that he had been oblivious to before. He failed to sell any trucks, though, and soon moved on to an office job, where he stared in agony at the clock while 'trapped in his cage' all day every day. Repeatedly found asleep at his desk, instead of processing the required paperwork, which as far as he could tell nobody would ever even see, he professed amazement that anyone could cope with such a stultifying existence. He longed to actually live. His office career didn't last long, and with the end of his engagement he turned again to aviation, to which he would remain faithful for the rest of his life. He began working as a pilot for the burgeoning airmail routes of Aéropostale (later to become Air France). At a time when letters took weeks and months to get to the French colonies in Africa or South America, Saint-Ex joined a daring band of pilots prepared to take on the Pyrenees, deserts and oceans in primitive open-cockpit planes in order to quarter the time it took for the mail to arrive. An average of ten pilots a year lost their lives in the pioneering days of airmail.

It was while seeking to break a record flight time between Paris and Saigon for a prize of 150,000 francs that Saint-Ex and his navigator, André Prevot, crash-landed in the Sahara desert and had to trudge for three days before finding water. It was that event which inspired *The Little Prince*, the book for which he is most famous. It is a story about an aviator downed in the desert, who is kept from fixing his engine by a series of conversations with a little prince who has fallen down from the stars. The prince tells the aviator about the tiny planets he has visited before landing on Earth. What follows is a satire on the world of self-important adults blind to the real purpose of life. The first planet is inhabited by a king who is oblivious to the fact that he has no kingdom, the second by a vain man who only hears what he wants to hear, and the third by a drunkard who drinks because he is a drunk. On the fourth planet lives a businessman who is too busy counting the numbers on a sheet of paper on his desk to raise his head. The businessman tells the little prince that he owns the stars, 'those little golden things that make lazy people daydream'. The little prince asks what he does with them all. 'I manage them. I count them and then count them again . . . It's difficult work. But I'm a serious person!' On the sixth planet lives an academic, a geographer, who never actually goes anywhere but waits for people who have travelled to tell him what the world is really like. The only planet that the little prince considers remaining on is one inhabited by a man who thinks of things other than himself. It's not really a children's book and, if you haven't read it, I urge you to go out and buy a copy.

But Saint-Ex wasn't just a master of allegory. In terms of my journey it is when he turns his attention to machines that he really comes into his own, believing they evolved from the best of men.

> The more perfect machines become, the more they are invisible behind their function. It seems that all man's industrial effort, all his calculations and his nights spent poring over drawings, all these visible signs have as their sole end the achievement of simplicity . . . On the surface it seems that the work of engineers, designers and research mathematicians consists only in polishing and refining, easing this joint and balancing that wing until there is no longer a wing joined visibly to a fuselage, but a perfectly developed form freed at last from its matrix, a spontaneous and mysterious whole with the unified quality of a poem.

In Saint-Exupéry's view machines became an extension rather than an obstacle of man, one that enabled him to have a more intense relationship with the natural world.

> Today we forget the revolving of the engine. It is at last fulfilling its function, which is to revolve just as the heart goes on beating, and we pay no attention to our heart. The tool no longer absorbs our attention. Beyond and through the tool we are rediscovering nature as it was, the nature of the gardener, the navigator, or the poet . . . A plane may be a machine, but what an analytical instrument it is! It has revealed to us the true face of the earth.

Saint-Exupéry was dismissive of those who sought to blame machines for men's ills too, putting the blame for their misuse firmly at the feet of men, but, like Mumford, he saw mankind's primitive relationship with machines as simply the early stage in a connection that would one day transform the world. However, that relationship would have to evolve from one where machines served the work- and financially obsessed world satirized in *The Little Prince* and began to serve what it meant to be human instead.

> In the exhilaration of our progress we have made . . . use of men in the building of railways, the construction of factories, the sinking of oil wells. We have forgotten sometimes that these structures were meant to be of service to men. While we were conquering soldiers, we had the morality of soldiers. But now we must be settlers. We must bring life into this new house which as yet has no human face.

Aviation was undoubtedly part of Saint-Exupéry's humanity. As he recovered in New York after another crash, *The Little Prince* was published, to great acclaim, but he longed to get back in the air and protect his beloved France, which was still under a German cosh. Too old to serve in the French military towards the end of the Second World War, not to mention the fact that he was still hampered by his numerous crash-related injuries, he used his connections (most notably *Life* magazine photographer John Phillips) to persuade General Eaker, who commanded the Allied Mediterranean Air Force, to let him back at the controls of an aeroplane. He was assigned to fly reconnaissance flights for the Americans from Sardinia in 1943. On 31 July Saint-Ex flew towards France on one of these missions but never returned. He was forty-four.

Such a full life, ending so tragically, leaves fans of Saint-Ex to trawl through his work in the search of some greater meaning, and there is plenty to find. My favourite passage comes from the greatest of all his books, *Wind, Sand and Stars*, where he recalls the bus journey he took with miserable-looking commuters to the aerodrome for his first solo mail flight across the Pyrenees. It is a brutal passage, which in my view gets to the heart of the way most people forget how sacred life is. I realized, as my journey came to a close, that he is actually pointing out what befalls those who are only able to value the things in life that can be rationally measured, counted and quantified.

> Old bureaucrat, my companion here present, no man ever opened an escape route for you, and you are not to blame. You built peace for yourself by blocking up every chink of light, as termites do. You rolled yourself into your ball of bourgeois security, your routines, the stifling rituals of your provincial existence; you built your humble rampart against winds, tides and stars. You have no wish to ponder great questions; you had enough trouble suppressing awareness of your human condition. You do not dwell on a wandering planet, you ask yourself no unanswerable questions . . .
>
> No man ever grasped you by the shoulder while there was still time. Now the clay that formed you has dried and hardened, and no man could now awaken in you the dormant musician, the poet or the astronomer who perhaps once dwelt within you.

He touches on the concept of 'quality' or '*Spielzeug*' that we have learned about too. His little prince befriends a fox on his travels and, when it is time for them to part, the fox gives his new friend the gift of a secret, telling him 'It's quite simple: One sees clearly only with the heart. Anything essential is invisible to the eyes.'

It is surely obvious to us all deep down that it is the pilgrimage through all those unexplainable, immeasurable, wonderful things about being human that the focus of all our lives should be.

The sky was clear, with ghosts of cloud high above us. I looked left out of the window and saw Chichester harbour sweep away: the harbour the Romans had sailed up thousands of years ago, the harbour that would have greeted returning pilots in Spitfires from sorties across the Channel, the harbour I had sailed and paddled in as a child. The plane wobbled, and I stiffened with fear. Peter turned and looked at me. 'You're doing fine. Relax. We're just being buffeted by air, but your speed is good. Now, enjoy it.'

He then began to point out the landmarks that I had only ever seen from the ground. 'There's Bosham, we're going over it now.' I looked down to try and spot the house of a family friend, George Kingsbury, who had died a few years earlier. I remembered a conversation I'd had with him, while walking his dog Bella across a vast lawn, about me being too afraid to fly. 'I was afraid of flying once,' he confided to me, reaching out literally and emotionally in a way men of his time and of his age rarely did, 'but you've got to open yourself up to life, Dan, even when you are afraid.' I'd been glad of his words then, and they came back to me, through watering eyes, now.

Gazing down at the earth, I knew the fear had gone. I could hear it shouting at me vaguely from a distance, but the taunts were unintelligible now.

Peter began to urge me to turn in a huge circle to head back the way we had come. Banking left, the plane turned what felt like 45 degrees, but I'm sure it wasn't actually that steep. As I looked out to my left, the window was filled entirely with the earth. This is the kind of thing that would have seemed agonizing in a jumbo jet but, cocooned in that little plane, it was too beautiful to arouse complaint. I was more interested in spotting tiny cars heading along the A27, boats in the flat glistening sea, nature's carved coastline, the harbour, and then, with a flood of delight, I recognized the canal! It was the Chichester ship canal, where my journey had begun. Winding up towards the city, it was less than a ribbon, the faintest thread of blue that seemed so stunted from up there, so short, but it had led me such a long way: all over the country to a thousand feet above the earth and a perspective of enthusiasts that had finally become so clear. And then Peter told me all too quickly that it was time to head home.

'You can take her in to land, now you need to go right a bit, look ahead, can you see the airfield?' It was a tiny island of green, but I could just make it out. 'Now head right and begin to push the nose down . . . further . . . further . . . that's fine, hold it there.' We drifted down to the earth, and my brief glimpse of a new world began to filter away. We lost altitude quickly but with no hint of a fairground plunge and surged towards the ground, but still Peter left me with the controls. The trees regained their lateral shape, and the speed seemed to increase as we charged back to earth, and still I held on. The hedge loomed ahead and below us, 400 feet, 350 feet, 300 feet, 'Push the nose slightly further . . . airspeed good', and still I held on. It was the most exhilarating thing I have ever done. Andy was right. Computer games just don't come close. The hedge vanished, and I saw the control tower and still I held on, 'Steady . . . steady . . . now pull back, pull back!' and finally Peter wrenched the controls at the last moment and tugged them deep into his chest as we hit the ground. The rumble began as our airway was replaced with grass and earth. He stamped on the brakes, and we dribbled off the runway to the right so that another plane could take off.

The surge I felt next, as we taxied back, I simply can't explain. A thousand childhood hugs, catching a cricket ball on the boundary when I was six, my son's perfect newborn eyelashes, Rachel on our wedding day, a Matthew Le Tissier free kick . . . It was as though I'd never felt so purely and intensely me.

The next morning I woke on the start of a bright and sunny day. I went to the kitchen and immediately stared out into the sky, but before turning the radio on I heard the faintest buzzing sound. It was the engine of a plane. I looked up into the perfect clean blue and, without thinking, said out loud, 'You jammy sod.' I was up there in my mind, the sun glinting on the water a thousand feet below. The gentle buf-feting of the air, turned firmly into a road by our 80 knot speed. The slow, comforting response of the controls to a slight pull left and back to take us up higher into the sky, the tilt of the wing as we turned and the earth fell into place below. It was impossible not to be in awe of that machine as it responded to the slightest movement of the controls, built with as much hope and imagination as mechanical know-how. I remembered more of it then. I had flown over the flat where my granny had lived and saw the gardens where I played as a child. The Isle of Wight looked tantalizingly close too as we flew along, parallel with the coast. Everything else was forgotten, and I was just there. Peter had seemed far more relaxed than on the ground too. 'It's beautiful, isn't it?' I remember him saying simply, with the same watering eyes I'd found in all the enthusiasts I'd met on my way.

That morning I knew I had finally disentangled my own truth about why men love things that go. Aeroplanes may be machines, but the magic and poetry of flying a light aircraft had given me – and still gives me, even months later – a greater sense of being alive than any novel or book I've ever read. The process of getting up there told me more about myself and the human experience than any work of art or film I've ever seen. And it hit me emotionally more than any music I've ever listened to or any political speech I've ever heard. None of those things has ever expanded my horizons and shown me the wonder of what my life could be in the way that staring out over the wing as I turned the plane in a bold circle above my home did that day. I think it's safe to say I'd finally found the machine that 'did it' for me. It had taken courage to go 'over my limit', but I had done it and in doing so I had at last discovered my own 'quality' within a machine. One of those experiences that the rational world cannot explain – an indefinable feeling of pure joy that simply can't be counted, measured or plotted on a graph.

The secret at the end of my quest, then, was surely very straightforward. Enthusiasts are said to have an 'irrational' love of machines by those that don't understand them. I had come to realize that this is because the very beauty or 'quality' enthusiasts experience through machines simply is irrational.

Epilogue

After a great deal of searching I had arrived at a conclusion, or rather an experience, that felt like a meaningful end to my quest, but I am aware of the convenience in settling on an answer that is, by definition, indefinable. Some might even go as far as to call it a cop-out. It is for that reason each chapter has the title it does.

Some people clearly love machines because they allow them to escape, others because certain kinds of machines have integrity to their construction that touches them deeply, while many love machines because they evoke their curiosity. Then there are those who love machines because they allow them to access a greater sense of adventure and freedom. Power, as it is defined in the dictionary, means 'the ability, skill, or capacity to do something', and many machines offer that rare luxury of engagement with the world too. *Spielzeug* is my own personal favourite, and there is no doubt in my mind that a vast number of enthusiasts love machines because they spot something magical within them that was not written down or drawn in on the blueprints, while for others machines turn the experience of being alive into pure poetry. I'm sure for some the answer will be a combination, if not all, of those things.

I always find myself coming to bold conclusions when I venture into the ever-increasing world of my own ignorance, but the titles of the eight chapters of this book are some of my very favourite words and I think it's worth looking at them, briefly, again.

Escape. Integrity. Curiosity. Adventure. Freedom. Power. *Spielzeug* and Poetry.

Surely most people would agree that these things are the very blood of life, and yet every one of them is largely missing in the way we live today, or where it exists it is despite, rather than because of, the structures that rule our lives.

You could write a book on the apparent demise of our ability to escape, or examining the fact that so many of us are desperate to leave the corrupted values of the way we live far behind. Integrity is largely non-existent in most spheres of life you care to look at, in a world where economic growth has become the only moral absolute. Curiosity is being stifled by the pursuit of only measurable success in our educational institutions, and true adventure now seems to be limited to a carbon copy of someone else's gap year. Freedom – well, we all seem to live with the assumption that we can only ever achieve that by becoming rich, so the route to our freedom itself becomes a cage. Power? Who has any sense of power these days? Not when you deal with your bank, your mobile phone company, or even through the government you voted for, when they are on the verge of bankrupting the country for generations to come in order to bail out the financial institutions responsible for the economic turmoil we are all now immersed in. There's not a lot of *Spielzeug* in the world these days either, just the ephemeral myth of it that the advertisers and marketing men spend so much money and effort trying to conjure into increasingly laughable vessels: razor blades, mobile phones, eye-liner or chocolate bars. But surely this indefinable feeling is what we're all searching for to make our lives more meaningful. Which leaves us poetry.

Well, there's plenty of other people's, I suppose, if you know where to look. But very few dare to risk derision by expressing their own idea of poetry any more. Perhaps it's because the inclination to be moved to think of life in poetic terms is so hard to secure.

The other noticeable feature of all these things is that none of them can be measured or displayed on a graph in any meaningful way, and, as we all know from painful experience, if something can't be measured, then today it is usually deemed to have no value.

That was certainly the most powerful idea I would take from my journey to try and understand the world of machines. Surely the biggest problem we face is that the rational framework inside which we all live is incapable of valuing anything that it can't measure, and as a consequence it vastly overvalues the things that it can.

Lewis Mumford saw the rise of machines as the inevitable consequence of this approach but also saw in machines hope for the future. So did Saint-Exupéry. Both looked ahead to the day when we will learn to use machines for a more profound purpose than merely increasing political power or economic wealth. They dared to imagine a generation of machines in the future that would allow us to explore more human qualities instead. But I was beginning to wonder whether those machines might already exist. The men I met had certainly learned to use machines for their own immeasurable human benefits rather than their purely functional ability to go from A to B. They had found in their machines something not apparent in the designers' original blueprints or the engineers' practical concerns, something that I had concluded bloomed from their own passion and lust for life.

The key to changing the machine of society we all live in, then, might be to find a way to restructure it in human terms rather than the purely measurable, economic values of today. The way to do that, I would suggest, is to stop paying so much attention to the leaders of the measurable society and follow the example of the machine enthusiasts instead. People who are not passive or complacent about their lives, but who actively engage with what it means to 'be'.

Picture Credits and Copyright Acknowledgements

on I. K. Brunel', given at Brunel University on 22 January 1958, by L.T.C. Rolt, are reproduced by kind permission of the History Press and Sonia Rolt. February 9, 2010 marks the hundredth anniversary of L.T.C. Rolt's birth and various events are planned to celebrate his life. For more information about this and the great man himself, please visit http://www.ltcrolt.org.uk/

Acknowledgements

First, in the words of Hunter S. Thompson, I would like to thank all the people who keep me mercifully unemployed. No writer could function without them: my agent Simon Benham and the team at John Murray, particularly Kate Parkin, whose idea it was for me to embark on a journey to try and understand why men are obsessed with machines. Second, my thanks to the enthusiasts themselves, who were kind enough to ignore my hopeless lack of knowledge about every one of their enthusiasms. I hope I did each of them and their various passions justice. Third, I would like to thank Rachel for her patience and kindness, and for listening to me drone on while pacing around the lounge in numerous fits of confusion. Lastly, I need to thank Wilf, three at the time of writing, for his astonishingly wise words of advice as I struggled over my keyboard one cold November morning. 'Don't worry, Daddy. It's only words.'